MANAGEMENT SKILLS FOR THE INFORMATION MANAGER

Edited by

Ann Lawes
Task Force Pro Libra

Routledge
Taylor & Francis Group

LONDON AND NEW YORK

First published 1993 by Ashgate Publishing

Reissued 2018 by Routledge
2 Park Square, Milton Park, Abingdon, Oxon OX14 4RN
711 Third Avenue, New York, NY 10017, USA

Routledge is an imprint of the Taylor & Francis Group, an informa business

Copyright © Ann Lawes, 1993

All rights reserved. No part of this book may be reprinted or reproduced or utilised in any form or by any electronic, mechanical, or other means, now known or hereafter invented, including photocopying and recording, or in any information storage or retrieval system, without permission in writing from the publishers.

Notice:
Product or corporate names may be trademarks or registered trademarks, and are used only for identification and explanation without intent to infringe.

Publisher's Note
The publisher has gone to great lengths to ensure the quality of this reprint but points out that some imperfections in the original copies may be apparent.

Disclaimer
The publisher has made every effort to trace copyright holders and welcomes correspondence from those they have been unable to contact.

A Library of Congress record exists under LC control number: 93187357

Typeset in 11 point Melior by Photoprint, Torquay.

ISBN 13: 978-1-138-32581-4 (hbk)
ISBN 13: 978-1-138-32587-6 (pbk)
ISBN 13: 978-0-429-45020-4 (ebk)

Contents

Notes on contributors   vii

Introduction   1

1 Recruitment and selection of staff   4
Susan Hill and Alison Jago

2 Motivation of staff   26
Beryl Morris

3 Staff training and development   40
Sylvia P. Webb

4 Marketing and justification of the information service   54
Colin Offor

5 The information audit   75
Feona Hamilton

6 Budgeting, financial control, purchasing and charging   97
Liz Chapman

7 Relationships with suppliers   114
Roy Adams

8 Records management or information management?   131
Veronica Davies

9 Your political base   139
Colin Offor

10 Time management   157
Beryl Morris

11	Self-development *Feona Hamilton*	179
12	Management concerns for the minimal staff library *Guy St. Clair*	193
	Index	223

Notes on contributors

Roy Adams ('Relationship with suppliers') went to the College of Librarianship Wales, obtaining his professional qualification in 1970. He also has a masters degree from Loughborough, and is a Fellow of the Library Association. He worked in a public library before going to college, and has subsequently had experience in industry and in further and higher education. Since 1979 he has worked for Leicester Polytechnic, first as Head of Technical Services, then as Second Deputy Librarian, Deputy Librarian, and currently as Head of Library and Information Services. He has been active in research and development since the 1970s, working on one of the first computer information dissemination systems in the UK and carrying out research in the field of library user education. From 1983 he developed the AIM interlibrary loans administration system, which is now the leading seller in the field. He has also carried out research in the areas of local area networking and decision support. His current interests include the use of artificial intelligence systems for decision support, and methods for predicting the development of information technology applications in libraries. He was the founder and is manager of the COPOST electronic mail service, which includes LA-net. He acts as a consultant on communications and networking to commercial and public bodies. Mr Adams speaks regularly at meetings and conferences on information technology, particularly wide and local area networks and technological futures. He has written over 50 articles and contributed to several books. In addition, he has written two books on the impact of information technology on the communications and information chain.

Elizabeth Chapman BA MA DipLib FECert FLA ('Budgeting, financial control, purchasing and charging') is Librarian at the Institute of Statistics, University of Oxford. Previously she was Assistant Librarian at Brunel University. Liz has been closely involved with the National Acquisitions Group in the UK since its inception, and has contributed widely to the professional literature on library acquisition techniques including her acclaimed textbook *Buying for Libraries*. She is Editor of the Oxford University Libraries Bulletin, and Chair of the IT training special group for librarians in Oxford University.

Veronica Davies ('Records management or information management?') is Head of Information Services at Shell International, where she is responsible for the effective management and exploitation of information resources to meet the requirements of the Shell Group business activities. She has lectured and published widely on aspects of information management. Veronica is a graduate of London University, and holds a Diploma in Archive Administration.

Feona Hamilton BA MPhil MBIM ('The information audit' and 'Self-development') is Manager, Information and Corporate Communications at Bain & Co., the management consultants. Prior to taking up this post, she spent six years as a self-employed consultant, writer and lecturer in information management. Her career spans over 30 years in the information profession. Earlier posts include Information, Research and Consultancy Group Manager at Aslib, the Association for Information Management, and Press and Information Officer at the Library Association. Feona Hamilton is well known as a lecturer on introducing information management, and marketing, on which subject she has written a best-selling book, *Infopromotion: Publicity and marketing ideas for the information profession* (Gower, 1990).

Alison Jago ('Recruitment and selection of staff') is a qualified librarian, and holds a Diploma in Personnel Management. She is also a Fellow of the Institute of Personnel Management and a Member of the Institute of Training and Development. Her early career was spent in university, public and special libraries. More recently, she has specialized in management training, developing particular expertise in training in recruitment and selection techniques. Alison is now a Recruitment Consultant at TFPL, where she is involved in a wide range of recruitment and training activities, including compilation of TFPL's *Business Information Salary Survey*.

Susan Hill ('Recruitment and selection of staff') is a member of the IEC and has worked in the information world for 20 years. Since becoming a Director of Task Force Pro Libra Ltd six years ago to take responsibility for its growing recruitment division, she has been active in helping both candidates seeking work and clients wishing to find new staff. She lectures extensively on curriculum vitae production and interview technique to potential employees, and on the complexities of recruiting new staff to employers.

Ann Lawes (Editor) has nearly 40 years' experience in libraries and information departments. She began her career at the Science Museum Library but quickly moved into the chemical industry. There she worked on competitor intelligence and marketing information systems – manual versions of today's EIS programmes! Ann then moved into advertising with spells as a one person library, as librarian at the Advertising Association and finally as Head of Information at Lintas Ltd., then part of Unilever. At Lintas she developed the subject specialist approach to information handling and coordinated a world-wide network for the exchange of advertising, marketing and product information.

Moving on to the Food Drink and Tobacco Industry Training Board as Information Manager, Ann led a service providing personnel and training information to those industry sectors. During this period she was elected Chairman of the ASLIB Midlands Branch and consequently became a member of ASLIB Council, serving 10 years in total. When the Food Drink and Tobacco ITB was closed by the Government in 1982, Ann elected to become a consultant undertaking a number of projects involved with the management of small special libraries. Her interest in the training and development of staff crystallized during her time at the Food Board and she was able to build on this by developing a programme of public courses and conferences for Alan Armstrong and Associates Ltd., a specialist bookseller serving the industrial library and business information market.

In 1987, when TFPL was set up as an independent company, Ann joined the company as a Director with special responsibility for courses, conferences and seminars.

The TFPL programme is designed for records managers as well as for library and information personnel. It operates at all levels providing some 80 events per annum ranging from First Steps

Introductory courses to continuing education in areas such as Implementing CD-ROM systems, and management education with courses in people skills such as Performance Management and operational skills such as Project Management. Seminars are run regularly on topical issues, such as QA for records managers, and the conference programme includes the European Business Information Conference held each year in a different European centre.

A feature of the TFPL programme lies in cooperation with other information bodies, and events are regularly held with IIS, HERTIS, DPA and CD-ROM SPAG.

Today, in addition to her roles as a Director of TFPL and Head of Training, Ann lectures widely and undertakes consultancy work associated with the development of small special libraries and information units.

Beryl Morris ('Motivation of staff' and 'Time management') is now an independent consultant, having previously been Head of Cultural Services for the London Borough of Newnham. In that post she was responsible for more than 200 staff working in arts and entertainment, community centres, libraries and a conference centre. Previously she held posts with Manchester Polytechnic and the Polytechnic of East London. Her professional interests cover the management of change, communications skills and people management. She is a consultant to a number of organizations helping people to maximize their skills.

Colin Offor ('Marketing and justification of the information service' and 'Your political base') was Head of Information Services at J Walter Thompson, the international advertising agency, before moving to Warwick University to establish the fee-based business information and statistics service. In a move to 3i he became Market and Information Service Manager, investigating and reporting on companies seeking venture capital in the marketing services, publishing and information industries. As an independent consultant he was involved in evaluative work on the Public Library Development Incentives Scheme for the British Library. He is currently Chief Executive of Milton Keynes Business Venture Ltd, an enterprise agency supporting the creation and growth of small businesses in Milton Keynes.

Guy St. Clair ('Management concerns for the minimal staff library') is President of OPL Resources, Ltd., a management consulting firm located in New York. OPL's work is focused in three areas: the presentation of seminars and workshops for practising librarians and information specialists; consulting with management about library problems; and the publication of the monthly periodical *The One-Person Library: A Newsletter for Librarians and Management*. Guy St. Clair is the one person recognized internationally as the authority on the need for, the organization of, and the growing usefulness of the one-person library.

Sylvia P Webb BA FLA MIInfSc ('Staff training and development') is now an independent consultant operating in the fields of training, research and writing. She is a well-known author and lecturer on various aspects of information management, and her first book, *Creating an Information Service*, is still one of Aslib's bestsellers, selling in over 40 countries. She has worked in a variety of business environments in both the public and the private sectors, joining MSL International from Stoy Hayward, a leading firm of accountants. Previously, at Ashridge Management College, she had a dual role as College Librarian and Lecturer in behavioural sciences, specializing in management and interpersonal skills. This led to her interest in personal development, the subject of her second book, *Personal Development in Information Work*, also published by ASLIB. As well as being active within the Library Association, her own professional activities include membership of several government advisory bodies and considerable involvement in professional education. She is a former Vice-President of the Institute of Information Scientists. Her most recent book is *Using Professional Advice* (Director Books, 1990).

Introduction

Ann Lawes

Those people who have so generously contributed to this book have a common concern – the professional management of information within organizations – and a common aim – that information plays its rightful role in the successful operation and development of those organizations. We make no apology for stating the obvious: that sensitive, efficient management is the key to success.

The starting point for this book was TFPL's management training programme. Whilst many information managers obtain their training with peer groups in their employing organizations, many find themselves learning 'on the hoof' with a strong 'do-it-yourself' element. Recognition, therefore, of individual strengths and weaknesses and the ways in which management training can help becomes essential. Equally important are informed decisions as to which management techniques are the most appropriate and helpful to the management of information.

Most of the contributors to this book have, at one time or another, been involved with TFPL's management training programme. Most knew each other and have respect for each other's views. Not exactly a book written by a group of friends, but as near as one can come.

The elements of management development chosen for inclusion in this book reflect the contributors' experience of what is needed, backed by response from participants in the TFPL training programme. It is therefore hoped that the choice of topics is both relevant and timely.

A typical profile of the participant in a TFPL management training course would be someone who:

- has recently assumed supervisory responsibility for staff
- has been appointed manager of a small information unit
- has some experience of management but recognizes the need to develop additional skills.

Therefore these are the people that we had in mind when this book was written.

It is important the reader understands that there is no finite point at which one says 'I am now a good manager'. There is always, always, more to learn, particularly about people; new techniques and approaches present themselves daily (for example, the current interest in contracting out and Total Quality Management). Experience is building in both these areas, and this will eventually lead to accepted standards of excellence.

This book is therefore a starting point. Some readers will want to look at certain issues in more depth, and hopefully the reading lists will aid in that process. Others will find there are management issues not covered here where help is needed. Some of that help can be found in the management literature produced specifically for the information sector, but it is also possible to adapt and learn from much that has been written for the more general manager. This literature is even more relevant today as information units of all types become more commercially aware, often to the point of operating as businesses in their own right.

The information world has changed beyond recognition in the past decade. Computers have revolutionized our ability to manipulate and analyse large amounts of data, and online systems have made information accessible at a speed undreamed of in the professional lifetime of many readers. Changes in communications technology have revolutionized document delivery and personal networking.

Such developments have happened during a period when the actual volume of information generated has grown to an almost uncontrollable extent. Costs in all areas have risen to the point where sophisticated measurements of value for money and cost benefits are essential. Information now makes a substantial contribution to the costs of almost all organizations. Consequently, the belief that information should be freely available to all is increasingly being overturned by the necessity to charge for services.

A further key change has been a blurring of the divide between information in the public domain and that generated internally by organizations. This has largely been brought about by the application of information technology, and it can be illustrated by, for example, the growth of Executive Information Systems.

Users of information have also changed. They expect higher

standards of expertise from the information profession. Time spans are shorter, and an understanding of the ramifications and implications of information provided is routinely expected. It is no longer acceptable simply to provide lists of references on given subjects – value must be added, whether it be in the form of analysis, evaluation or recommendation.

The contribution of the librarian, information scientist and records manager in terms of information management is now widely accepted. The importance of information to the health and prosperity of organizations is increasingly recognized. Professional expertise and standards are already high, but they need to be matched with management expertise in terms of self, people and resources.

# Recruitment and selection of staff

Susan Hill and Alison Jago

- Personnel departments
- Job description
- Person specification
- Finding the right candidate
- The interview
- The selection process
- Sample job descriptions and person specifications

Without doubt there have been many changes in recent years. Recessions have come and gone, employment or unemployment has been through highs and lows, and the demographic changes resulting from fluctuating birth rates have taken effect and altered the numbers of people in different age groups available for work. Recruiters have generally come to realize that they can no longer pick and choose; the right employees can be difficult to attract, and the old methods of recruitment need to be updated. Criteria may need to be modified or changed. Stability is as important as ability, and personal skills and attitudes may be more realistic requirements than academic qualifications alone. When recruiting it is necessary to market the credibility of the organization, the value of the job, and the pleasant work environment.

What is different about recruitment for the library and information profession? Some aspects, certainly, but in general the steps and procedures are similar for recruitment in all areas.

Differences that we have noted over the years might also apply to other fairly small and closely knit professions. Library and information personnel tend to take their professional responsibilities very seriously. Indeed, because of the very subject of their specialism – information – they need to continually keep up to date and remain professionally aware. This means that they often belong to a number of different professional groups, and quite possibly know the very people whom they may be about to recruit. Sometimes this is an advantage, at other times it is not. There are well known examples of organizations having difficulty in recruiting because it is common knowledge within the small sector of the profession to which they belong that the head of department has a bad reputation.

It is a pity to miss the opportunity created by a vacancy to develop departments, import technological expertise, service new specialist areas of interest, and so on. Perhaps recruitment is a way in which to bring the implementation of new technologies forward? People can be frightened of change, and incorporating changes in technology when planning for new staff often makes the transition easier.

To avoid problems in the selection process later on you must know from the start:

- What the job involves   **Job description**
- What sort of person could do it **Person specification**

This is the professional approach, and there are no short cuts. Every professional, whatever their field, has to follow a pre-determined number of steps to arrive at the end result; e.g. an architect has to draw (or describe) a building and then select (or specify) the materials with which it will be built. It not only enables you (and, if applicable, your personnel department) to more accurately assess interviewees, but it is also of great value to potential candidates who will be better able to assess their interest in, and their ability to do, the job available.

Taking short cuts at this stage can both put good candidates off and upset and alienate your personnel departments. If you advertise without adequate preparation you could be advertising your ineptitude to your peers, and of course you could end up with the candidates that you do manage to attract gaining a poor opinion of you and your organization.

◆ Personnel departments

Procedures for recruiting vary greatly from company to company. If you do not have a personnel department then the task in hand is likely to be your responsibility. Should you have a personnel department this could still be the case, but in most cases the recruitment of library and information staff will be a combination of joint effort and cooperation with the personnel department. The first priority should be to discuss your requirements (using your prepared job description) to establish first the protocol and then the procedures that you will use.

It is important to establish a good relationship with your personnel department – even before you have a vacancy. There are many ways in which they can help you. Once you have a vacancy, keep them informed from the outset and they will always be on your side. Do your homework *before* you enlist their help. Establish the parameters within which you will search, and hand them a full job brief including job description and person specification. They will welcome your initiative because their job is to help with the mechanics of recruitment, not to know how your department runs. If you produce a clear brief you are more likely to get what you want.

◆ Job description

A job description defines the tasks which make up the job. It records facts about job *content*, not the job holder. It should include:

1. Job title
2. Reporting relationships – up and down
3. Overall purpose of the job
4. Short description of main activities listed under 'responsibilities'

The job description provides the basis for deciding what sort of person could do the job.

You *must* have a job description before you can prepare the person specification.

Before looking at the component parts, think about the reasons for the vacancy. Is it a new post, a replacement, or is some short-term help needed? If it is a new post you have probably reviewed the structure of your department and in doing so realized the need to create the new post. Why not use the same process for replacement help? Is it time to recruit a European language into the department? Should you try and import new skills?

You should look at the job description and person specification of the person leaving and see if they are still valid. Perhaps you could replace a full-time person with a part-time person? Perhaps you will need to replace them with one and a half or even two people? What about job sharing?

Can you promote one of the junior staff into the position, or move someone across from the same level? This can be beneficial in a number of ways: helping further job satisfaction, training in new facets of the work, producing an interchangeable team. Should the job be graded at a higher (or lower) level? Is there anyone in another department or team you can move to this post?

WHAT'S IN A NAME?

Every job should have a job title. When describing a job to a potential candidate it is normal to start by telling them the job title. This should indicate both the level and nature of the job. A poorly chosen job title may be detrimental to the recruitment process. The number of people who lose interest after just hearing the title, or who read no further after seeing the advertisement heading, can be surprising.

Personnel departments often describe a job accurately but need specialist advice on a suitable job title. This is understandable, as they may not be experts on the subtle differences between, for example, assistant librarians and library assistants.

WHO'S DOING WHAT WITH WHOM?

Candidates are as concerned about who they will report to as they are about who will report to them. An interview is not the best time to start casting around in your mind to see if there are any staff that the interviewee might be able to manage, or be allowed to have control of in order to increase interest in the job on offer.

WHAT'S IT ALL ABOUT?

Apart from paying out a salary and having another smiling face around, there should be a fundamental reason for the job, i.e. an overall purpose. This can usually be summed up in one or two sentences. (See sample job descriptions at the end of this chapter.)

RESPONSIBILITIES

This needs to be an itemized list of the main activities of the job. Be concise – it is a mistake to put too much in – but keep some flexibility as a very strict and regimented list of responsibilities may cause an employee to refuse to operate outside the boundaries of the job description at a later date. A 'catch all' phrase such as 'From time to time any other duties necessary for the smooth running of the department' is useful.

◆ Person specification

This describes the person not the job.

A traditional technique widely used in the preparation of a person specification is the Seven Point Plan. This provides a useful framework to identify what is required for the job holder to carry out the job. It covers seven aspects of the individual:

1. Physical makeup
   – appearance
   – health
2. Attainments
   – education
   – professional qualifications
   – job experience/practical experience and achievements
3. General intelligence (e.g. numeracy, flexibility, ability to think quickly)
4. Special aptitudes (e.g. computers, languages, entrepreneurial flair)
5. Interests
   To what extent should interests be practical, intellectual, professional, physically active, social?
6. Disposition
   Friendly? Approachable? Methodical? Attention to detail? Analytical? Outgoing? Confident?
7. Circumstances
   Ease of access to work? Availability for hours of work, overtime, etc?

When preparing the person specification, consider what is essential and what is desirable, and using the Seven Point Plan as a framework, divide each factor on your person specification into two sections: one for **essential** attributes, the other for **desirable** attributes (see sample Person Specification on pp.22–25):

- **Essential** These are the attributes without which the candidate would not be able to do the job.
- **Desirable** Those qualities and skills that are not vital to the job, but would be useful. Desirable attributes enhance both the candidate's chance of getting the job and the range and scope of skills existing in the department.

Think carefully about this. Take languages, for example: which ones, how many, what level – fluency or knowledge of? Are languages essential for the job, or merely a useful addition, or do you know that they won't really be needed at all? Unfortunately, fluency in languages wanes if they are not used. A candidate with good languages wanting to continue to use them will think differently about the following descriptions:

'Must have fluency in at least one European language'
'Knowledge of European languages useful but not essential'
'Foreign languages an advantage'

◆ Finding the right candidates

By now you know what the job involves. You know what sort of person you need to do it. How do you find them? There are two main ways – advertising and recruitment agencies.

WHERE TO ADVERTISE

Professional journals circulating within the library and information profession may take advertising, indeed they may have special supplements for job vacancies, and they have the advantage of precise targeting.

Newspapers, on the other hand, reach a far wider audience, and may well attract responses from unlikely sources. Remember that newspapers may carry specific types of job vacancies on certain days of the week. Find out in advance which day is appropriate for your vacancy.

Timing may be an important factor in your choice of advertising media. Newspapers will of course bring fast results. Weekly, fortnightly and monthly publications can delay the appearance of your advertisement by a further week, fortnight or month if your timing is wrong.

DESIGNING A JOB ADVERTISEMENT

The aim of a good advertisement is to produce, at reasonable cost, a field of applicants capable of doing the job to the standard required. If care is not taken to ensure that the advertisement is clearly laid out and well designed, the impact could be non-existent, particularly if it is lost amongst pages of other advertisements. Above all, it must be relevant, factual and avoid ambiguity.

The advertisement should:

- identify the organization (including size, future projects/development, innovation, expansion, specialization)
- convey the flavour of the organization
- identify the main purpose of the job and the key components (from the job description)
- specify essential requirements of the applicant (from the person specification)
- specify incentives such as pay, benefits (bonus, company car, private health insurance, etc)
- include any unusual aspects (evening and weekend work, overseas travel)
- give directions to the applicant to write or telephone

The response to any advertisement can vary because of circumstances beyond your control (e.g. strikes/hurricanes). These you cannot eliminate, but you should try hard to avoid any other circumstances that will bring in a paucity of response (such as advertising on a bank holiday).

Timing can often affect the type of person you are seeking. If you need a new graduate in Librarianship or Information Science, check when their courses finish. And there are other aspects of timing which are important. Speed of response to applicants can subtly alter their impressions of you as an employer. Time and time again, good candidates withdraw because of an overly long recruitment period, or because of ominous silences between responding to the advertisement and hearing about an interview, between first and second interviews, and even between a second interview and a job offer. If there is a typing backlog you can always make contact verbally and confirm in writing later. If there is an unavoidable delay, let the candidate(s) know.

ALTERNATIVES TO ADVERTISING

- specialist recruitment agencies for professionally qualified or experienced information specialists
- local or general agencies for junior non-professional staff
- employee introduction schemes
- staff noticeboards
- in-house magazines
- university noticeboards
- speculative letters from candidates
- radio or television
- exhibitions

SPECIALIST RECRUITMENT AGENCIES

A good specialist recruitment agency will:

- offer immediate access to a wide range of qualified and experienced candidates
- have interviewed *all* the candidates on their books, and will be able to discuss each candidate with you individually
- work with you to identify the skills, knowledge and experience required for the job. They will take the time to visit you and your organization to discuss the job thoroughly. This may include the preparation of a job description and person specification, and salary advice based on specialist knowledge of the market. This can be especially helpful with a newly created post
- do the sifting for you (saves time and money), and draw up a shortlist of suitable candidates with the appropriate skills, experience, qualifications and personality for the job
- when appropriate, advertise on your behalf in a selected newspaper or specialist journal, deal with the response, carry out preliminary interviews, and draw up a shortlist or sometimes advertise (at no cost to you) in one of their general advertisements
- provide a totally confidential professional service

It is advisable to find out the terms and conditions before using a recruitment agency. Some offer a free service to candidates and clients, and a fee is payable *only* when there is a successful placement.

INFORMATION FOR CANDIDATES

Before candidates attend your organization for interview, make sure they have received a job description and background information about the organization. A map may also be useful, particularly if your organization is in an out of the way location. Of course, a keen candidate will also do their own research on your organization.

It is in your interests to ensure that a candidate is well informed about your organization before attending the interview. There is an element of self-selection involved which means that a sensible candidate will withdraw at an early stage of the selection process if the job or organization appears unsuitable. Also, better use can be made of the interview time if the candidate already has a clear picture of both the job and your organization.

PLANNING THE INTERVIEW AND CHOOSING WHOM TO INTERVIEW

It is very important to plan the interview. The aim is to find the right person for the job. You decide whom you are going to interview from the application forms and CVs. At this stage the information on the application forms or CVs is probably all you know about the applicant. Check each form or CV against the person specification, and draw up a list of those that most closely match your requirements. You may have a second list that you might want to look at again. Keep these, but put firmly in the reject pile those you know are not suitable. It is probably fair to them to write a rejection letter immediately.

Presentation of application form, letter and CV is important. Is it roughly thrown together, badly laid out, full of errors? A CV may be so beautifully done that you suspect it may have been prepared by a third party? Does it ramble on inconclusively for ten pages? (no good if you are looking for a clear concise writer and thinker). Are there unexplained gaps? Check carefully. The applicants may have had a nervous breakdown or merely over-edited the relevant section in the wordprocessor. Is the handwriting legible? If not, will it matter in the day to day execution of his or her work?

Once you have finalized your shortlist of candidates for

interview (probably not more than six people), you should then contact them to arrange an interview, remembering that their applications should be treated in confidence. Try to plan your time so that you can offer to see some people in the early morning, lunchtime or after work. Not everyone is able to take leave at short notice to attend interviews.

If travel expenses are likely to be incurred, make your company policy clear. The timimg may mean an overnight stay. You may need to recommend a nearby hotel in the allowed price range, and reimburse first or second class rail travel, or offer a car allowance.

Re-read all of the applications carefully, and note any gaps in the recorded history that need explaining. Check each candidate's details against the person specification, and make a list of those things that you want to find out. This should be done on a clean sheet of paper, not scrawled on their form or CV (remember that smart people can read upside down!).

You should then plan the questions you intend to ask, and the order in which you will ask them. Until you are well practised in interviewing it is probably a good idea to have them written down. Start with the easy questions and leave the more difficult and personal questions to the end.

Care should be taken to ensure that no questions are included that could be construed as illegal (particularly in respect of any type of discrimination). If in doubt, seek advice.

CONTACTING THOSE YOU WISH TO INTERVIEW

It is important to pay great attention to when and where candidates can be contacted. The knowledge that they are job hunting could certainly prejudice their present employment. Again, you must be careful. If you have details from a recruitment agency you should contact the agency and tell them whom you wish to interview. They will know how and when to get in touch with the possible candidates. They will arrange a mutually convenient appointment for the interview, thus saving you valuable time.

PLAN THE PHYSICAL ENVIRONMENT

First you need to book a room, or make sure that you can clear your desk. Before the candidates arrive make sure that there is a comfortable chair, and plan whether you wish to sit at a desk, beside a desk, at a coffee table or in a boardroom. It is important to ensure that you are not disturbed (including telephone calls). Again, remember that the interview should be confidential.

Don't forget to notify others who may need to be involved with the interviews. If a panel is involved, try to allow time to meet the panel members and to discuss your requirements with them. See that they are given the job description, person specification, and a copy of each applicant's details in advance.

If you offer the candidate tea or coffee, try to arrange for someone to bring it in. If possible, borrow a clock so that you can keep a check on the time without looking at your watch. It can have a devastating effect on a candidate, particularly if you have a watch that needs a long hard look.

Make sure that your receptionist, or the first person who will greet the interview candidate, knows their name and the time of their appointment. Check that there is a pleasant place where they can wait (preferably well out of earshot), and that there is up-to-date, interesting reading matter available. If you have company details then these can be given to the candidate. If you have to keep candidates waiting, make sure that they are fully informed and that tea, coffee or a cool drink is offered.

A recent survey by the UK employment agency, Reed Employment, showed that such simple courtesies were often overlooked, and tended to give a bad impression of the company. To recruit successfully, companies need to market themselves as caring employers from the outset. A surprising statistic showed that while 4% of candidates said they had been late for interviews, 33% of employers admitted to being late. Worse still, nearly 40% (virtually three times the number of candidates) had either forgotten, misspelt or mispronounced the candidate's name. Over one fifth of employers confessed that they had spent less than ten minutes on preparation for the interview. An interview is a type of test, or examination, and there is no doubt that the better prepared you are, the better the interview will be. A comparatively small investment of your time at this stage could have the effect of saving hours of time and money at a later stage.

The library information world is not overly large. There is a good chance that you may know, or know of, your interviewee or their colleagues. Likewise, they may well know you, or know of you. It cannot be said often enough that job applications should be treated in the utmost confidence. Candidates are known to avoid applying for jobs in certain organizations where there are known contacts between their manager and the manager of the department with the vacancy, because they are terrified that comments will be made. It is important that you respect that confidentiality, but do not be afraid to ask for the same courtesy in return. You may not wish it to be known publicly that you are recruiting.

HOW LONG SHOULD THE INTERVIEW LAST?

This is a difficult question, and often has no bearing on the final decision. It could last anything from 20 minutes to one and a half hours, depending on:

- the level of seniority of the candidate
- the amount of work experience
- the number of applicants you have to see and the time you have available

There may be times when tests need to be completed, or personnel officers need to see the candidates which will add to the time spent. Inform candidates in advance, and if you want candidates to bring examples of their work to the interview, tell them beforehand.

It is extremely important to give yourself enough time between interviews – again, ensuring that you are not interrupted – to write an interview report on the candidate you have just seen. Note any points or areas you omitted to cover so that you can pick them up next time, and any particular comments you have about the candidate while everything is fresh in your mind. Then prepare for the next candidate by familiarizing yourself with their details. After a day of interviewing it is easy to confuse one candidate with another. There is always the nightmare that you will not be able to recall anything about an individual ('He was a tall short woman, with dark grey black hair and a bright red blue suit' is the classic jumbled picture that springs to mind!).

◆ The interview

You should try to establish a rapport with the interviewee. Be polite, friendly and welcoming. Try to relax them. If they are relaxed they will reveal more about themselves. A good icebreaker is to ask questions that are not related to the job such as 'did you find us all right?' You can always resort to discussing the weather if you are really stuck.

Start by outlining the interview plan and reminding them of how long you expect it to take. Make it clear that they should do most to the talking ('First I'll ask you to tell me about yourself, then I'll tell you about the job and answer any questions you may have'). You can save valuable time and tedious repetition by having sent as much information about the job and the organization as possible in advance.

Try not to take too many notes. Use the time you have allowed at the end to write a useful summary. If your head is down while you scribble during the interview you will be in danger of losing the rapport you have worked to establish, and you will not be able to listen to what they are saying. It is polite to ask the candidate whether they mind you taking notes.

INTERVIEWING TIPS

- Ask **open questions**. Open questions elicit more than a yes or no answer. 'Tell me about . . .' is the most valuable phrase you can use. Others are 'What is your opinion of . . .', 'Why do you like/prefer/want to . . .', and so on.
- Don't be afraid of **silence**. Open questions can cause the candidate to stop and think. Even a few seconds may seem intolerable to the interviewer, but allow your applicant time to think. Resist the urge to leap in with another question to fill the gap.
- Ask **follow up questions** (sometimes called **probing** questions). Second or third questions on a topic may yield valuable information about the applicant. Don't hesitate to ask further questions if you feel the answer to your first question is still incomplete.
- **Show interest**. A smile and a nod where appropriate will greatly encourage the candidate and help to allay nerves.
- Use the **candidate's name** during the interview. Make sure that you get it right. Calling them by the wrong name can be devastating.
- Don't ask **leading questions**. They usually indicate the answer that you expect, e.g. 'We use on-line sources a lot. You can use

TEXTLINE, can't you?' The candidate may be tempted to answer 'yes' even if it is untrue.
- Don't interrupt unless you feel they are waffling about something completely irrelevant. Some candidates like to give very full answers to open questions. Interrupting will throw them completely, and you might miss something important.
- The **over-talkative** candidate may need to be interrupted. Try to do it at the end of a sentence. Useful phrases include: 'Thank you, that was interesting, but can we now turn to . . .' 'Can I ask you to move on to . . .'. It is usually easy to spot an over-talkative candidate at the outset. Try asking them for a *brief* account of . . . .

CLOSING THE INTERVIEW

Consult your interview plan before you draw the interview to a close. Make sure that there are no gaps in the information you have requested.

Remember to give information about the job, hours of work, pay, etc. This can be left until the second interview, but no later.

It is important to be aware that the interview is a **two way process**, therefore you should ask the candidate:

- do you have any questions?
- is there anything else you would like to add?

If you feel confident that the candidate is good and that you will want to see them again, it may be sensible to show them the work environment at this stage. Candidates often assume that if they have not seen the work place then they are not in the running. Candidates are certainly taking a risk if they accept a job without seeing where they will work. One information department, with high staff turnover, never showed candidates the information department in advance (choosing to interview them in the plush surroundings of the company boardroom), because they knew that they would not be so keen once they had seen that it was in a windowless, unpainted basement.

Summarize briefly the details discussed, then tell the candidate when you will be in touch, whether there will be a second interview, and so on. See the candidate to the front door.

Now, sit and make a summary of your notes. In particular, go carefully through the person specification. Note any particular comments about the candidate while they are fresh in your mind. Try to be objective. You should also note any points or areas you wish to explore further so that you can pick them up if you choose to interview the candidate a second time.

If you are seeing a few people on the same day (three is an optimum number, four the absolute maximum), then it is a good idea to make notes on what they wore and their physical appearance (some personnel departments now take a polaroid photograph of all candidates, just as an *aide mémoire*).

◆ The selection process

Only you will know which candidate best fits both the job and person criteria you have drawn up, so sit down with your interview notes and your immediate summary and make a checklist. Select those candidates who most closely match your person specification. Remember that some requirements are more important than others. It is important to try to remain objective. Avoid assumptions. Look for evidence from their application details or your interview notes to back up your conclusions.

Sometimes you will find that you have difficulty in choosing two or three candidates to invite for a second interview. On occasion one candidate is clearly ahead of the others, at other times no particular individual shines through, and you really do have to make a hard choice between two or even three evenly matched candidates.

No one can really help you in this situation. Take some quiet time and go through the details again. Look more closely at the desirable requirements.

If no candidate measures up to your requirements you have to decide whether to 'make do' – often a recipe for disaster – or whether to start the whole recruitment process again. It is often a good idea here to reassess your criteria and see if you can make any sensible compromises.

MAKING THE OFFER

The initial offer can be made verbally, and should then be followed by a written offer that includes the following details:

- job title and reporting structure
- start date
- the starting salary, and frequency and method of payment
- any benefits applicable
- hours of work
- holiday entitlement
- sickness pay
- confirmation of any specific details such as shift work

This letter forms part of the contract of employment, and it is essential to get the details right. Make it clear that candidates should contact you if there are any queries.

REFERENCES

You *must ask the candidate's permission* first. People have lost jobs or chances of promotion purely because of the unprofessional conduct of possible future employers.

References can be taken up before offering a candidate the job. If taken up after you have offered the job, then you may want to make the offer conditional upon the receipt of satisfactory references.

There are four main types of reference:

- testimonial (written statement of good character)
- letters to candidates' referees
- structured reference forms
- telephone references

Ideally, you are seeking confirmation of a candidate's period of employment with the company in question, the position they held, an indication of their standard of work, and such details as honesty, punctuality and, perhaps most interesting, whether or not they would re-employ them.

Remember that this can be an imposition on people's time. It is courteous to include a stamped addressed envelope if you expect a written reference.

REJECTION LETTERS

These are never pleasant letters to write. You should remember to reject all of the unsuccessful candidates at each stage as you eliminate them. Do not, however, reject those who you felt were a possible choice until you have a written acceptance from your number one choice. You may need to tell these candidates that the decision has been delayed, but it is better than telling them they are effectively second-best. Letters should be courteous and gentle, encouraging unsuccessful candidates and wishing them well in other job applications they may make.

RECRUITMENT COSTS

The direct costs are easy to quantify:

- advertising
- agency fees
- postage/photocopying costs
- travel expenses where appropriate
- relocation costs

The indirect costs, though, are hard to estimate. Some are more indirect than others:

- planning time – to prepare job descriptions, person specifications and write advertisements
- time taken to read through applications and respond appropriately
- booking specific interview rooms and completing the actual interviews. To this should be added the time of any other people involved.

Getting it wrong can cost a fortune. It can affect tempers, morale in the department, and can occasionally cause other staff losses. This can do untold harm to the department's (or even company's) image and undo previously good public relations.

RECRUITMENT MISTAKES

The statistics of those new recruits who leave their new employment within months, weeks, or even days, of commencing can make depressing reading. The normal reasons are failure to 'fit in', uncertainty about the work required of them, resentment of management style or, worst of all, a feeling of having been misled at the interview stage.

The underlying cause of a recruitment failure almost always arises from a series of false assumptions being made both by candidate and organization. The employer may not have thought through clearly what the job involves and what sort of person is needed, and consequently selects the candidate on the basis of inaccurate or inadequate information. This may be compounded by poor interview techniques, where the employer assumes (wrongly) that the candidate is suitable, without objective and thorough questioning at interview stage. Likewise, the candidate, keen to get a job, assumes without further investigation that the organization and position are just what they are looking for.

INDUCTION – FINAL STAGE OF THE SELECTION PROCESS

It is tempting to skip induction on the basis that newly appointed staff are almost always desperately needed and therefore required to be productive from day one. However, it has been proven time and time again that a good, timely induction programme reduces staff turnover.

Induction is covered by Sylvia Webb in her chapter on 'Staff Training', but here are a few pointers. Help the new candidate settle in. Make sure all your own department are fully informed. Where possible, let others in the immediate area, or contact areas, know as well (security, reception, mailroom, etc.). Ensure that the new candidate's desk is clear, and that new pens, pads, etc, are available. See that a colleague is assigned to show them the facilities.

Try to make sure that new staff are introduced to as many relevant people as possible on their first day. Be friendly and welcoming, and encourage colleagues to be the same. Make the new person feel part of the team. You need their loyalty and commitment from day one.

Nothing is more satisfying than observing a cohesive, productive, happy team of people at work, except perhaps, knowing that you have successfully recruited them yourself.

◆ Sample job descriptions and person specifications

JOB DESCRIPTION

Job Title: Librarian/Information Officer

Location: City of London

Responsible to: Manager Information Services

Main Purpose of Job: To assist in the provision of an information service to the Corporate Finance Department, and to deputize for the Manager Information Services

Responsibilities:
- Identify and access appropriate sources of hard copy and on-line information (using a wide range of hosts in response to enquiries received from the London office and other offices located in Europe)
- Manage journal and book acquisitions
- Catalogue/classify internal information resources, reports and presentations
- Develop and use internal databases (Inmagic, Paradox, Wordperfect, Lotus 123)
- Enhance specialist collection of European financial information
- Train staff in use of databases and other information services
- Deputize in absence of Manager Information Services, including some supervision of library assistant

PERSON SPECIFICATION

Job Title: Librarian/Information Officer

1. **Physical**
   Essential: No requirement other than normal good health
   Desirable: Non-smoker preferred
2. **Education**
   Essential:
   Desirable: Professionally qualified librarian or information scientist
3. **Experience**
   Essential: At least two years' relevant library/information experience. Knowledge of business information sources
4. **Skills**
   Essential: On-line searching experience
   Good keyboard skills
   Good knowledge of at least one (preferably two)

European languages, particularly French, Italian, Spanish or German
Good communication skills

Desirable: Knowledge of Inmagic, Paradox and spreadsheets
Familiarity with Datastream and Textline

5. **Personality**
   Essential: Outgoing, resilient, good team worker, able to handle pressure and work to deadlines
   Desirable:

6. **Intelligence**
   Essential: Flexible, quick thinker
   Desirable:

7. **Circumstances**
   Essential: Able to work additional hours (e.g. evenings) if required
   Desirable: Reasonable commuting distance of City of London

JOB DESCRIPTION

Job Title: Assistant to Records Manager

Location: Nottingham

Reporting to: Records Manager

Purpose of Job: To assist the Records Manager in the day to day running of the Records Management Service

Duties:
- Receiving data from within the organization for addition to company records
- Recording and updating holdings of company records on the CAIRS database
- Using word processor (Wordperfect) to update and circulate retention schedules
- Identifying records due for review and destruction
- Maintaining file retrieval system on the CAIRS database, including chasing up overdue records
- Dealing with enquiries and requests for records from within the organization
- Assisting in operating restricted access to records, including handling of confidential information

PERSON SPECIFICATION

Job Title: Assistant to Records Manager

1. **Physical**
    Essential: Must be physically fit and able to lift boxes of files, plans, etc.
    Desirable: Non-smoker preferred
2. **Education**
    Essential: Educated to O-level or equivalent standard
    Desirable: Willingness to study for the City & Guilds Records Management Certificate is an advantage (the employer will encourage and support an employee working towards this qualification)
3. **Experience**
    Essential: No requirement for previous experience
    Desirable: Some previous office experience, especially of filing systems, would be an advantage
4. **Skills**
    Essential: Accurate keyboard skills 30–40 wpm
    Helpful telephone manner
    Desirable: Knowledge of WordPerfect
    Knowledge of CAIRS database
5. **Personality**
    Essential: Must be methodical, well organized, with attention to detail
    Desirable: Able to work unsupervised
    Ability to communicate with people at all levels within the organization
6. **Circumstances**
    Essential: Able to work 9.30–5.30 Monday to Friday
    Desirable: Within commuting distance of Nottingham

◆ UK Recruitment law

1. **Data Protection Act 1984**
    Regulates the use of automatically processed data relating to individuals and the provision of information from such data.
2. **Disabled Persons (Employment) Acts 1944 and 1958**
    Enables persons who suffer certain types of disability to find work suited to their abilities and general qualifications.

3. **Employment Agencies Act 1973**
   Regulates the licensing and conduct of employment agencies.
4. **Equal Pay Act 1970**
   Provides a policy of equal pay for equal work, and aims to prevent discrimination against women workers as regards terms and conditions of employment.
5. **Race Relations Act 1976**
   Makes it unlawful to discriminate (either directly or indirectly) on grounds of colour, race, nationality, or ethnic or national origin in the employment field.
6. **Rehabilitation of Offenders Act 1974**
   Provides protection to previously convicted persons by forbidding unauthorized disclosure of their previous convictions after a certain length of time, thus making it easier for the ex-offender to obtain employment.
7. **Sex Discrimination Act 1975**
   Makes discrimination on the grounds of sex or marital status unlawful.

◆ References

Courtis, J. (1985) *The IPM Guide to Cost-effective Recruitment* (2nd edn), London: Institute of Personnel Management.

Mackenzie Davey, D. and McDonnell, P. (1975) *How to Interview*, London: British Institute of Management.

Plumbley, P.R. (1980) *Recruitment and Selection* (4th edn.), London: Institute of Personnel Management.

Ray, M. (1980) *Recruitment advertising: a means of communication*, London: Institute of Personnel Management.

Reed Employment (1990) *Successful recruiting*, Tolworth, Surrey: Reed Employment Marketing Department, 1990.

Rodger, A. (1970) *The Seven Point-plan* (3rd edn.), London: National Institute of Industrial Psychology.

2 Motivation of staff

Beryl Morris

- What is motivation and why is it important
- Motivation theories
- Practical methods of motivation
- The manager's role in motivating staff
- Motivation and the poor performer
- What else should managers be doing?

Staff motivation is one of the greatest challenges facing library and information managers today. As staff become more scarce and the pressure to make optimum use of this key resource increases, the importance of making the most of our staff will become paramount.

Motivating staff becomes more difficult at times of change. A characteristic of library and information work over the past decade has been the pace of change in terms of both technology and demand – and this in a situation where many of the organizations employing librarians and information professionals are themselves undergoing extensive change and cut back.

Much research has been carried out into what makes people motivated and helps them work well. This chapter examines some of this theory in terms of its usefulness in the library/information context. There is also consideration of some of the factors that contribute to people's motivation, and the need to tackle so-called 'poor performance' is briefly addressed.

◆ What is motivation and why is it important?

We are motivated when we freely pursue goals with energy and enthusiasm. The key question is whose goals? For most managers, the challenge is to help match an individual's goals with those of the organization.

Related to this, we often assume that someone who is performing less well than they might – for example, persistent absenteeism or lateness – is suffering from poor motivation. This may be so, but as we will see, motivation is a complex subject, and it is dangerous to leap to such speedy conclusions.

◆ Motivation theories

Although motivation is very complex, numerous writers have attempted to understand what motivation is and why it is important. And over the years, a number of theories have been propounded which shed light on the motivation of staff.

Prior to the 20th century it was felt that employees had few rights, and that paying staff a wage was enough to ensure their loyalty and commitment. This notion was refined by Frederick Taylor, an American, whose theory of Scientific Management suggested that staff (men in this case) were motivated purely by money. They did not want responsibility and needed close supervision to ensure that they did not slacken. Taylor took this view a stage further and propounded that the work could be narrowed down to specific tasks and the men could be trained in these tasks until they were proficient. Taylor's approach, which laid the foundations for piece-work, was very influential, and although it has largely been discredited it still appears to be alive and well in a number of organizations.

The more modern work on motivation commenced in the 1920s, also in the USA, and tends to be known as the 'human relations school of management'. Perhaps the first to recognize the importance of people in the work process was Elton Mayo, who carried out a series of experiments at the Hawthorne Works of the Western Electric Company in the US. Mayo was attempting to determine the effects of changes in the working environment on productivity. For example, it was felt that if the lighting was improved, the rate of work should also increase. What Mayo's research found, however, was that the control group also experienced an increase in productivity without any change in conditions. It was deduced from this that taking an interest in staff was much more important in encouraging motivation than a change in environment.

Mayo also discovered that most employees have a need for a

stable and social work group, and that the group had a more significant effect on the staff's behaviour than the formal messages emanating from management. This relates to Maslow's findings which are described below. Mayo has been criticized for being somewhat selective in reporting his findings. However, his work did refute the work of Taylor, which assumed that the use of incentives would be sufficient to improve productivity and is very important in terms of practical motivation, as we shall see later in this chapter. It also gave the phrase the 'Hawthorne effect' to the English language, meaning that the results of an experiment can be distorted by the attention paid to the subject.

Following the Second World War, the work of the Human Relations School became more influential. Abraham Maslow, a researcher in the USA, developed his theory of human needs. These were not just work-related, but were important in determining what helps people to work well. Maslow suggested that humans have a hierarchy of needs. These range from the basic need for survival to the need for self-actualization. His hierarchy is shown in Figure 2.1.

Maslow's lower order needs relate to our need for survival and to shelter. The saying 'man does not live by bread alone' is true unless there is no bread! According to Maslow, if our lower order needs are not fulfilled we cannot aim any higher, so we will never feel a sense of achievement or attainment. As we shall see, this is important to staff motivation at work. Maslow also drew attention to people's need for love and affection, i.e. to belong. This echoes the Hawthorne experiment, and again it is important to remember.

At the top of Maslow's pyramid is the need for self- and others' esteem, as well as the need for self-actualization or ego. These needs are very complex and probably the most difficult to attain. Also, it has to be emphasized that we are all different, and what motivates one person may not have a positive effect on others. Similarly, it is suggested that different factors motivate us at different times. The only certainty is that there are no easy answers with anything to do with people.

Another theorist who had a significance in the 1950s was Frederick Herzberg. Herzberg interviewed a number of professional staff – engineers and accountants – and asked them about incidents at work that made them feel positive or negative. From their responses he developed lists of positive and negative factors. The negative factors (which he called **job dissatisfiers**) were:

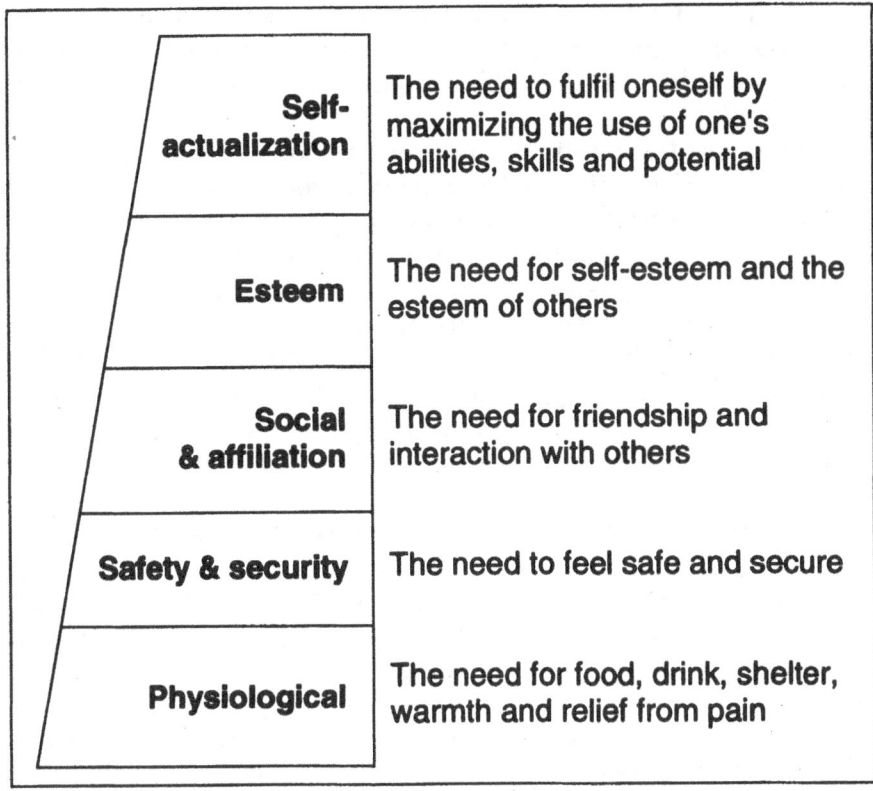

Figure 2.1

- policy and administration
- supervision
- relationship with supervisor
- work conditions
- salary

The positive factors (called **motivators**) were:

- achievement
- recognition
- the work itself
- responsibility
- advancement

Herzberg's dissatisfiers became known as **hygiene factors**, i.e. they fulfill a preventive function but not a curative one. To take salary as an example, Herzberg suggested that a low salary would act as a demotivator. However, if the salary were increased, in the long term it would cease to be important, rather than motivate positively.

Herzberg restricted his theory to work motivation, and although he, too, has been criticized for using a very small and selective sample, his findings do bear a remarkable similarity to those of Maslow. His **motivational factors**, as they are called, equate to the top two levels of Maslow's pyramid, and demonstrate the importance of giving staff responsibility and recognition as well as a say in their work. Herzberg also identified the importance of the supervisor in motivating employees, which suggests that all staff in a management role should have training that includes a discussion of motivation and an awareness of the practical issues which need to be addressed.

The other major writer on motivation was Douglas McGregor, a professor at the Massachusetts Institute of Technology. McGregor developed Maslow's work, and suggested that successful managers take human nature into account when managing their staff. McGregor identified two distinct management approaches – theory X and theory Y.

McGregor's theory X relates to Taylor's work in that employees are regarded as being basically lazy and need to be watched constantly. The theory X manager believes that people lack ambition, are resistant to change, dislike work, and avoid it at all costs. A theory X manager assumes total control for his or her staff, directs all their work, and leaves no scope for initiative or responsibility.

The theory Y manager, on the other hand, believes that, with enough support and encouragement, people are capable of motivating themselves. In this case, the task of the manager is to provide the right sort of atmosphere to support staff in their work. They also pay attention to staff training needs, particularly those aimed at helping staff achieve their potential, and they spend time helping staff to reconcile their own goals with those of the organization and encouraging them to become more involved in their work.

Theory Y is clearly an optimistic view of people. There are those who would say it is naïve, unrealistic, and only appropriate to staff in more senior positions. However, one particularly important aspect of McGregor's work is the notion that we actually get the staff we deserve! Because a theory X manager emphasizes control, he or she is likely to get staff who are less confident and therefore need more supervision, whereas a theory Y manager will encourage staff to give their best. This self-fulfilling prophecy is also important in terms of practical motivation.

Finally, the last theory of motivation to be outlined here is the equity theory. This has received much attention lately as it suggests that our own motivation is tied up with our observations of others. In a library and information context, this can be important as staff are often lower paid and treated less well than other groups of staff. This seems to be a particular problem in education and the public sector, where library and information staff may be on lower salary scales and receive fewer benefits than other groups, yet they may also feel they are working longer hours and are very visible. The equity theory is complex, but it relates to Herzberg's **hygiene factors** which suggest that attempts to improve conditions, salary, etc., only go so far, and may be important to bear in mind when considering comparability.

◆ Practical methods of motivation

Practical methods of motivation are complex, and some demand a considerable investment of time and money. They fall into several areas.

HYGIENE FACTORS/BASIC NEEDS

Although attention to environmental and other matters may not positively motivate staff, if we ignore people's needs in this area we are likely to be creating problems for ourselves in the long-term.

Of course, staff are entitled to a decent working environment. This includes attention to health and safety issues, but it also means ensuring that offices and other work areas are clean and welcoming. This is essential for those organizations with customers in any case, but it is often the case that conditions for staff are far worse. The investment needed is sometimes very little, but it does demonstrate that staff actually matter, which is an important factor in encouraging commitment.

Other basic needs include a decent salary. According to some management texts, no one in work is short on their physiological needs. But library staff are not always well paid, and if we believe that equity with others is important, salary becomes significant. Other aspects of work relating to this area may include adequate catering provision, particularly important if staff work in the evenings or weekends; help with accommodation if necessary, and a safe working environment. Sadly, this is becoming increasingly problematic as staff in the public sector particularly are subject to verbal and physical abuse. Some organizations have developed special strategies to help with this issue.

Safety needs include attention to health and safety (as mentioned above), pension and sickness provision, and job security, although this latter seems to be increasingly difficult to guarantee.

A less obvious, but important factor that contributes to an individual's security is basic training, which helps staff to feel competent and confident at work. This should include induction training to introduce individuals to the organization and make them feel more secure. Information, too, is important to people's security, and attention to communications systems, particularly those encouraging communication upwards, is an important consideration.

BELONGING/SOCIAL NEEDS

Managers often think that belonging refers only to a work group or team. However it is much broader, and includes the need to make people feel part of the organization by involving them in the decisions which affect them. Participation is often neglected, with the consequence that staff feel no commitment to what is proposed. If consultation is not feasible because of time or other constraints, there should at least be adequate communication of not just what is going to happen, but also why it is going to happen.

Other activities that can help staff feel they belong include in-house training, but only after the member of staff feels secure in their work group. Team working and a recognition of the importance of informal groups and social events also help the feeling of belonging, although these activities can also be threatening for staff if not handled well.

Staff working in isolation may have particular problems in feeling that they belong. Line managers need to make a special attempt to involve such staff, and to make sure that communication is frequent. Staff themselves might find it useful to find a network or support group either within the organization or outside that relates to their professional interests.

REWARD AND RECOGNITION

Tangible rewards such as a pay increase may be difficult to offer, although there is an increasing use of performance related pay in a variety of organizations. However, it costs nothing to say, or write, thank you to staff, and making those thanks public through newsletters, etc., can be even more motivating. Thanks and recognition must be genuine: staff will see through such gestures if they are given for the wrong reasons. Performance appraisal is also covered in Sylvia Webb's chapter on training.

Training can also be seen as a reward, although as with all examples of recognition, one always has to be careful to be fair. It is easy to reward the person who is good at selling themselves. Staff who are less forthcoming should also be singled out, although it may be more difficult to become aware of their achievements. Appraisal schemes can help in this respect, but they need to be carefully designed so as to remove any element of threat.

SELF-ACTUALIZATION

According to Maslow, this is the most difficult need to attain, and is probably the most personal. However, work that helps staff to develop their potential and which is meaningful and interesting is likely to help. Training can help, but other methods such as shadowing, secondments and personal development projects may be more useful in the long-term.

Tom Peters (1988) stresses that if we are able to engage people through the use of training, the impact on them and, in turn, the organization is immeasurable. One organization that has taken this on board is the Ford Motor Company. Their EDAP (Employee Development Assistance Project) allows all employees, at whatever level, to receive funding for further education which does not have to be job related. To date, a large number of employees have taken advantage of the scheme, and Ford have found that not only are staff more motivated, but that it is helping them to recruit and retain staff within the organization.

Another UK-based organization that offers staff secondments as a boost to their motivation is the John Lewis Partnership, which is making a particular effort to train and develop older workers. Staff over 50 are eligible to take a six month sabbatical, which can either be work related or for non-work reasons such as for travel. This not only helps the individual, but it provides valuable experience for someone to cover their work while they are away. A number of other organizations are also looking at these options.

Other approaches that can be used to help staff develop their skills and so attain more job satisfaction include job rotation and job enrichment. Job rotation entails giving people a variety of work by swopping responsibilities on a regular basis. This means that the person in charge of serials swops with the person responsible for inter-library loans, thus gaining experience of both. In many small libraries, job rotation probably happens by default as there are too few people to allow a rigid demarcation. In other libraries, there would be trades union opposition to such a suggestion.

Job enrichment is a broader approach, and involves giving staff additional responsibility which helps them develop their skills and confidence. Examples include looking at ways in which to promote the library or information service, or researching a specific topic such as performance related pay. Writing and presenting the report is an important part of the process. As with all attempts at motivation, it is vital to avoid exploitation in the negative sense, so that staff are not being paid for the work they carry out.

◆ The manager's role in motivating staff

If we believe Herzberg, the manager has a crucial role to play in motivating staff. Many of the points made above relate to organizational activities, but what can the individual manager do to make their staff feel more committed?

First, the manager must be aware that staff are probably their most important resource. Certainly, this is likely to be true in cost terms, but it should also be true in achieving the organization's objectives. A manager who takes an interest in their staff, who says thank you for a job well done (and genuinely means it!) and gives adequate help and support is more than half way there, whereas a manager who is dismissive of staff effort is unlikely to receive the staff's support and help when it is important.

Other activities that can help include 'Walking the Job' or 'Management By Walking About', i.e. getting out, visiting and talking to staff in their place of work. MBWA was coined by Tom Peters but was pioneered by Hewlett Packard, amongst others. It is a definite move away from ivory tower management which sadly has been practised in a large number of organizations, including libraries and information units, in the past.

MBWA is an important and necessary way of keeping in touch with staff (and with customers), and helps to lessen the 'them and us' attitude. The object of MBWA is to observe, listen and praise. It is not to criticize or to check on staff. For it to be successful it needs to be regular: it is imperative to schedule time in busy diaries or the impetus will be lost. Making the visits informal helps to avoid the 'visiting Royal' approach, although it is only polite to tell the local manager when you have arrived! Seeing and being seen is one of the most important aspects of motivating staff.

Another aspect is leading by example. If, as a manager, you make pronouncements about attitudes towards customers, lateness, style of dress, etc., you will do tremendous damage if you are seen to flout your own advice! Staff will soon learn to do what you do, not what you say, so your own role is very important. As someone once said, 'His (sic) actions were talking so loudly, they couldn't hear what he was saying.'

Other activities managers should do to help motivate their staff include taking staff concerns and doubts seriously. Our own perspective is bound up with our experience, and it is easy to dismiss staff complaints as histrionic when we know more or are not putting up with the same problems every day. However, putting yourself in other people's shoes is often very salutary, and can help make you more receptive to others' fears and doubts. Remember also Maslow's Hierarchy: if staff feel that their security or livelihood is threatened, it is very difficult for them to be motivated.

Similarly, many managers tend to oversupervise their staff. By constantly checking people's work, such managers find mistakes, enabling them to believe their staff are useless and cannot be trusted, thus becoming part of McGregor's self-fulfilling prophecy. Staff, in turn, become obsessed with detail, and eventually lose their confidence and commitment. This has led writers such as Tom Peters and Sir John Harvey Jones (1989) to suggest that there are no poor staff, only poor managers. This may be considered as too extreme, but most writers on motivation suggest that positive reinforcement is far more effective than constant criticism. This is easier if managers walk the job as suggested above, as this gives opportunities for thanks and praise. Similarly, getting to know the staff helps to recognize their achievements. Of course, poor performers will still exist, and the following section examines this problem in more detail.

Finally, another important aspect of the manager's role is to eliminate demotivating factors. Titles such as junior staff (who may have been in the service for 40+ years) are insulting, as is the use of the term 'non', e.g. non-professionals or non-academics. In British universities, the traditional hierarchies such as access to senior common rooms seems barbaric, and must undo many attempts to make staff feel they matter to the organization. In any organization there are rules and rituals that make at least some staff feel inferior. Make an effort to identify these rules and tackle them if you can.

◆ Motivation and the poor performer

As we have already seen, according to some writers there are no poor performers, only poor managers. Others put it down to inefficient recruitment and selection procedures. Whoever is the culprit – and it is usually a combination of a number of factors – poor performance must be tackled. Not only does it cost an organization a considerable amount of time and money, but the effect on other employees is very negative, which in turn has an impact on the total organization.

The stages in tackling poor performance are clearly laid down by Stewart and Stewart (1982), but they stress, as would all other writers, that prevention is always better than cure.

DETECTION AND CAUSES

Detecting poor performance is easier in some areas of work than in others. Bad customer care, for example, may be evident very quickly if the number of customers diminishes. Giving someone incorrect information, on the other hand, may not manifest itself for years, if at all. This section looks at ways in which to determine poor performance, but it must be stressed that it only scratches the surface.

Persistent absenteeism and lateness are two of the most common examples of poor performance. Others include the quality and quantity of work falling off or being low in comparison with others. Dishonesty, conflict with managers, public or peers and a lack of commitment all have a negative effect on the organization, and must be tackled. Other forms such as an inability to delegate, poor decision making and 'attitude' problems are more difficult to measure, and may well be the result of a lack of confidence and relevant training as much as anything else.

Methods of detecting poor performance include performance appraisal. This is probably too infrequent to be truly effective, but it does give an opportunity for an employee and his or her manager to discuss the individual's work.

Analysis of data is probably more useful, but only applies if the person's work is measurable in productivity terms. Standards of performance are useful and, at present, all too rare in library and information units. They do, however, give concrete information that can be used to measure a person's work.

The causes of poor performance are legion, and reflect the complex nature of the individual as stressed under motivation theory. Sometimes, the person's ability is inadequate for the job and any amount of training and coaching will make little difference. The 'Peter Principle', where someone has risen beyond their level of competence, is an illustration of this. Those who subscribe to McGregor's theory Y find this view disturbing, as McGregor suggests that anything is possible with the right help and support.

Similarly, a person's skills or experience may be insufficient for the work they are expected to do. Here, attention to training and confidence building should help. In addition, some form of mentoring and support may be useful.

Non-work difficulties can cause a reduction in performance. Most people find it difficult to completely divorce home from work, so problems with partners, children, debt, etc., can manifest themselves in the work place. Similarly, alcohol and drug abuse, often the result of other problems or concern about health matters, can all cause a person's commitment to slip. The organization can also be a contributing factor: if an individual feels that his or her work is of little value, or the work group is hostile, the work carried out can be affected. This can be a particular problem for minority groups who may suffer from harassment which affects their work and saps their confidence and self-esteem.

Conditions of work can also be a cause of poor performance.

Long working hours and poor health and safety conditions tend to undermine people's confidence and commitment, which brings us back to the importance of Maslow's basic needs.

WHAT CAN BE DONE ABOUT POOR PERFORMANCE?

If staff are performing less well than they might, the manager must tackle the problem at the earliest opportunity. The tendency, though, is to leave matters and hope they improve. This can be dangerous as other staff can then begin to feel aggrieved if the problem is not addressed. There are various stages in addressing poor performance. It is important to keep discussions with the person concerned confidential, to concentrate on action and regular review rather than blame. However, records should be kept in case further problems occur. Where a system of performance appraisal is in operation, this should of course be used as part of the manager's armoury of techniques to combat poor performance.

It goes without saying that criminal activities, assault or harassment should be treated very seriously.

Other factors include having guidelines on absenteeism, etc., so that all staff know the standards that are expected. However, these should not go to extremes. There are organizations where the disciplinary and dismissal procedures are longer than the training policy. This could be construed as having one's priorities mixed up!

◆ What else should managers be doing?

As we have seen, motivation is a complex issue and takes time and effort to effect changes. Also, it is important to reiterate that what motivates one person will not automatically motivate another. This point is important for managers to accept, as they sometimes expect staff to have a similar commitment to their own. Bearing this in mind, effective strategies are those that recognize this individual nature, and treat staff with respect.

Training for managers is also crucial, and needs to be on a regular basis, not just when a manager joins the organization. Communication, too, is important both in terms of information about developments within the organization, and in clarifying individual roles. An enormous number of misunderstandings happen because people are not clear about what is expected of them.

Other strategies for making more effective use of staff include seeking their involvement and advice, particularly when new systems or approaches are considered. It is particularly important to ascertain staff views on issues that affect them, and it is management's responsibility to do this.

Finally, it is important for the manager to maintain his/her own motivation and commitment, for most staff will take their lead from their managers. This can seem difficult when resources are scarce and time is limited. Try to see the positive aspects of the job, clarify your own goals, and see problems as broadening your own experience. Above all, keep a sense of perspective: in that way you will be motivated, and your staff should be likewise.

◆ References

Harvey Jones, Sir J. (1989) *Making it Happen: Reflections on leadership*, London: Pan Books.

Herzberg, F. (1966) The motivation/hygiene theory. In Pugh, D.S. *Organisation Theory: Selected readings*, London: Penguin Books.

Jones, N. and Jordan, P. (1987) *Staff Management in Library and Information Work* (2nd edn.), Aldershot: Gower.

McGregor, D. (1960) *The Human Side of Enterprise*, New York: McGraw-Hill.

Maslow, A. (1954) *Motivation and Personality*, New York: Harper & Row.

Peters, T. (1988) *The Customer Revolution* (Video), London: BBC Enterprises.

Rooks, D. (1988) *Motivating Today's Library Staff*, Pheonix: Oryx Press.

Stemp, P. (1988) *Are You Managing?* London: Industrial Society.

Stewart, V. and Stewart, A. (1982) *Managing the Poor Performer*, Aldershot: Gower.

There are numerous books on motivation and management theory. The work of Tom Peters is probably of most practical help.

3 Staff training and development

Sylvia P Webb

- The induction process
- Training for all
- Training objectives
- The training and development schedule
- The importance of wider professional involvement
- Evaluation
- External courses
- Managing your own training

Managers not only need to recruit but also to retain staff with the potential to help take the library/information service forward and to make the right impact on the organization. If this objective is to be achieved, effective staff development throughout their careers is essential. Development is a broader process than training, concerned with motivation, attitude and personal qualities, as well as with job related skills. The skills themselves may be put into place through training; building on and adding to what has been acquired represents development, which is a continuing process leading to the realization of an individual's full potential. It is also a lifelong process that contributes to personal as well as professional advancement. Those involved in seeking, finding, organizing and managing information, usually on behalf of others, require certain basic personal qualities as well as professional and technical skills and qualifications. Consider some of the recent job advertisements that you have seen – there is likely to have been just as much emphasis on personality and creative thinking as on technical and professional ability.

In 1989, A McDougall and R Prytherch observed in their preface to *Co-operative Training in Libraries*, 'Training has become established in most libraries as a primary activity affecting all areas of work. General staff morale, attitudes to users, competence, awareness and efficiency can all be enhanced by a regular and systematic scheme of training for all levels of staff.'

While agreeing with the latter part of this statement, it is doubtful whether a majority of managers would accept as accurate the initial comment. Also, while all types of libraries and information services undoubtedly benefit from the encouragement and support of staff training and development, managers in special libraries need to make a strong individual case for training in the absence of group or co-operative schemes.

◆ The induction process

So as a manager where should you start? As the King in *Alice's Adventures in Wonderland* answered, 'Begin at the beginning'. The total process of staff training and development starts on the day that a new member of staff joins the organization. If they are to be successful they will need to learn about the organization they are joining, and the environment in which it operates, as well as the specifics of the library and information department of which they are to become a key member. All staff should be encouraged to view their role as a key one, otherwise they and others might ask why it exists at all.

You will have started to consider the training requirement with your new recruit before the first day at work – in fact, you may well have discussed it during the interview. It may be that there is a standard training programme in place either for every new person who joins the organization, or for each new recruit to the library and information service. Whatever else exists, the starting point should be the induction programme. Although the format may vary between organizations, the purpose will be the same: to familiarize the new recruit with the organization, its activities and the way in which it operates. The content of the programme can be grouped under four main headings: the organization (what it does), the people (who does what), the surroundings (what is where), and the job (what the individual will be doing). It is important that the induction process begins as soon as possible. Even if the formal organization-wide programme is held only at certain times throughout the year, you as a manager can start the process on the first day. If new recruits are not given adequate information at an early stage, they may make assumptions and take actions which are inappropriate, possibly leading to difficulties which could have been avoided. It can be much more difficult to undo early misunderstandings than to provide accurate information at the start. Although it may be followed by a much more complex training and development programme, the induction process itself is a straightforward one. The first step will usually take place on the first day, and ideally should involve a discussion with a personnel officer, who will be able to present the organization and its work in general terms. This session also provides the new recruit with an opportunity to raise any questions relating to contractual matters or of a personal nature, and to seek any clarification which may be required. It is helpful for the personnel officer concerned to have some idea of the degree of detail that you think would be appropriate for this first meeting, given your own initial session with your new member of staff and any subsequent input planned by the personnel department, perhaps on the formal induction programme.

On this first day it is often best for the manager, as head of the department, to start with a brief meeting, introducing the new member of staff to the rest of the department as early on as possible. This can be followed by a more detailed discussion of the job and the department later in the morning. First, get the new recruit settled in. Show them where their desk is – personal space is important. To help them feel part of the team it can be a good idea for another member of the department to have the responsibility for a partial tour of the building, pointing out key areas, including the cloakrooms, and making a few initial brief introductions – not too many and not too detailed at this stage. Lengthier meetings with other departments and staff should be set up as a later part of the overall induction process. The main aim of the first day is to make the new person feel welcome and useful, so have some tasks planned so that he or she has an early opportunity to actually operate in the new work setting. This gives them a reason to familiarize themselves with the stock and systems, rather than just looking around without a direct purpose. It is important to strike the right balance between pointing out key elements of the service and how it operates, and allowing early participation. The first day will have a lasting effect, so you need to get it right and allow the new member of staff the opportunity to make the right impression.

Following the first day there will be a gradual build-up in the familiarization process, which will be greatly helped by the formal setting up of a number of meetings for the new employee, allowing them to meet colleagues and learn about the different functions within the organization. It is important that these are put into diaries and the people involved are briefed as to what you require of them. This also helps to indicate how important it is for information staff to be fully integrated, and to be aware of what is going on throughout the organization so they can provide the most appropriate service. Such meetings need to be properly paced, not all crammed into the first week, or left so long before they take place that their original purpose is lost. The number and depth of these meetings will vary according to the frequency and detail of the organizational induction programme, and should be arranged accordingly. Only in this way will new recruits be able to grow to understand the organization as an integrated whole, and to see how their role fits into it. This will then in time lead them to see how best to carry out their work so that they make the best possible contribution to the organization as a whole.

◆ Training for all

So far the discussion has centred on a new member of staff. That person will quickly become an established member of the department and, along with your other staff, needs to receive regular training, counselling and appraisal as part of their longer-term career development. Each individual will work in a different way; perhaps with a different level of responsibility. Therefore, although a common core of training will exist, there will in addition be specific areas where there are separate individual needs, requiring a different approach. How do you set about identifying and assessing the training needs of each individual and drawing up a schedule which will ensure that both the common core and the individual needs will be covered in a way most relevant to the organizational needs? Depending on the type of organization in which you work, there may already be a career structure in place for all staff. The training process would be part of this, and there are probably standard stages through which to proceed. Within that process there will need to be points at which specific individual requirements can be catered for. If you operate within an organization where the prevalent discipline is not that of librarianship and information science, but another professional field such as accountancy or law, then a modification of the standard company training programme may not be appropriate. If to date there has been no separate library and information training programme, one will have to be established.

IDENTIFYING TRAINING NEEDS

How do you set about designing appropriate training for all members of your department? There are a number of considerations which together could provide a starting point:

- what expectations are there of the job which the individual has taken on?
- what experience and abilities does he or she bring with them?
- what relevant in-house training is already available?
- who carries out that training?
- how much time does it take?
- what does it cost?
- is there money set aside in the budget for this purpose?

The responses to such central questions need to be thought out from both an organizational stance and a departmental viewpoint. Changes within an organization will lead to a different training philosophy, as illustrated in Leinbach (1990). Although it is necessary to identify the training and development needs of the individual, these should also be viewed in the wider perspective so that the outcome of such training will be part of a co-ordinated approach towards ensuring provision of an effective and efficient library and information service by all members of the team.

The two mechanisms most widely used in identifying and analysing staff training needs are the simple act of noting gaps in the individual's range of competences through daily interaction with that member of staff, and the performance appraisal or progress interview. The first should not just be left to chance – management awareness is a technique that needs to be worked at and built into the manager's daily routine until it becomes second nature. What sort of competences will you as a manager be looking for? The list will differ from individual to individual, from post to post, and from time to time, but the grouping in Figure 3.1 may provide useful pointers.

It is important to remember that effective management is not just concerned with cost-effectiveness; productivity is achieved where those managed feel that somebody cares. Motivation and self-esteem come about through knowing that those who have responsibility for your work also have concern for your well-being.

APPRAISAL

The second mechanism in identifying training needs for staff, the performance or progress appraisal or review (the words are used in various combinations to describe the assessment of an individual's performance at work), has been used very successfully in both the private and the public sector, although not necessarily at all levels or across all functions. The appraisal, if regularly and well conducted, does offer the individual the opportunity to have a strong involvement in his or her own development, helping in the assessment of future personal training and development needs on a continuous basis. The appraisal needs to be seen as a positive and constructive activity both for the manager and the individual being appraised. As such, both parties need to prepare, with the appraisal candidate being given, about two weeks in advance, a checklist of questions and ideas to act as a focus for that preparation. At the same time, the purpose of the interview needs to be put forward with the emphasis on the fact that it provides an opportunity for an exchange of thoughts on the way forward for the service as well as the individual. The appraisal, unfortunately, is still regarded by some as threatening, by others as a waste of time (often for the same underlying reason, even if not the stated one). This underlines the importance of careful scene-setting and management using a range of skills, not the least of which are listening skills and objectivity. The appraisal process as a whole has a number of objectives; for example, assessing the potential and suitability of an individual for longer-term promotion in any part of the organization, but here we are looking purely at its role in identifying training and development needs relating to a specific job within the library/information function.

Appraisals should take place at regular intervals, six months being the preferred timing, although twelve months may be the norm in a number of organizations. The appraisal should be seen rather as a formal co-ordination and culmination of other regular interaction which has taken place between the manager and the

1. **Professional skills**
   Enquiry work
   - telephone
   - face-to-face
   - external/internal
   - sources (use of)

   Classification
   - includes knowledge of subject areas

   Scanning

   Online searching

2. **Technical skills**
   - use of equipment
   - searching techniques
   - physical organization of resources
   - display work
   - non-book material

3. **Communication skills**
   - written
   - oral
   - aural

4. **Management skills**
   - note-taking
   - filing, e.g. invoices, correspondence
   - innovatory
   - administrative

5. **Personal and interpersonal aspects**

6. **General review of progress/training**

Figure 3.1 Discussion points for library staff appraisal interviews (Reproduced from Webb, S. P. (1991) *Personal Development in Information Work* (2nd edn.), London: ASLIB, with permission of the author and ASLIB)

member of staff during the period following the last appraisal, rather than the one and only chance for the individual to discuss his or her future. Intervening discussions will have been both formal and informal, may have included counselling or coaching sessions, and are likely to have been both long and short in duration.

However, when it comes to the appraisal plenty of time needs to be allowed. One and a half to two hours is normal, with the slot in the manager's diary best left open-ended to avoid putting either of the participants under pressure of time. This could result in the loss of discussion of perhaps the most important point which the appraisee has been mustering up the courage to raise. That diary slot should also be regarded as sacrosanct – nothing suggests a lack of caring more than the late postponement of an appraisal for which preparation has been made and expectations set.

In some organizations the appraisal process might include some form of self-appraisal. This usually involves the completion of a standard in-house form, and is likely to take place as part of the appraisee's preparation. The completed form would then be passed on to the interviewing manager to be considered in their own preparation for the appraisal.

The value of the trainee's as well as the manager's involvement in this process is that after open and regular discussion both will be able to understand and agree exactly what is required. This dialogue will give you as a manager valuable insight into the potential of each member of your staff and enhance relationships, as well as often acting as the trigger for your own thoughts on particular aspects of the service. It is important that the detail and outcome of the appraisal is recorded. This is necessary for the manager's personnel records and planning, and equally important as feedback for the individual on their performance. It should include a set of goals and objectives upon which to act.

The performance appraisal will also provide a natural means of formally assessing and evaluating overall the training that has taken place to date, with regular monitoring and supporting counselling at various appropriate points in the intervening period.

ORGANIZATIONAL IMPACT ON PLANNING TRAINING AND DEVELOPMENT

Training and development needs can also be identified through a number of broader observations and involvements by the manager, other than those relating to gaps in the individual's knowledge or skills or experience. These are likely to occur in the following areas:

- new activities within the organization
- new activities/services within the department
- the introduction of new equipment/technology

- reorganization of administrative systems (manual and/or automated)
- reorganization of library/information systems/procedures (manual/automated)
- as part of the formal training requirement either of the employing organization or of a professional association

◆ Training objectives

Given this wide-ranging set of possible reasons for training and development, attention needs to be paid to setting out the specific objectives for each requirement. What does each piece of training or development activity seek to achieve? It is against such objectives that any later evaluation will be measured. Any programme which you draw up or buy in needs to start with a clear statement of its objectives. This does not necessarily have to be a long statement; in fact, a few short sentences stating the key aims is usually preferable. The content and detail of the programme will vary considerably according to whether it is a single course or a long-term training programme that is being designed. The level of the envisaged participants, and whether this is to be a standard training programme for regular use, or to meet organizational requirements or those of a professional association, will also determine what should be included and how it should be covered.

◆ The training and development schedule

Having defined the objectives the next task is to set out the actual schedule of training and development events that the employee will follow. The schedule should follow a logical sequence in terms of building on earlier learning, and particularly in the initial stages be related to the day-to-day tasks which the individual will be performing.

The success of the programme will depend very largely on the support and encouragement given by the manager and other members of the department, a supportive climate within the employing organization as a whole, and the methods of training used.

As part of the decision-making process in selecting the most appropriate training available, for example, films, distance learning packages, on-line tutors. The method of training makes a tremendous difference to the trainee's perceptions of a subject or activity. Training methods need to be varied and participative, including visits and external courses as well as guided reading and learning on-the-job, and all need to be firmly underpinned by regular counselling.

◆ The importance of wider professional involvement

One aim of professional training and development is to create a broader awareness in the candidate of the profession as a whole, not just one small part of it. This means not only seeing others at work, handling different information sources and organizing and using them in different ways, but also getting involved in professional activities like those that form the basis of the various special interest groups that exist. These range from economic and business information interests to promotion and public relations, and provide a very direct means of learning about the subject, as well as providing the opportunity to form professional contacts and become part of a network. Both formal and informal networks are at the very heart of the library and information profession. By encouraging the new trainee to participate in such activities you will be introducing them to a range of potential longer-term career benefits. The effect of such participation is also likely to be seen quite quickly in the increased confidence and broader approach that will be exhibited by the trainee. With that sort of outcome, evaluation of that particular part of the programme should not be too difficult.

◆ Evaluation

However, the evaluation of training is not easy, as what is being sought, as well as justification for the expenditure of time and money, is a means of measuring the effectiveness of the training which has taken place. Evaluation takes a considerable amount of time, and is a somewhat imprecise process. It relies on subjective judgements rather than scientifically measured units of outcome. If you ask the questions 'Is the trainee working more effectively? Is he or she exhibiting new knowledge or skills?' you are evaluating the person, but not necessarily the training. The person's performance could have improved despite the training as well as because of it. So what practical means are there by which the training itself can be evaluated? A much used method in relation to courses and seminars is the post-course questionnaire. This can then be matched to a pre-course questionnaire which may have been completed by the participants about the hoped-for outcome of the course. An alternative or addition to the use of the post-course questionnaire is to ask the trainee to write a short report on the course and how it has or has not met their objectives, but the trainee would need to be carefully briefed about this in advance of the course and advised on the criteria by which he or she might judge the course's effectiveness and suitability. The timing of completion of such reports and questionnaires is also important in that enough time needs to elapse to allow the trainee to sit back from the course and view it objectively, but not so much that elements of the course are forgotten.

FEEDBACK

Discussion of, and feedback on, each piece of training is essential for both the manager and the candidate, and such interviews form another part of the evaluation process. In addition to any written comment made by delegates, they should be encouraged to discuss with their manager their feelings about the course, especially any highlights or problems. It may also be possible to have comment from the trainer involved about the individual's response and level of participation – this is especially easy to arrange if it is an internal course with an in-house trainer. From such feedback and discussion, the manager will be able to tease out those areas that need further attention, or those which may suggest that the individual is ready to take on new responsibilities. The trainee will feel involved in planning his or her own future, and may also take the opportunity to suggest initiatives which could benefit the service as a whole.

OBSERVATION AND COUNSELLING

Discussion forms a central part of the evaluation process, but so does observation. Two questions raised earlier were said to relate to evaluating the individual rather than the training. Having said that, it must also be said that the manager cannot fail to observe the outcome of the training as being successful or not. If the latter, then it is time to look at the method and execution of the training to assess its suitability for the candidate, before assuming that the individual has not absorbed the training. Of course, there may be personal learning difficulties in certain areas, or other reasons outside the work environment which may have influenced the individual's response to the training. This is the time for counselling to try and get at the underlying problem, and to assess whether a different approach would be more suitable. Prompt follow-up on feedback is important if the overall training process is to maintain its momentum for the individual who could feel vulnerable in such a situation.

◆ External courses

As well as taking advantage of any in-house training opportunities that may be available, it can be of benefit to the trainee to participate in externally organized courses, thus meeting and exchanging ideas with people of varying experience and representing a range of different organizations.

Organizations offering short courses of interest to librarians and information professionals vary widely. Most of the professional organizations are active in the field, as are the various educational establishments with library/information faculties. Additionally, there are private commercial organizations offering programmes designed to meet the needs of the profession.

It is also worth remembering that most short course organizers are able to run their existing courses or adapted courses or totally new courses, in-house. Whilst this method loses the benefit of views/ideas from outside one's own organization inherent in a public course, it can prove more economic and provide more closely tailored training.

◆ Managing your own training

What about the manager's own training and development needs? Who will look after those? The further up the hierarchy that you move, the more it is likely to be left largely in your hands to suggest what you need, to monitor the training press as well as the library and information journals and see what is new, what may be relevant and what is available. (Feona Hamilton, in her chapter on self-development, also contributes ideas on the manager's own development.)

Opportunities for your own development and training are likely to be identified in the light of developments within the organization and the sector within which you operate. However, it is equally likely that you will have your own regular appraisal during which your training needs will be discussed. This will take place with the partner or director to whom you report, but could also involve a member of the personnel department. It is the personnel department to whom you might turn should you feel the need for career counselling, which is another service some professional associations and specialist recruitment agencies offer.

One of the routes that a number of managers have chosen to pursue in seeking personal development is that of studying for a further qualification in librarianship or information science. Other options may be available through part-time study and distance learning. Those managers who already hold a qualification in the library and information field may decide to move outside it for their development, perhaps looking at the possibility of a management or computer studies qualification. For others, a well structured series of short courses, perhaps incorporating the use of multimedia distance learning packages, may provide a more appropriate path.

Whatever route you would like to pursue for yourself and your staff, the choice will be in part governed by what is available on a part-time or occasional basis, possibly locally in the case of a regular day release arrangement, and what is dictated by organizational policy and related support. The latter is essential to training and development of all kinds and at all levels if staff are to reach their full potential and their employer is to reap the benefits in terms of a highly motivated staff able to provide a dynamic and relevant service.

◆ References

Advisory Conciliation and Arbitration Service (ACAS) (1985) *Induction of new employees*, Advisory Booklet No. 7. London: ACAS.

Advisory Conciliation and Abritration Service (ACAS) (1988) *Employee appraisal*, Advisory booklet No. 11. London: ACAS.

Baker, D. (1986) *Training Library Assistants. Guidelines for training in libraries 6*, London: Library Association.

Conyers, A. (1986) *The evaluation of staff training (2nd ed.), Guidelines for training in libraries 2*. London: Library Association.

Hellen, B. (ed.) (1988) *Survey of Training Materials*, London: Library Association.

Lawson, I. (1987) *Appraisal and Appraisal Interviewing*, London: Industrial Society.

Leinbach, P.E. (ed.) (1990) *Personnel Administration in an Automated Environment*, New York: Haworth Press.

Long, P. (1986) *Performance Appraisal Revisited*. London: Institute of Personnel Management.

McDougall, A. and Prytherch, R. (eds.) (1989) *Cooperative Training in Libraries*, Aldershot: Gower.

Nicholson, H. (1991) *Staff Development: Getting it done. Personnel Training and Education*, 8(3), 65.

Webb, S.P. (1991) *Personal Development in Information Work* (2nd edn.), London: ASLIB.

4 Marketing and justification of the information service

Colin Offor

- What is marketing?
- Finding out about the market
- Marketing strategies and plans
- Pricing
- Promotion

At first sight the title of this chapter is rather odd. The juxtaposition of marketing and justification may seem to support the view that a high profile and good publicity, or the generation of high volumes of use, can of themselves be a basis on which a case for service financing can be built. Those of us who have been at the receiving end of cut-backs, redundancies or closure will attest to the fallacy of that argument.

However, there is a deeper sense in which the connection is real, and it relates to consideration of what we mean by 'marketing'. To those who have studied the subject this may seem obvious. Nevertheless, it is worth spending time ensuring that marketing is properly understood, if only because common usage is such that it is easy even for practitioners to use it as a synonym for promotion.

At a recent small business training weekend devoted to the concept of marketing, everyone acknowledged the significance of understanding customers and the broad range of thinking and disciplines that make up marketing. Asked at the end to write on a flipchart what the first marketing related activity each would do when they got to work on Monday, the answers which came back were along the lines of 'redesign our brochures'. This may be more of a comment on the quality of the trainers, but I think it is because the debasement of the work has become ingrained in our thinking.

So in this chapter we will look at:
- what marketing is
- finding out about your market
- marketing strategies
- pricing
- promotion

◆ What is marketing?

Let us start with a definition of marketing – that promulgated by the Institute of Marketing:

> 'Marketing is the management process responsible for identifying, anticipating, and satisfying customer requirements profitably.'

Inevitably, such a definition, in order to be brief, sums up some very large ideas in a few words, so it is worth looking at the key words in the definition in some more detail.

- **Identifying** It is a marketing function to find out who the customers and potential customers are, and what needs they have which the product or service can satisfy. This can pose something of a dilemma for the service department in a company – who is the customer? Is it the user or potential user, or is it the budget holder who pays the bills? This is an issue we will return to later in the chapter.
- **Anticipating** It is a marketing responsibility to examine and monitor trends so that the service is not overtaken by events, and doesn't go on providing the same service year in year out regardless of how the user's needs, working methods and environment may have changed.

These two points will, it is hoped, surprise no one. They are broadly in the market research area. But the next key word in the definition is:

- **Satisfying** I would imagine that many people would say that that is the professional part of the job, equivalent to that of a production department in a manufacturing company. Hardly a marketing role. But that is to ignore perhaps the most important phrase in the definition, which is
- **Customer requirements** Marketing is about putting customers and their needs at the centre of all aspects of the business. An understanding of all of the benefits and satisfactions which the

user wants from your service, and the structuring of all aspects of its operation and delivery to meet those needs is at the heart of real marketing. It has been summed up as the concept of 'making what you can sell instead of selling what you can make'.

Making the customer, and the satisfaction of his needs, the focus for the structuring and delivery of the service, and for the application of its resources, is where marketing and justifying the existence of the service come together.

It is worth noting that customer requirements apply not only to functional activities. This is perhaps rather easier to understand in relation to consumer products, where brand values are often little to do with actual performance.

It used to be the case, for example, that the washing powder brand Persil was bought by people who held traditional, family-based values, while the Ariel brand was bought by working women with more 'modern' values. If true, then this was no accident. Their respective marketing executives had identified groups of consumers within the overall market whose buying decisions were influenced by such considerations. Considerable investments in package design and promotion built these perceived values into brands to exploit the desire for such identification.

Do such non-functional values exist among information service users? I suspect that they do, although they are difficult to identify and even harder to exploit.

The Chief Executive of one company for which I worked had considerable academic pretensions. He had many honorary degrees, sponsored a chair at a major university, and went regularly to Harvard Business School. He encouraged a culture which valued and rewarded a thoughtful, almost philosophical approach to the business. His successor was more inclined to a streetwise, hard-nosed, dealer mentality. It is perhaps unsurprising that the library service flourished rather more under the former. I have never quite been certain whether by adjusting the service, products and promotion we could have changed the perception of the library's contribution to appeal as strongly to the latter.

A frequently used model to illustrate the way in which all aspects of any business should be organized around its customers is shown in Figure 4.1.

The final element in the Institute of Marketing's definition is:

- **Profitably** Clearly, formal marketing disciplines have been

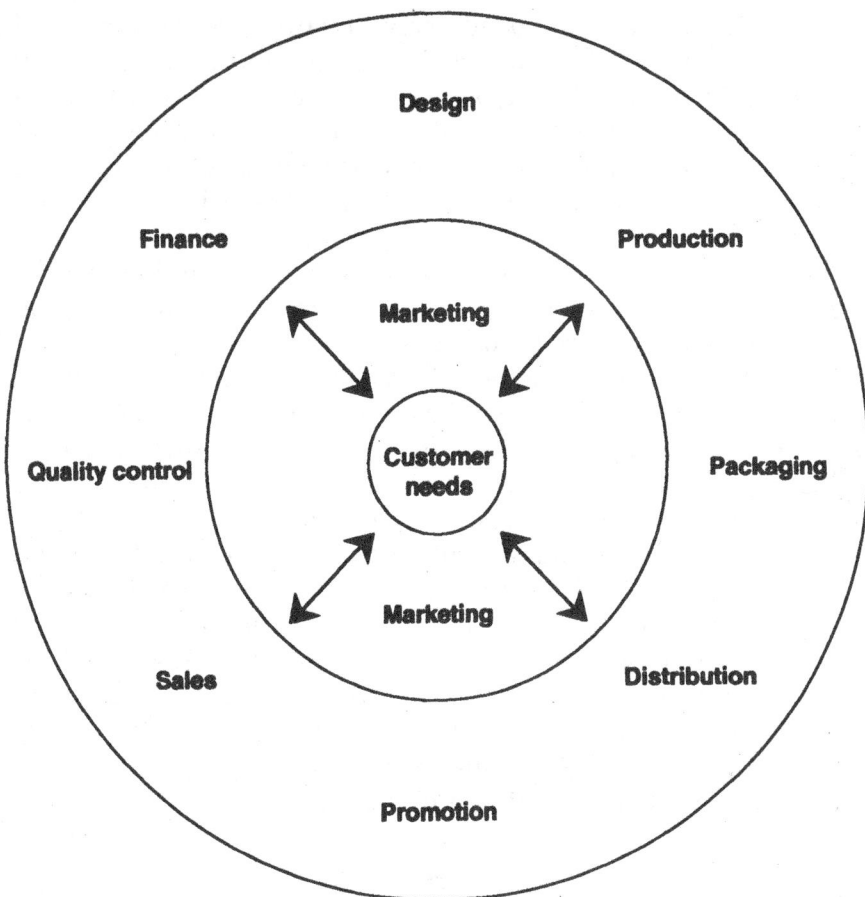

Figure 4.1

developed in a commercial environment where profit is the most obvious measure of success. Profit arises when customers buy, and go on buying, the product at a price advantageous to the supplier. Ultimately, this is the return which the investor gets for his investment in the business.

What the manager of a service department within a business can use as a substitute measure of return is by no means clear. Most frequently, information professionals are given to collecting statistics on usage levels. This is equivalent to a company measuring sales volume or market penetration. They are undoubtedly useful figures, but what would be the point of Persil achieving higher and higher sales if in so doing it traded at a loss?

Information academics spend years pursuing the 'holy grail' of value measures for libraries, usually based around the unproved and probably unprovable hypothesis that companies with good information services (whatever that means) perform better than those which do not have such services. The notion of profit has the advantage of putting the value judgment where it belongs – with the customer.

Those library managers who need to earn their budgets by charging user departments have some advantage in this respect. That the departments are prepared to go on paying is a measure of the value they place on the benefits which they obtain in return.

For those who are funded as a business overhead, or whose costs are borne by a particular budget, some alternative measure relating to the budget holder's perception of value must be found. In this context, continual improvement of service performance in relation to cost is generally a useful approximation to the concept of profit.

These theoretical ideas are all very well, but what are the practical issues which ought to concern the marketing-oriented professional? The textbooks usually refer to something called the 'marketing mix', by which they mean the aspects of a product or service offering that need to be individually and collectively managed in order to achieve marketing objectives.

Conveniently, the marketing mix is made up of four Ps:

Once again, notice that the customer is at the centre of the diagram. After all, nothing happens in any business until and unless there is a customer.

It is the management of all those features of the product which are designed to produce benefits to the customer, i.e.:

- how it is designed and made
- how much it costs

- how it is distributed and promoted

which characterizes the market-led organization.

◆ Finding out about the market

There is a popular misconception that all market research is about questionnaires. In reality, what we are concerned with is sound information about customers – how it is gathered is a secondary consideration. (Feona Hamilton's chapter on Information Audit is also relevant here).

First, it is important to consider two apparently obvious but often ignored questions – which customers, and what are we trying to find out?

Some of the main reasons for market investigations are to:

- understand existing users
- identify potential users
- test assumptions
- test new product/service ideas
- monitor progress

We have already noted that in almost every marketplace there will be a great variety of customers whose requirements, perceptions and attitudes will differ markedly. One objective of market research is to identify these factors in a way that makes it possible to divide customers into (as nearly as possible) homogeneous groups, classified by the usable characteristics. This is the process known as **market segmentation**.

In almost any industrial information environment the initial segmentation is likely to be some sort of grid, with departmental or functional roles on one axis and possible information use or attitude indicators on another. A simple grid might look like that shown in Figure 4.2.

Of course, life is rarely so simple, and a number of such grids will usually need to be overlaid to obtain a usable segmentation. Some other axes that may need to be considered relate to required response times, depth of data analysis, significance of comprehensiveness, quality of presentation, acceptable cost, and not forgetting political status. After all, one of the most important market segments is that which guarantees continuation of funding. If those

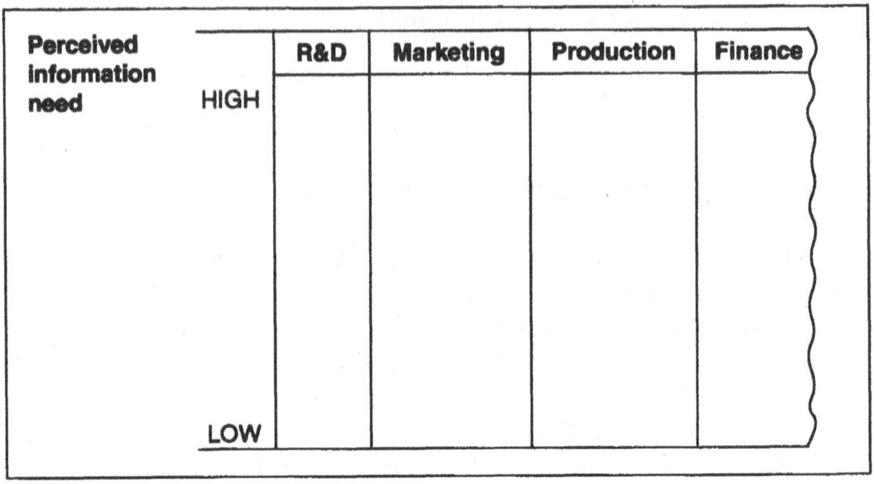

Perceived information need		R&D	Marketing	Production	Finance
	HIGH				
	LOW				

Figure 4.2

key budget holders find their needs satisfied – including value for money – the future of the service is unlikely to be threatened.

Much of the information required to complete such a picture will already exist. Just as businesses frequently use systematic analyses of sales records to reveal trends, so can the information department. If good records of use are kept. . . .

A simple example of how such analyses can help arose in a UK-based company with a large regional branch network. Analyses of the usage levels by the branches over time revealed an erratic picture. For example, the Brighton branch was a high user over an extended period and then quite suddenly became a low user, while the reverse happened in other branches. In this instance, the cause was not too hard to find; tracking use by individuals revealed a lesser inconsistency, and it was very soon apparent that the branch pattern reflected movements of managers around the network.

This was a valuable input into the market strategy of the service, since it revealed the significance of the manager to usage by staff, allowed further investigation into the reasons why two people doing the same job in the same place approached information use in different ways, and allowed the targeting of key individuals to discover gaps in market awareness of the service, or weaknesses in the service offering.

A key benefit of the regular analysis of good usage records is that it provides a quick awareness of changes in demand patterns which allows the service to react and be seen to be reacting to changing circumstances. From the same UK-based company, such analysis revealed a marked increase in the use of urgent company searches. By immediately setting in place procedures to handle the change in demand, the service was able to satisfy the need without a deleterious impact on other work.

The value of good user records analysed on a regular and routine basis should not be undervalued.

I am often surprised at the information world's obsession with 'user studies', though I have always wondered why so few people ask the obvious question, 'What about the non-users?' Why do so many professionals assume that the way forward is to improve what they already do for existing users? The most significant contribution which the library could make might well be for potential users who, for any of a number of reasons, do not find the existing services of value.

There are two basic approaches to researching the market – **qualitative** and **quantitative** techniques – and both have their place.

Qualitative techniques, often known as **focus groups**, have their main application in establishing hypotheses about users and their needs, and in testing reactions to products and promotions. Quantitative techniques have their main benefit in confirming hypotheses and establishing volume implications.

Setting up group discussions is generally straightforward, although it does require a high degree of cooperation and self-discipline. In principle it involves getting two or three groups of between six and ten people, chosen to be representative of an assumed market segment, to discuss, generally for no more than an hour, the issues, services or products under research. If you can afford it, such groups are best led by someone experienced, for there is a high degree of expertise involved in keeping the discussion on track and preventing it from being dominated by one or two outspoken individuals. The objectivity of an outsider as discussion leader means that the group will not get sidetracked into questioning you about aspects of the service, and you will not be tempted into justifying or explaining.

A number of groups should discuss the same issues, first to ensure that there has been a reasonable opportunity for all opinions to be heard, and also to check that the strength of feeling in any one group is in fact representative, and not the result of a particularly opinionated individual dominating the session.

Interpretation of the results of such discussions is critical. Without the objectivity of numbers which quantitative work provides, it is essential that complete notes – preferably recordings – of the discussion are taken. Phrases in a report such as 'a significant minority...' and 'well over half...' should be viewed with some suspicion.

An alternative to group discussions is one-to-one interviews. Unless you have a great deal of time this can only be a very limited exercise. For consistency, as with the group discussions, an open-ended questionnaire should be used to track the discussion.

Quantitative techniques generally mean a widely distributed questionnaire, with statistical analyses of responses. Time spent here discussing sample sizes or statistical significance, tolerance levels, and so on, would not be worthwhile. Those who need that level of sophistication will no doubt use an expert, or study the appropriate textbooks, (see the references at the end of this chapter). For most internal surveys the rule that the larger the sample and the better the response rate the more reliable the result is a good and obvious guide.

The value of such surveys is in the comprehensiveness of the picture they give. They can provide confirmation of hypotheses arrived at from group discussions, help to prioritize services, show what benefits users value most, highlight discrepancies between how users rate your performance and what they regard as important, and so on.

Questionnaire design needs some thought. A few useful pointers are given below.

Avoid questions which imply value judgments. For example, it may be that the answer to one question prejudices an open reply to a following one. A crude example would be a question such as "Do you regard good information in decision making as very important, moderately important, unimportant?" It would take a very strong minded respondent to admit that he regarded it as unimportant. Having answered this question positively, subsequent answers will be coloured by this one.

Use attitude scales. This is the technique whereby, for example, a particular service element may be rated on a scale from:

essential
very important
important
unimportant
inessential

Care must be taken to avoid a bland middle – the lazy respondent will go down the questionnaire ticking the mid-position.

Interpretation of such surveys is often most valuable where graphic representations of the results are made, particularly overlaying related issues such as user's desired benefits and perceptions of your performance.

Once this information has been gathered and analysed, it should be possible to make decisions about the content, structure, style, delivery and promotion of the service on the basis of what the customer needs rather than what professional training or established practice indicates.

◆ Marketing strategies and plans

Without a strategy and a plan to implement it, any service will carry on aimlessly doing what it has always done. It will react, usually late, to changes in its marketplace with inconsistent and uncoordinated initiatives. It is perhaps a cliché, but one with some value, to liken such a service to a boat without a rudder – at the mercy of whatever wind or current prevails.

Planning, however, should not be so rigid as to be restrictive and inflexible. A plan which does not permit creativity is just as bad as the undirected and random application of inspiration.

There is a useful sequence of questions which can be addressed to help in arriving at a strategy and a plan:

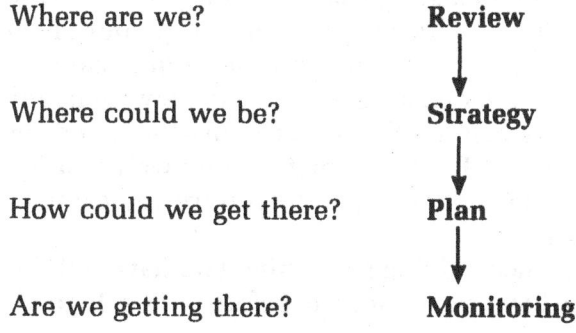

Where are we?	**Review**
Where could we be?	**Strategy**
How could we get there?	**Plan**
Are we getting there?	**Monitoring**

The final question indicates that the plan should not be a static, one-off action, but a cyclical activity constantly under review.

WHERE ARE WE?

As with the planning of a journey, it is as important in the planning of the route to know the starting point as it is to know the intended destination.

The starting point of the planning process is a realistic assessment of the current state of the service, its resources of expertise, staff, materials and budget. Just as important, though, is an appraisal of its standing in the marketplace. What services does it currently offer and to whom? What does it not do, and whom does it not serve? What alternatives do some people use – including doing without information – and why? What does it do well and what less well?

Much of this can be discovered by using a technique known as a SWOT analysis. SWOT stands for Strengths, Weaknesses, Opportunities and Threats. This assessment starts to provide the clues for the next step in the process.

WHERE COULD WE BE?

The review of the skills and resources available, together with the SWOT analyses, will indicate a number of choices available for the future development of the service.

These will broadly fall into four kinds of choices, shown in Figure 4.3.

It is important to understand the characteristics of each of these kinds of choice. Doing better those things that you already do for customers you already serve is clearly a low-risk exercise. Developing new services for existing users is not much more risky. You have customers who are already predisposed in your favour, and whose needs and information behaviour you understand.

It is a big jump even to offer existing services to new users. Why have they not been users before? You don't know them and they don't know what to expect of you. No matter how well you have done your market research and testing, until you try you cannot be sure how they will respond.

The fourth class of choice – doing something you have not done before for people you have never served before – is a high risk

		CUSTOMERS	
		Existing	New
S E R V I C E S	Existing	Product Improvement	Market Extension
	New	Product Development	Diversification

Figure 4.3

activity that requires a considerable degree of reflection and planning.

At the end of this part of the process a set of objectives will have been established, and the next step is to work out . . .

HOW COULD WE GET THERE?

This is the plan. It is the statement of what needs to be done to achieve the marketing objectives. And it is here that the concept of the marketing mix becomes of use, because how we get there is by putting together the total service offering around the benefits which it seeks to provide:

Product — Service specification
  Target response times
  Resources to be used
  Presentation style

Place — How does the user access the service?
  Is it delivered by phone/fax/on-screen?

Price — Is there a charge?
  How much?
  How is it levied?

Promotion — Advertising
  Public relations
  Presentations
  Personal selling

For each of the components of the strategy, specific actions under headings such as these will need to be agreed.

ARE WE GETTING THERE?

A key part of the plan involves the setting of performance measures against which the progress towards the achievement of objectives can be monitored. A number are possible: **market penetration** is a measure of how many of the potential users of the service have actually used it. However, some more qualitative measures based on sample user reponses will be needed to assess whether the anticipated benefits are being delivered effectively.

◆ Pricing

Pricing is one of the most difficult disciplines in any marketing exercise. For an information service there are added complications – the price of any service delivered is not generally paid directly by the user in relation to any one transaction.

Nonetheless, any product or service has a price, and one which at the very least the information service manager should understand. Costing is dealt with elsewhere in this book, but it bears repetition that pricing each particular service is a key element in satisfying the customer's (i.e. the Company's) needs.

Market pricing – using price as a mechanism to position a product in the marketplace – is something for which there is limited opportunity for in-house services. Where the opportunity does exist, though, it should not be dismissed.

Increasingly, companies are giving discretion to managers to source competitively. This means that where they can buy a service in the open market which is better or cheaper than the in-house provision, they are free so to do. This has had a significant impact on information services in such companies. They now have to compete for business, a situation generally unfamiliar to most professionals. Pricing is one of the key tools in competition.

Charging based on 'cost plus' is the most commonly used system in such circumstances. It has some significant drawbacks, the main one being that it restricts the opportunities to use price strategically. This is what is frequently described as 'pricing at what the market will bear'. Most markets will in fact bear a range of prices for any given product or service. As the price increases through the range, so fewer customers will regard it as good value, and usage will fall. By the same token, reducing the price will increase the levels of usage.

What the manager has to decide is the level of profit, or contribution to overhead, that he/she seeks and at which point on the price scale that is maximized. Nevertheless, he/she may decide to sacrifice profit for the sake of winning a contract which is vital to the servicing of the core overhead. This is what is known as 'penetration pricing', using low pricing to secure a desired market penetration.

This has its dangers, though. Once a price expectation for a particular product or service has been created, it is extremely difficult to then increase it.

◆ Promotion

And now, at last, we come to that activity which so many people think of as marketing – promotion. How do the considerations of customer-centred product development help to plan appropriate promotion?

First, of course, if the services have been planned, developed, designed and priced around the satisfaction of customer needs, then you have something to promote which you know your users want. This does not mean that there is no need to promote, though.

In an American advertising directory from the end of the last century there is a little verse which sums this up quite well:

> 'He who whispers down a well
> About the goods he has to sell
> Will never make the silver dollars
> Like him who climbs a tree and hollers!'

A homely little truth, perhaps, and a silly rhyme. But it is surprising how many professionals find themselves uncomfortable with selling. It is somehow regarded as not quite nice. The American poet e. e. cummings wrote a poem that started with the lines 'A salesman is an it that stinks to please'. Yet I'm sure he was glad that someone took the trouble to promote and sell his books.

In a market survey recently I spoke to four professionals who were involved in delivering an information service. All independently said that they would resign rather than take on a sales role. I wonder why? They were happy to service the customers, and be paid for doing it, yet were contemptuous of the role of winning the customers in the first place.

There is a responsibility for the provider of any service to keep the users aware of what benefits it can provide. It is a responsibility because the budget for the service has been created so that the organization's information needs are serviced. If those needs go unmet in part of the market for lack of awareness of the service, then clearly it has failed in part of its job.

Promotion presents an additional opportunity, however, which is to take control of the users' perception of the service. Do you want to be regarded as glossy and high profile or utilitarian and value conscious? The style and content of your promotion, which is under your control, can be designed to reflect the desired 'non-functional' values which you want to embody.

Let us get down to practicalities. First and foremost is the consideration of what is being promoted, and to whom. Referring back to the concepts introduced at the beginning of the chapter, libraries, like any other service, exist only to provide benefits to customers. Promotions which lead by demonstrating the benefits customers will receive are far more effective than those which describe the features or resources of the service.

Yet how often one sees library and information service promotions that extol the wonders of the collection, the number of directories and splendid reference books, the amazing databases with millions of entries, and all available at the touch of a button. Well, as a customer, I say 'So what?'

Customers care about solutions to their problems, how they are solved is entirely secondary. If you can supply me with the right data, in the right format, at the right price and within my deadlines, I am unlikely to care whether it came from a whizzo new CD-ROM or from an old-fashioned book.

And since the required benefit will change from user group to user group, so the promotion should not try to be all things to all people. If for one group fully comprehensive data is more important than speed, or vice versa, then the ability to have all the data, or some data now is what should be promoted.

There is a story told, probably apocryphal, that Land Rover used to sell in all markets under the 'all terrain' message. So buyers in Iceland were told about its desert capabilities, and those in the Middle East were told about how well it copes in snow. Now those in the Middle East didn't care much about how it coped with snow, and probably thought that this compromised its efficiency in the heat, or at least that the price must include features they wouldn't need. The answer for Land Rover was to promote the same vehicle as the Snow Rover and the Desert Rover.

Before looking at a variety of promotional techniques, it is important to realize that there can be a number of different promotion objectives. Promotion should not be done for some vague notion of bringing in customers. Consider some examples of different kinds of advertisement. Is the advertisement in *Flight* magazine extolling the virtues of the Tornado under the headline 'All weather strike . . . under the curtain' trying to do the same job as the *Daily Telegraph* reader offer 'Warm and cosy coat only £27.95', or the British Coal advert 'We won't ask your children to pay the earth for today's energy'? Clearly not.

Promotional objectives can range from the creation of an immediate sale (*Telegraph* coat), to changing perceptions of a product (British Coal), to maintaining market awareness (Tornado). In fact, it is possible to look at a spectrum:

Promotion objectives

Immediate
↕
Long-term
strategic

- direct sale
- initiate trial
- get on the 'shopping list'
- change customer perceptions
- remind of product values
- maintain corporate values

This is not mere academic analysis. When creating a promotion you should always have in mind what response and what action you want the recipient to take.

Now let us look at some of the techniques available.

Branding It became very fashionable during the 1980s for information services to create an internal brand image. This was manifest in a logo, often a varient or addition to the corporate logo, and in a standardized style for the presentation of all material from memos, compliment slips, publications, and so on.

This is certainly a very powerful tool, establishing values and acting as an identifier for the service. Good branding incorporates the desired values — compare the logos of banks, which try to convey solidity, age and respectability, and those for design companies, which say creativity and style. An information service may want to say something about wisdom or knowledge, as did J. Walter Thomson's London Information Centre with their stylized owl.

I believe that the opportunity to use such style devices is becoming more limited, because companies are themselves becoming more precious about their total corporate style. Corporate style manuals are designed to ensure that everything, whether in internal or external communications, conforms to a standard. However, if the opportunity exists it has some very powerful advantages.

Advertising   Opportunities do exist inside some organizations for advertising. Display advertising in in-house newsletters, posters and on-screen announcements through networks have all been used. They tend to be most effective for promoting special events, launching new services and announcing changed arrangements.

The most commonly used form of advertising for in-house information services is the production of leaflets and brochures. Most of the ones I have seen, though, are extremely dull. Often the problem is that in trying to tell everything on one publication it becomes so general as to be meaningless, or spends too much time on the service features so it fails to sell the benefits.

In preparing any piece of promotional literature, thought must be given to the target reader — who is it being written for, in what context will it be read, what is likely to ensure that it is noticed and read, what do you want the reader to think, feel or do, having read it?

Very often, such brochures are published to give to new employees in 'starter packs' or at induction courses. The worthy full brochure is unlikely to make an impact on the new starter — there is so much more of obvious and immediate significance such as how to claim expenses or who maintains the company car fleet. The most effective leaflet I have seen in this context was a 'teaser'. This was a single sheet with some vital questions about the company's marketplace, clients and competitors. There were questions with obvious clues to the company culture and politics, such as 'what is the trade magazine most frequently read by the members of the Executive Committee of the board?' For the answers to all of the questions, recipients were advised to telephone an individual on a particular phone number. The library was not even mentioned.

Induction and other training courses provide a key opportunity for the information service manager. Identifying the training manager, and ensuring that a slot is available on all appropriate courses, should be straightforward. It is always easy to make a case for a slot on a course – the sources of information relevant to the topic is always good for 20 minutes. However, you should not make the mistake of thinking that that is what you are there to talk about. It is the opportunity to make a sales presentation.

The distribution of any publications also requires thought. If you consider how you react to the promotional material which lands uninvited on your desk, you will have an idea how yours will be received – generally, these items go straight from the in-tray to the waste bin. Worse, they often don't get past the secretary. To be effective in reaching the individual and attracting his/her attention they have to have some reason for their existence. This can, of course, be a borrowed reason. One company for which I worked published a series of official 'Management communications'. Not only were these physically distinctive, but they contained vital procedural information, changes in reporting lines, amendments to manuals and so on. By publicizing a particular service in the form of such a communication, not only were we guaranteed that it would be read, but the choice of medium created the opportunity to write the use of the service into the company procedures manual. I have to say that persuading the relevant authorities to permit this was no easy task, but one which eventually proved highly effective.

Public relations There is a wide range of activities which can be undertaken under the loose definition of PR. Most often it is associated with getting editorial coverage in the press. For an internal information service there are many possibilities here, and it is an important part of keeping the service in the forefront of users' minds. It has the additional advantage of helping to create a high public profile. Those who ultimately make decisions on funding may not themselves be users, and to these people the activities, services and promotions will be largely invisible. A well conceived programme of PR will ensure that the department is seen to be vital and outgoing.

In many companies the major opportunity will be through the medium of the in-house newspaper or staff magazine. As with all other aspects of marketing, this is something which benefits from analysis and planning. What image of the service is it that you are trying to convey? What is the readership of the magazine, and what is its editorial style? Many are gossipy papers, concerned with births to staff members, photographs of retirement parties and the like, while others are heavyweight vehicles for perpetuating the corporate culture.

In the case of the former, I have come across a number of information services which, rather than participate in the trivia, use such papers by having a regular quiz column, exploiting the 'fun' style while demonstrating the knowledge base of the department. The most successful of these generated considerable interest by the simple device of offering a bottle of champagne as a prize! At £15 per quarter the cost is trivial, but the attention generated is considerable. Further mileage is gained by photographing the presentation to the winner.

Those organizations with a more serious style of magazine often use book reviews, information updates or articles summarizing the latest developments in a particular field drawn from the literature. From my own experience, these rather more 'worthy' approaches require more planning and preparation to be effective, for they can so easily become extremely boring.

Other aspects of public relations can be activities which draw attention to the services offered without specifically promoting their virtues. One very effective tool I came across was a 'lunch club'. The library invited prominent speakers in issues of current concern to address members and to participate in a buffet lunch. Speakers were generally economists, analysts, academics or politicians – this was, after all, in a bank. Club membership was by invitation, thus making it apparently exclusive, although of course invitations were issued to anyone who wanted them. Clearly, a prominent banking institution has key advantages in attracting high profile speakers, but the approach does have wide application even if the detailed arrangements need to be altered to suit the particular organization and the library's objectives.

Some years ago the library of an advertising agency which published a daily bulletin based on scanning the daily and weekly press asked the scanners to start collecting the more humorous little snippets they came across. They arranged to have these illustrated with cartoons and published it as a booklet on April 1. This was so well presented that it got a mention on the local radio station which read out extracts throughout a whole day.

Reminders Information is a very difficult concept to sell. In many environments, recognizing that there is an information need or a simple resolution of it does not happen automatically. While a scientist or engineer may be unable to progress a project until certain questions are answered, the businessman can progress without even realizing that he has made assumptions that could have been improved or even radically altered with better information.

In such circumstances, the first task of the information professional is to try to build in 'trip wires' which ensure that progress cannot be made. These are often procedural: for example, in an investment company, procedures are such that a credit search must be made immediately before the completion of any deal.

However, this will not be possible in all circumstances, so 'reminders' can be introduced which serve to keep the information service and its potential value regularly in the forefront of users' minds. These can range from stickers to put on to the users' telephones to on-screen menus on networks, from desk calendars to bookmarks, from mugs to pens. What works in any one context will depend on the culture – and budget – available. Prestige items generally work better than high volumes of cheap items because they tend to stay on the desk. The cheap plastic pen with a printed message will join thousands of others in the back of a drawer. Such promotional items need not be expensive. Creativity is generally more important.

Very successful, inexpensive desk calendars often work if they are witty or unusual, for example.

Customer care I make no apology for including customer care as a promotional tool. It is a generally accepted rule that while one customer expects to be satisfied and so tells no one, one disgruntled customer moans to at least half a dozen colleagues. If each of these passes on the story to a couple of others, then negative views spread very quickly.

Customer care means training all staff to make the user and attention to his/her needs more of a priority than an insistence on applying the rules. It also means having a strategy for dealing with complaints. A user who has complained and had that well dealt with and his/her problem put right often becomes a more loyal advocate of the service than the customer who never had a complaint in the first place.

The Scottish Tourist Board recently published a leaflet for Guest Houses on handling complaints. It was called *How to stand tall while bending over backwards* and encapsulates the philosophy that a complaint is a golden opportunity – it presents us with an immediate focus for improvement to the service. More than that, it creates a situation in which you can influence that most elusive promotional tool – word of mouth.

Customer care sums up what marketing is all about – the old-fashioned notion that 'The customer is always right'.

◆ References

Arnold, S.E. (1990) Marketing electronic information in the 1990s. *The Electronic Library*, **8**(5), October, 350–358.

Cronin, B. (ed.) (1991) *Marketing of Library and Information Services 2*, London: Aslib.

Curtis, J. (1985) *Marketing Services: A practical guide*, London: Kogan Page (for British Institute of Management).

Edsall, M.S. (1980) *Library Promotion Handbook*, Phoenix: Oryx Press.

Hamilton, F. (1990) *Infopromotion: Publicity and Marketing Ideas for the Information Profession*. Aldershot: Gower.

Kies, C. (1987) *Marketing and Public Relations for Libraries*, New York: Scarecrow Press.

McCaughan, D. (1991) Brand strategies and libraries. *Special Libraries*, **82**(3), Summer 178–182.

McCaughan, D. (1991) Ingratiating yourself to all and sundry . . . or how I crawled my way to notoriety. *Special Libraries*, **82**(3), Summer, 183–188.

Mills, C. (1991) Changing perceptions: making PR work for an information service. *Special Libraries*, **82**(3), Summer, 189–195.

Pymm, R. (1990) Marketing and special libraries. *Australian Special Libraries*, **23**(1), March, 7–13.

Unruh, B. (ed.) (1989) *Information Marketing Handbook*, Philadelphia: National Federation of Abstracting and Information Services.

Yates-Mercer, P.A. and Steward, Y.F. (1991) The marketing of internal business information sources. *Journal of Information Science*, **17**, 221–233.

5 The information audit

Feona Hamilton

- An era of change
- Why audit information resources?
- How to do an information audit
- Presenting the report

'Auditing' has long been a term associated with accountancy – but what does it actually mean? Dictionaries will give definitions such as 'the inspection, correction and verification of business accounts', which is a polite enough way of saying that an auditor is there to make sure you're not being dishonest. But that's not what it's all about. An audit is a means of helping the Directors of a company to make sure that they've given a proper value to the company's assets.

These assets may include some fairly nebulous items, not just the buildings, furnishings, stock, and current orders on the books. The best known of the more shadowy assets is **goodwill**. An amount to indicate that goodwill, which is part of a business, is often included when putting a selling price on a company. After recent legislation in the UK, goodwill can now also be included in the annual accounts.

In the last few years the importance of information has also been acknowledged as a company asset. It is surprising that the absolute necessity of good information in order to function successfully has not been recognized long before this. After all, no matter how much money or how many staff may be available, and no matter how large the premises, no organization will survive without accurate, timely information. In fact, information is very much a – if not the – core commodity.

Obviously, such an important part of the company should not be ignored. It makes sense to include it as a function which should be audited – i.e. inspected, corrected and verified – but how should such an audit be undertaken? Many companies have never seen information as a commodity. If the word 'information' was used at all, it was probably in conjunction with two others: information and technology (i.e. the computer centre) or information and services (i.e. the library).

The split between these two functions – information technology and information services – is one which has been allowed to develop because of the perceived difference in use. IT people were traditionally the computer specialists devising complex computer programs, or sophisticated hardware. The results of their endeavours were too often reams and reams of computer printout, containing long columns of numbers, or names and addresses with spelling mistooks.

The information centre, on the other hand, was simply a different name for the library (and was still usually referred to as the library). The staff were very nice and very helpful. They lent you books and circulated journals. Sometimes they ordered your newspaper for you and could also get hold of microfiches if you needed them. The railway timetable and maps were the other reasons for visiting the library, especially if you were going on holiday. Some very advanced places had Prestel sets in them, with the latest cricket scores or share prices displayed all day.

◆ An era of change

That may have been the situation 20 years ago, but it certainly is not now. Today the main search tool for the information centre is the PC, with a modem for on-line searching and/or a CD-player for the growing number of services available via CD-ROM (Compact Disc – Read Only Memory). Books, other than directories and standard reference works (e.g. tax manuals and legal tomes), have ceased to be the major information sources. Journals are still an important part of the stock for many information centres, although even these are less in favour than they were.

Perhaps even more importantly, information centres have become involved in joint systems with their IT colleagues – systems designed, for example, to enhance competitive awareness, capture know-how and so forth. It is also aiding the synthesis of internally generated information (records management) with information in the public domain – the traditional area of operation for the library or information centre. Thus we now have the tools available for total information management within an organization. (For more on this integration of companies' information resources see Veronica Davies's chapter on records management.)

Why has this change happened? In the financial sector, particularly, with its emphasis on a swift response time and the most current information, the reliance on on-line services has increased at the expense of hard copy. This is necessarily so, as the frequent updating of such services makes their currency undeniable. The increasing sophistication of telecommunications, with the use of satellites for 'bouncing' information from one side of the globe to another in milliseconds, means that events are being reported as they happen. Compare this with the earlier system of foreign correspondents taking notes, then having to find a telephone to dictate their article to someone furiously taking more notes at the other end of the line.

The growth of information sources via on-line searching has put vast amounts of information literally at the fingertips of anyone able to tap the appropriate keys on a computer. Such skills are acquired by means of a two- or three-day course at the most – and such courses are included in the initial subscription charges levied by those supplying the service – the hosts, as they are called. Once learned, the minor changes in command structure needed to access other hosts can often be self-taught in a matter of hours, although every course offered should always be attended by new users if possible.

Once familiar with the use of computers in this area, many information staff found how simple it was to use computers for other reasons, such as library housekeeping (with specially designed, more or less successful software), or budget control and the production of standard documentation (with equally standard software such as spreadsheets and word-processing).

The generation which learnt its computer skills this way probably picked them up backwards, but still found them fairly easy to grasp. The new generation, having had access to computers since schooldays, has even less trouble picking up all the related skills needed to run what has become a highly automated service.

◆ Why audit information resources?

The point of all this is to indicate how foolish it is to still consider the IT function separately from the IM (information management) function of any organization. Not only is it a false division of function, it is also an inefficient way of managing the information resources of any one organization. At the most basic level, a lack of awareness of the equipment used by the staff in both sections or departments could lead to unnecessary duplication. With the spread of the 'screen on every desk' attitude to the use of PCs, such a lack of awareness could deprive other staff of access to large amounts of information of vital importance to them in their work, simply because they will be unaware of it themselves. Apart from the IT/IM functions, there are all the administrative and support tasks carried out in all departments, especially accounts and personnel. The files resulting from such work are all information resources, and should be included in the audit.

Computers are not the only equipment used in information management, of course. How about the photocopiers, the telephones, the typewriters which are all used in the gathering and disseminating of information? What about the filing systems, the shelving, the cabinets, the dark and dingy basements used exclusively for storage? Is there an external secure archive facility, or is a commercial archiving firm used? Once started on listing the facilities actually used in the management of information in the widest sense, it is difficult to draw a boundary; yet another indication of the importance of information to the organization.

If a proper, complete picture of the information resources within an organization is to be obtained, the only way to do it is by carrying out an information audit. The initial results of such a project can be quite startling. Many organizations, whether companies or professional institutions, research bodies or charities, really have no idea of the basic facts connected with their use of information. They do not know:

- precisely what are the information resources in use?
- how are they used?
- what are the results?
- are there any marketable products resulting?
- what is the equipment and who has it?
- exactly how much is it costing?
- what is the value to the organization?

It is difficult to think of any other function where such ignorance would be acceptable.

Complete knowledge of information resources is also important for the personnel involved in providing those services. The realization of the vital importance of these services, of the skills needed to provide them, of the amount spent on necessary equipment, cannot fail to raise the standing of information professionals. Often, for the first time, they are truly acknowledged as possessing an expertise unknown to anyone else. They are seen as part of the overall IT/IM picture, and the need for both kinds of skill in operating computer systems is at last recognized. It is an opportunity which should not be missed.

◆ How to do an information audit

The best way of approaching a new project is to prepare a good proposal. This will be the means by which you persuade the powers that be that it is a good idea to undertake an information audit in the first place, so it must be properly put together and look professional. On gaining acceptance, the proposal will then become a very useful guide to actually carrying out the project. It follows that it must be put together in a logical order, and explain, in some detail, precisely what it is you are going to do.

If you are part of an organization which offers consultancy services, then you should follow the house style when compiling your own proposal. If not, there is an accepted order in which proposals are put together, no matter what the project. Although there is some flexibility as to content, the order goes something like this:

Title of proposal – including the word 'proposal' to show that this is what it is, and not, for example, a finished report.
Introduction – a short section giving some indication of what the project is about, and the events leading up to it.
Methodology – i.e. how you're going to do the audit, item by item. In this case it will include something about interviewing, building a database, giving estimates of cost and value, and so on.
Staffing – indicate how many people will be involved in the project and what their specific skills and input will be.
Timescale – give some estimation of how long it will all take, item by item. Include desk research (which includes finding out what you're supposed to be doing!) and slippage (which means

allowing for unforeseen holdups, like everyone going off sick, or the computer packing up). Allow ample time for writing the report itself.

Costs – give some estimation of how much it will cost, including any external consultancy fees, visits to other offices, extra software, purchasing relevant texts, and so on.

(N.B. Be generous in your estimations of time and cost. It creates a much better impression if you finish earlier and within budget than if you overshoot in both areas.)

Finally, make sure that the proposal is produced using a word-processor rather than a typewriter, and don't use a dot-matrix printer. This has got to look seriously professional and not like something produced by an amateur, so take time with selecting typefaces (e.g. bold and upper case for section headings) and setting it all out with wide margins and double spacing. This practice is not simply to make it look longer than it really is, but to allow room for scribbled notes in the margin.

AFTER THE GO-AHEAD

Before beginning any data gathering, it is advisable to spend some time preparing the ground. Basically there must be:

- a properly designed questionnaire for use in interviews
- a record format for each database compiled
- staff with the necessary skills in interviewing/analysis/report writing/forecasting
- a mixture of IM and IT specialists so that both sides of the project are properly understood.

Finally, it must be borne in mind that this is a time-consuming exercise requiring a great deal of concentration. It cannot be picked up and put down at will. Some organizations decide to use an external consultant as a project director, sometimes a complete team is brought in. There are advantages to this approach. External consultants have no vested interest and cannot be accused of trying to empire-build. They see matters objectively because of their distance from the first, lack of interest in and knowledge of office politics, and so on. On the other hand, they may take longer because they have to learn about the organization. An existing member of staff carrying out an information audit has the advantage of already knowing many of the people who should be interviewed, the structure of the organization and, hopefully, a great deal about information and equipment used, costs, and budgets. Both ways of dealing with the project have advantages and both have drawbacks. The decision on how to approach an information audit can only be taken according to individual circumstances. If you are proposing to do it in-house, what follows will guide you through the exercise.

QUESTIONNAIRE FORMS

It is not easy to devise a form suitable for face-to-face and postal interviews. One of the basic rules is always to keep it as short as possible. The example given in Figure 5.1 was used for face-to-face and telephone interviews only. It covered only one side of a sheet of A4 paper, although the back was used for making notes if needed.

The headings were used as talking points, i.e. the questionnaire could not have been filled in by anyone without the interviewer being there. This was deliberate. Sending a form like this through the post always risks it landing in the out tray (also known as the waste paper basket) and never being returned to you. Many market researchers and mailshot users don't expect more than a 10% return on postal questionnaires. This is definitely not good enough for an information audit, when you need a 95% return at the very least, and 101% would be better. Incidentally, the headings did not tie in with the field names used in the record format because of the questionnaire being used as a prompt, rather than giving a tight structure.

This was the main questionnaire, used for finding out about the actual information resources being used. Naturally, it was also necessary to know more about the equipment that was being used. Although there was a central point for co-ordination of IT use throughout the organization, the nature of the beast, with its many individual offices, meant that equipment other than that available centrally was also in use. The IT staff were aware of its existence, but unable to gain any specific details, because their enquiries were naturally seen as interference. The same enquiries made by a consultant, concerned solely with this one project, and unattached to any department, received a very different response.

Another questionnaire was compiled – with an explanatory

Questionnaire (Face-to-face/telephone interview)

Name: **Tel:**

Location:

Databases:

Other:

Training:

Comments:

Figure 5.1 Questionnaire (Reproduced by kind permission of Grant Thornton)

Computer use

Please indicate which of the following you use:

Hardware

BM XT   IBM AT   IBM PS/2   OTHER IBM
COMPAQ III   COMPAQ SLT286   COMPAQ SLT386
OTHER COMPAQ

Other PC compatible (Please state name and model)

Other PC (Please state name and model)

GT Network   Yes/No

Software

CBEAM   IDEA   CAS
TAXPOINT   TAXPARTNER   TAXWATCH   TAXSOFT
LOTUS   LSD   DW4   DELTA 4.3   DELTA 5

Other software
(Please list other software giving name, supplier and cost if known)

Figure 5.1   concluded

memo – and sent to every office. This time the questionnaire was to be filled in by the recipient and returned to the consultant. As the example in Figure 5.1 shows, the emphasis was on 'Yes/No' responses, or ticking a specific item. Only the last item needs actual words to be inserted to any great degree. There was a 100% response to this questionnaire, with only one person telephoning to ask 'why his time was being wasted, when the information was available elsewhere'. The explanation that it wasn't and that answering would give him better access to more information than he currently had was sufficient to calm him down and persuade him to fill in the form and return it.

SELECTING INTERVIEWEES

It is important to select the right people to talk to if you are to gain a full picture of the information resources in your organization. The firm's telephone directory is a good starting point, especially if it gives details by department (and the hierarchy within that) as well as a straight A–Z listing of names. If the telephone directory is not put together in that way, try a staff handbook. This should certainly give details of the different functions carried out by the whole organization, and often gives the names of Heads of Departments as well.

Setting up appointments with the relevant people can be quite time-consuming itself, but it pays off to do it properly. This will mean drafting a memo, giving brief details of what it is you are doing, and stating that you will be contacting the addressee (or their secretary) to arrange an interview. Explaining that this will only take a short time is another means of making sure you do get some time with them. If you address the memo to the Head of Department – which it is courteous to do – you may be referred on to someone else in the department. This is not a rebuff – the person you are referred to will probably be the one who can help you most anyway. For example, there may be someone with responsibility for computerized systems in the department, or someone who represents the department on a Library Committee, if you have one. The point is that you have told the most senior person in the department what you are doing, so that he or she does not hear from someone else, or suddenly come upon you 'prowling around' (as it may be seen).

You should quickly be able to spot where the same functions are carried out in a standard manner. Taking the accountancy firm example, all offices will have audit and tax functions, so you won't need to talk to every auditor or tax specialist in the firm. If, on the other hand, there are people who act as experts in a specific industry sector, and are already used to giving advice on that sector to other members of staff, obviously they should be included in your list. In the firm Grant Thornton, for example, where an information audit was carried out during 1990, there were such specialists. Some were industry specialists (e.g. brewing, agriculture), and some were specialists in particular accounting areas (e.g. estate planning, corporate finance), and all had knowledge of the appropriate information sources. They also had their own files and, in some cases, networks of contacts, both internal and external.

DON'T INTERVIEW – CONVERSE!

Using a questionnaire which prompts you, the interviewer, rather than simply demanding a response, should result in an interview which bears more resemblance to a relaxed chat than a formal, structured session. If you ask someone a narrowly focused question, you only get a narrowly focused answer. As an example:

Q. Do you use IBM machines here?
A. Yes.

Instead try:

Q. What PCs are you using here?
A. Well, I've got an IBM M55 and Jim's using a Mac. The secretary's on the 5520 at the moment, but we're getting an AS/400 in this office soon. Do you want to know what the others are using across the hall?

and so you're launched into a conversation. At this point, if you have someone who's really keen on equipment, you can find yourself on the receiving end of a lesson in the use of software and relevant hardware in the company. Don't stop the flow – it will probably add to your knowledge as well, and meanwhile the interviewee is relaxing and feeling great as he/she shows off how much they know.

Similarly, encourage people to tell you about their job and the way in which they use information while carrying it out. They will proudly show the 'office library' (no comment) and their filing systems, including the card index on which they list all their contacts. Often, they will teach you a thing or two about keeping records, or give you their extremely useful thoughts on centralizing functions. Only stop the flow if it's imperative for you to get to another appointment, otherwise you could miss a vitally important piece of the jigsaw. Sudden thoughts just as you are about to leave are common – make a note if it's a short thought – ask if they will jot it down for you, or if you can ring them if it's longer.

Another advantage of visiting people and spending time talking to them in this way is that they will tell you not only about information resources which you didn't know existed, but also suggest who else you should speak to. If it seems to you that this might prolong the project unacceptably, it won't necessarily be so. A pattern can emerge quite early in the project, and indicate similar usage of information resources in several departments. Confirmation of the pattern can cut down on the original list of interviewees, leaving time to see others not included before, but who turn out to be vital to the completion of your task.

SETTING UP DATABASES

Obviously, all the information that you are collecting by means of your interviews must be loaded onto a database. This database, if properly constructed, becomes an important information tool itself for the whole organization. It will (probably) be the first really comprehensive index to the firm's information resources. After the audit has been carried out, this database should be made available – either by network or in hard copy, for distribution to everyone. For that reason, when setting up the record initially, bear in mind that it should be easily understood and capable of being referred to, as a standard library catalogue should be.

It seemed sensible, in the project used here as an example, to use the database management system (DBMS) that was standard throughout the organization. In this case it was Delta 4.3, a transactional database. Using this particular software meant that the majority of people within the organization who already had access to computerized systems would understand and be able to access the index with a minimum of training. The disadvantage of this particular DBMS was that it was not relational, i.e. only one database could be searched at a time, rather than being able to search across several. This lack of flexibility was a problem during the carrying out of the project. Finding the disadvantage, and knowing that Delta 4.3. was the recommended DBMS, led to a recommendation that Delta 5 (or another relational database) should be used in future. Thus from the start of the project it was possible to justify the work being carried out and to show the benefits of such a study!

Defining record files is one of the most frustrating things any computer user ever has to do. The important thing to realize is that you must expect to have to adjust and revise the fields in the record, before you get the format right. The more experienced you become at this, the more you will understand how much care it needs. It will take at least three days of steadily increasing tension and bad language before you come anywhere near the ideal. No one else's format will precisely meet your needs, so the example given in Figure 5.2 will definitely need to be adapted – you cannot use it as it is; it simply worked very well for one project. (If all this reads like someone writing from very bitter experience – it is!)

Believe it or not, one of the best ways to start devising a record format is to write it down on paper. List the headings you think you will need. Some are obvious, like a unique identity number for each record, the name of the person who gave you the information, where they are situated, the location of the information resource. The example also has some indications as to the category of resource (in this case, a source, a system, or a service), the type (manual or automated) and the security level. This last was vital for this particular project. Assuring people that there would be a level of confidentiality in what they were disclosing if they so wished, meant that they told of resources which they considered to be absolutely confidential to themselves or the department in which they worked. These included items such as the files relating to compliance matters, or court cases, personnel files and lists of personal contacts (although many people said they would be quite happy to share the names on their contacts lists, under certain circumstances). The security levels decided upon were:

1. Available to anyone (e.g. public reference library)
2. Available to all staff (e.g. National Information Centre)
3. Available to this department only (e.g. work in progress)
4. Confidential to interviewee (e.g. legal adviser's files)

No one who agreed to be interviewed subsequently refused to talk about their files once the confidentiality had been explained.

INFORMATION RESOURCES INDEX

ID Number:

Category: Type: Security level:

Resource Name:

Location:

Contact name:

Description:

Used for:

Used by:

Access method:

Equipment:

Computer literate:

Training:

Supplier:

Cost: Value:

Future:

Comment 1:

Comment 2:

Comment 3:

Comment 4:

Figure 5.2 Questionnaire on information resources (Reproduced by kind permission of Grant Thornton)

The second group of field names in this case were concerned solely with the resource in question. The name given by the interviewee was important, as that made it recognizable if, in future, someone else enquired about it. A contact name and the location were also basic needs. In case the original interviewee left, there was a brief description of the resource, to help in tracing it, or to help in searching for a group of related resources. The use made of the resource, and who were the users, was information needed to assess whether the resource was necessary, or whether it duplicated information held elsewhere. Finally, the access method was given – i.e. did you have to be on the network, or was it available as hard copy or in a manual file?

This was all that was needed for this particular database, although there were other fields added that were not used. They were included because they related to sections on the main questionnaire that had led to considerable discussion during interviews. The responses to these questions were comments, opinions and suggestions rather than hard facts. Nevertheless, since these unused fields were subsequently rehashed and formed two other databases – one on training in computer skills and one on suggestions for the future – it had not been a waste of effort to include them in the original design.

KEYING IN AND WHEN TO DO IT

What you read in this section may seem to be so obvious as to be unnecessary. On the other hand, if you've never carried out a task of this sort before, it will seem like pearls of wisdom.

It is extremely important to key in information from completed questionnaires as often as possible, and certainly not less than every three days. There are good reasons for this – one of which is connected with the type of interview described above. Chatting to people, rather than asking questions and getting the answers, does elicit much more information. The problem is that it is easy to forget to note something down, or to simply run out of space. Many people will testify to having thought 'I don't need to write that down – I'll remember it', only to forget about the whole matter in a few days. That is why it is so vital to keep keying in the results of your interviews as quickly as possible.

The frequency with which you can do this may be dictated to a certain extent by the availability of the people you wish to interview. If you are working in an organization where people are frequently out of the office during the course of the working day, you must be prepared to be flexible, where possible. In the service sector, for example, the client/customer always gets priority. Frustrating as this can be, it's no use getting annoyed about it. Be aware, instead, that those clients contribute to your earnings, then you'll find it easier to agree to a change of appointment, or a change of interviewee (as might well happen).

Whoever you see, and however you get hold of the information you need, time for returning to the office and keying it in must be put in the diary as well as the interview appointments. Try and keep these times sacrosanct – e.g. agree to an altered appointment on another day, rather than leaving yourself no keying in time for a whole week. Even if there is a team of people involved in this project, keying in from interview sheets should be done by whoever conducted the interview. Such sheets handed across to a secretary, for example, may be virtually meaningless, again because of the informal nature of the interview.

As the number of entries mounts you may find that slight differences creep in which will have to be ironed out. You will need a form of 'authority file', such as is used in cataloguing and classification, to indicate the preferred form of entry. For example, if you are working in an organization with offices all over the country, how do you enter the location for a specific information source: is it 'London – Insolvency' or 'Insolvency – London'? The earlier you can make such decisions and note them down for the enlightenment and guidance of others, the easier it will be to create a consistent pattern of entry. This makes it easier to understand when in use as a search tool by others.

It is also helpful to do a few test runs by printing out the database when it has only a few entries in it. Between ten and twenty is a good number, as this is long enough to get the flavour of the finished product while being short enough to alter the record format (yet again) if necessary. It is surprising (and depressing) how often a format which seemed ideal when it was first set up looks less pleasing when it has some entries in it. This is a necessary test for a database which is to be produced in hard copy. Running off a short test run will also ensure that you have really designed the record correctly, and that you are able to enter all the items which you need. Remember that you will also want to search the database when it is complete, as it will form part of the basic search tool for your own information when compiling your report.

◆ The cost of information

The most difficult part of the information audit process is trying to compile accurate costs. It may not seem to be complicated at first – the information centre itself will have a budget, and there will be the invoices from online hosts and other suppliers such as booksellers available, so it is a simple matter of looking at these – or is it?

No. The information centre budget and the invoices really only start things off. This is an audit of *all* information resources in use throughout the organization, a very different matter from the cost of running the information service. What about the cost of journals and books bought without your knowledge by other departments or offices within the organization? What about IT costs generally? What about the costs involved in training people in computer skills, especially all the different software packages they need to use – word-processing, DBMS, spreadsheets, the organization's own network?

There are also the added complications of costs that are passed on to clients. For example, if someone in the information centre carries out a search, they may charge for:

- the on-line search costs
- telephone costs
- cost of using an external information broker
- staff time (at so much per unit of 15 minutes)

and inform the enquirer of the total cost. The enquirer subsequently passes that cost on to the client for whom he needed the information. The charge made by the information staff will normally have an in-built profit margin, and the charge made to the client by the in-house enquirer will certainly include a profit margin for his or her work. Strictly speaking, the information was not a cost, but made a profit. Is that how you assess it?

If that was done for every enquiry and strict records kept, then again it would be easy to cost out information services and use. Information services don't work like that. A number of enquiries which come to the information centre will be answered free of charge. These are the quick enquiries, such as supplying a telephone number, or an exchange rate for a particular currency, a share price, or the address of an association. The administrative costs of charging for such an enquiry – and the goodwill and 'repeat business' engendered by not charging – make it inappropriate to do so. Over the year, the cost of these 'free' enquiries will add up to several thousand pounds, at least. There will be other items of a similar nature – perhaps ordering a second copy of a directory at the same time as you order one for your own department, as a favour to another department. (The following chapter by Liz Chapman, on 'Budgeting, financial control, purchasing and charging', contains further in-depth material on costing.)

Outside the information centre, costing for information use is even more complicated. Again, you have the actual costs for IT equipment and staffing (if a separate department). General administrative costs for information functions carried out in other departments will, however, have to be estimated.

It should be clear by now that the costing of information use throughout the organization will have to be based on what information is available, plus a best guess (an estimate in 'business-speak'). A session with the accounts department, and preferably the chief accountant in the organization, is the only answer. The one comfort you have in all this is the knowledge that, since there are currently no accounting standards that can be applied to information resources, your estimates are as good as anyone else's. Perhaps before long, such standards will appear – which may or may not be a good thing, depending on the complexity of such standards.

THE VALUE OF INFORMATION RESOURCES

The argument about how to value information resources is an intense one. The book *InfoMap* by Burk and Horton (1988) has an interesting chapter on this subject. It gives tables of the attributes which may be considered as values and applies them to many different information resources. It takes some study to grasp the essence of what is being said, but once grasped it makes complete sense. It also forms an excellent basis for assessing the values of your own information resources. The problem of a lack of standards applies to valuing as much as to costing.

When valuing information services for the purposes of an information audit, it must be made clear that it is simply not possible to put a monetary value on anything – unless it is a service for which a charge is made. This might be a publication, or an on-line service produced in-house. Even with such items, care should be taken not to just assign a monetary value. Information resources are used for many purposes, which may in themselves generate cash at the end. The information itself has value by:

- being good publicity
- enabling new markets to be entered
- enabling existing markets to be expanded
- giving contacts
- giving expertise
- bringing together diverse items to make a coherent whole

but it does not itself have a cash value (unless you're a spy with a state or industrial secret to sell).

WHAT NEXT?

When all the interviews have been carried out, all the resulting information keyed in, and all the costing and valuation done, what do you do with it? You analyse it and compile the final report.

This is possibly the most daunting part of the whole operation. In many information centres it is the point at which, in the normal course of answering an enquiry, the work stops. The information gathered is passed on to the enquirer, who does with it whatever he or she wishes. Now it's your turn.

It will not be as difficult a task as it may seem when simply reading about it in a chapter like this. One advantage will be that, having spent weeks, if not months, steeped in the project and concentrating on nothing else, you will have much of the information at your fingertips. You will also have determined patterns of information flow, noted gaps in provision and unnecessary duplication, during the course of your questioning and visiting.

I can only explain the way I do these things myself: frankly, I let it fester in my mind for a couple of days or so. There is a Video Arts film – one of a series on management skills – which refers to the importance of thinking time. It shows John Cleese apparently gazing idly out of the window. His secretary tells someone that he is not available, even though he is visibly alone, 'because he's thinking'. At this point in an information audit you will realize how necessary thinking time is. If gazing into space is not an acceptable action in your organization, and you have the misfortune to work in an open-plan office, you can overcome the problem in two ways:

1. Sit at your desk with an open file and a pencil in your hand
2. Book an empty meeting room or find an empty office

and sit and think. I find that after a couple of days at the most, my ideas have reached boiling point and it all spills out onto the paper.

Work straight through the report and edit it later. The order in which you write the report will be dictated to a certain extent by the order in which you carried out the project. There will be amendments to add afterwards, of course, and the finished product should also have a more or less standard structure, as with the original proposal.

What you have at the end of writing should include some or all of the following sections:

- Summary of main points (compile this at the end of writing)
- Introduction (what the report contains)
- Brief explanation of the concept of information auditing (if necessary)
- Details of the information resources and how they are used in the organization
- Cost and value of information resources
- Samples of questionnaire forms used
- A list of people interviewed
- A copy of the original proposal

The main section, detailing the actual information resources in use, should be divided into manageable sections. It is possible, if you have designed your database correctly, to simply run it off in hard copy and use that. It will certainly give all the details you need and, with a key at the front, provide not only an overview for senior managers but also a resources index for distribution throughout the organization.

The section on cost and value of information resources will need to have considerable and careful explanation of the difficulties in carrying out these particular assessments as a substantial part of the whole. There should be no difficulty in having this accepted as there are manifestly no established standards to be referred to, and no one, no matter how hard they look, will find any.

This is where you point out any duplications or gaps in service provision. You can also take the opportunity to make a few recommendations, although, strictly speaking, an audit is simply an accounting function and not an opportunity to comment. Nevertheless, since one point of carrying out an information audit is to see where improvements might be made, it would be foolish to simply list everything without comment.

Sample questionnaires and a list of those people interviewed should be added to indicate the thoroughness of the job which has been done. A copy of the original proposal is also attached to remind everyone what the exercise aimed to achieve at the outset.

◆ Presenting the report

The opportunity to present a report should always be eagerly grasped. After conducting an information audit, especially for the first time, it is important there should be an opportunity to explain everything to those above you in the hierarchy. When making the presentation, bear in mind that you are the expert and they probably won't fully understand what you're talking about. Bearing this in mind greatly boosts self-confidence.

Presenting a report usually means simply talking through it, with everyone having a copy open in front of them, section by section. This is the occasion on which you explain why you undertook to put the questionnaire together as you did, why the record format was designed as it was, and any difficulties you encountered, either expected or unexpected. It is also an opportunity to acknowledge help and interest shown, especially if it came from surprising quarters.

Sometimes the finished report shows that the project did not keep to the original proposal, and presenting the report provides an opportunity to explain what happened to change the project's direction. It does not mean that the original proposal was wrongly put together. It does mean that, while carrying out the project, it was realized some tasks would need to be included that were not known about at the beginning. There is nothing wrong with that.

Those people listening to you will also take the opportunity to ask questions. This may be because they are striving to understand, or because of some internal politics within the group of which you are unaware. Don't try to be clever – just answer the question!

Presentations usually last from about 30 minutes (a little short) to an hour and a half, depending on the priority given to the subject. You may not get any feedback at the presentation; that will come later when there has been time to digest what you have written. Silence for a few weeks does not mean that all your efforts have been wasted.

AND THERE'S MORE ...

Carrying out an audit of information resources can be shown to be the first step in a programme that can lead to the formulation of a corporate information strategy. This is not something of interest to large companies alone, but to all organizations, whatever their size or interest. Nor is it merely a question of cutting costs, and should not be promoted as a means of saving money. Turn the idea on its head, and promote it as a way of increasing competitiveness and grabbing a larger share of the particular market in which your company operates – or of penetrating new markets – by means of having in place a strategy for developing information resources over the coming years: a five-year plan for information management, as it were (no longer – remember, this is a rapidly developing area).

Even if a corporate information strategy is not required, the information audit will certainly be a useful basis to use as a starting point for putting together your own development plan. This plan could contain recommendations for the future enhancement of the information services available within the organization. What about suggesting the merging of the IT department with the Library to form an Information Resources Department (with you as Director)?

◆ References

Burk, C.F. Jr. and Horton, F.W. Jr (1988) *InfoMap: A Complete Guide to Discovering Corporate Information Resources*, New Jersey: Prentice Hall.

Orna, E. (1990) *Practical Information Policies: How to Manage Information Flow in Organizations*, Aldershot: Gower.

6 Budgeting, financial control, purchasing and charging

Liz Chapman

- Budgeting
- Accounting
- Purchasing
- Charging

The central planning document for any library or information unit is the budget. This chapter considers different ways of drawing up and keeping track of a budget, along with purchasing, and charging for your service.

◆ Budgeting

BACKGROUND TO THE BUDGET

Whether you are setting up a service from scratch or taking over the budget function, there are several points you must find out from your organization before drawing up any financial estimates. You should talk to the manager who has responsibility for the library budget, and to the accountant(s) and those people who actually handle payments on behalf of the library. On the whole, accountants have scant understanding of the multiplicity of orders and invoices involved in the provision of information, and a personal link will help ease any problems you may have in the financial year ahead.

Some of the questions you will need answers to are:

- Who has overall managerial responsibility for the library budget?
- Who has day-to-day responsibility for the library budget?

- Who has authority to sign invoices for payment for the library?
- Who actually handles the library's accounts?
- When (in the month) are invoices paid?
- Are payments sent electronically/by cheque?
- How do you get a cheque raised quickly?
- How do you get petty cash quickly?
- Is there a central purchasing department? (If so, how does it affect you? Are you obliged to order everything via them?)
- Is the library considered to be the central purchasing department for all printed material even if it is not intended for the library?
- What happens if you overspend/underspend?

With the answers to these questions, and any other information you may have already on library use (or non-use), you can begin to draw up a budget. Bear in mind what you already know about your organization in terms of which parts of it are flourishing and which are not doing so well. Try to align yourself with the first.

HOW MUCH MONEY WILL YOU GET?

Formula-funding represents perhaps the least complex form of funding, where the library receives a percentage of the income of the organization it serves, or perhaps a percentage of its research budget. This is not a very helpful way of funding, since it cannot take into account the particular needs of information units, as opposed to other parts of the organization, which have different responsibilities.

Lump sum funding means exactly what it says; the library receives the amount of money that the organization believes it deserves. The library will need to break it down into meaningful segments.

Incremental funding takes into account various factors; what happened last year, inflation trends, currency trends, the way in which the business is heading, financial constraints, and growth plans.

Departmental accountants and corporate planners can be very helpful by explaining current constraints and opportunities. However, librarians should not get too excited about their ability to actually influence the amount of money they get. You can only make the best case possible on your behalf.

DRAWING UP A BUDGET

Library budgets can range from the very simple (lump sum) budget to those which are broken down into a variety of different areas, heads, funds or account codes. Examples of different kinds of budget are given later in this chapter.

The method of budgeting used in other departments of your employing organization will probably also be used in the library. This may be line-by-line, performance budgeting, or zero-based budgeting, but it is worth familiarizing yourself with various types as each has useful attributes.

Usually, the librarian or equivalent will draw up a draft budget or estimates that will initially be discussed with the line manager who collates budgets from various departments. After any necessary changes it will go to higher management for approval. The library manager may be called on to defend the budgetary figures at this stage, so you must know what you are talking about.

Always draw up a clear and simple budget. Accompanying explanatory notes should appear on separate pages. Draw it up in a professional-looking way so as to influence decision-makers. Senior managers have enough negative feelings about the competencies of librarians without you adding to them. Always have plans ready for all contingencies:

- What you could buy with more money
- What you could cancel if necessary
- What plans you have for the future
- What was right/wrong with last year's budget
- What comparative units are spending elsewhere

Remember that bad news well presented will go down better than good news badly presented. Senior managers do not want surprises.

LINE-BY-LINE BUDGETING

Here is an example of a line-by-line budget for a commercial scientific research library:

1. Books and pamphlets   £ 45 000 ($ 81 000)
2. Periodicals   £100 000 ($180 000)
3. Microform   £ 1 000 ($ 1 800)
4. Binding   £ 3 000 ($ 5 400)

5. External information	£ 97 000 ($174 600)
6. Translations	£ 15 000 ($ 27 000)
7. Inter-library loans	£ 15 000 ($ 27 000)
8. Internal information	£ 25 000 ($ 45 000)
9. Private (i.e. not library) books	£ 13 000 ($ 23 400)
TOTAL	£314 000 ($565 200)

Line-by-line budgeting is also known as **incremental** budgeting, as it is simply extrapolating next year's budget from what happens this year. It is relatively easy to understand and draw up, however, it can allow for too much inertia and mask a lack of serious thought about the library service. It leaves little room for new developments or for contingencies, although new lines or codes can be added. It does ensure that money is allocated to existing known needs.

The example given has no figures for staff or their associated costs such as travel or training, since this is handled separately. Equally, there are no figures for capital equipment, furniture or maintenance. Again, these are usually kept separate, and new items to be purchased involve making a special case.

An even simpler example of a budget from a management consultancy information unit follows:

1. Library costs debit	£20 000 ($36 000)
2. Library costs credit	£20 000 ($36 000)
3. Data costs debit	£25 000 ($45 000)
4. Data costs credit	£25 000 ($45 000)
5. Journals and books (net)	£40 000 ($72 000)

Here, budget items mirror each other. The information unit charges out its services to the consultancy group, so as the library uses an information broker or an inter-library loan the cost is entered on line 1; when the charge made is recouped it is entered on line 2. Data costs for on-line searching are entered on line 3, while the recouped charges are entered on line 4. The money the unit may spend on books and journals is a net sum which cannot be billed out to clients. Actual estimates will show figures in 1 and 3 to be mirrored (reflected) in 2 and 4, respectively. Charging for services is considered in more detail later in this chapter.

PERFORMANCE BUDGETING

Budget examples given so far provide no evaluation of the service. They are concerned with input rather than output. Performance budgeting starts from a cost-benefit analysis of the service. Unit costs are developed for each activity, with emphasis being laid on effectiveness and accountability.

The first widely used type of performance budgeting was Planning Programming Budgeting Systems (PPBS). This provides an analytical approach to budgeting where the three elements of planning, programming and budgeting are integrated. For this system you have to develop clear objectives, identify outputs, measure these outputs, and analyse the benefits in relation to the cost. A general example could be:

INPUT COST	CATEGORY	OBJECTIVE
£8 000 ($14 400)	Current awareness service	Promote awareness of library services

OUTPUT	COST PER OUTPUT
60 bulletins	£8 ($14.4)

There are variations of this system available which, while they are time consuming in terms of preparation, will give a good indication of how the service is working and how much individual services cost.

ZERO-BASED BUDGETING (ZBB)

It is certainly no coincidence that zero-based budgeting came to prominence in libraries at a time when they were being squeezed, by and with their parent institutions in the 1980s. This system involves justifying all expenditure from scratch, or from a zero base.

Decision packages are prepared by looking at specific activities and their purpose or goal, and the advantages of retaining the activity or the consequences of stopping it are considered. Then a cost table can be drawn up showing cuts in the activity, retaining the status quo, and increases in the activity. An example hypothetical decision package framework is:

Name of Activity:
Purpose of Activity:
Advantage of Retention:
Consequence of Elimination:

Alternatives

Budget	Description	Cost
80%		
100%		
120%		

With this sort of form, which can easily be set up on a microcomputer with a spreadsheet package, you might, for example, have to consider the telephone provision of information to remote branches of your organization. Why do you do this? Would it be a good idea to continue? What would happen if you stopped? Then you need to cost out a cut in this provision (80%), the retention of the status quo (100%), and an increase in the service (120%). Of course, this presupposes that you already log all your calls and have worked out the cost of staff time involved. Nothing is ever as simple as it seems on a form.

ZBB is very time consuming, although it does have the advantage of making you look critically at the service. It is often forced on special libraries, particularly where managers have no idea what a library can provide, nor why this unkown provision seems to cost so much. Some employers take the system at face value and work up from a zero base: 'Imagine that the library budget is nil; how would you justify the purchase of x...?' It is to be hoped that you won't have to do this every year.

It is best, if possible, to combine elements of several types of budgeting: line-by-line budgets show how money will be divided up; ZBB provides criteria to justify services and, with performance measures, shows how the service is operating in terms of its aims and objectives.

◆ Accounting

THE FINANCIAL YEAR

Drawing up estimates and a budget is only the beginning of a process which goes on throughout the year. The financial year does not always coincide with the tax year – it may be January to December, or the academic year. However it is organized, you can expect to receive information on expenditure from your accounts department at least once a month.

A monthly statement should include 'year to date' figures, i.e. those showing how much you have spent so far this financial year. You should also receive 'current transactions', i.e. figures for credits and debits made since the last statement. The figures should be allocated to the various cost codes you have available for credit and debit. A final figure will indicate how much money you have left to the end of the financial year. Computer printouts seldom print in red. You will have to look for any codes that imply you have a minus sum left for the year.

If you have submitted detailed estimates, these may also be shown alongside expenditure figures, thus giving an idea of how accurate your estimates were and whether any funds or 'heads' should be delayed for a while, or stepped up.

The example in Figure 6.1 shows a monthly statement from the library of a research institution. Income codes are listed at the top first, and then expenditure.

Monthly statement	End of month 8		LIBRARY Estimates	
Library grant	£55046.00 cr	($ 99082)	£55046.00 cr	($ 99082)
Sales and services	£ 3537.18 cr	($ 6042)	£ 5000.00 cr	($ 9000)
TOTAL INCOME	£58583.18 cr	($105449)	£60046.00 cr	($108082)
Printing and stationery	£ 158.00	($ 18284)	£ 300.00	($ 540)
Equipment rental	£ 1589.57	($ 2860)	£ 1000.00	($ 1800)
Photocopying	£ 400.00	($ 720)	£ 500.00	($ 900)
Library books	£12139.00	($ 21850)	£20000.00	($ 36000)
Library periodicals	£12797.22	($ 23034)	£25000.00	($ 45000)
Binding	£ 1084.30	($ 1951)	£ 4000.00	($ 72000)
Non-book material	£ 397.53	($ 714)	£ 380.00	($ 684)
Information services	£ 6242.29	($ 11235)	£ 8866.00	($ 15958)
TOTAL EXPENDITURE	£34807.91	($ 62654)	£60046.00	($108082)

Figure 6.1

From the example, it can be seen that on the whole the budget is on target two thirds of the way through the financial year. Equipment rental and non-book material are overspent while binding is way below target. This is probably because the annual binding time has not yet occurred 'Charged for' services are also on target to create the estimated income, and possibly more. It looks as if only half the periodicals have yet been renewed for next year.

This is an example of a fairly helpful statement. You are just as likely to receive a statement which is covered with indecipherable codes, known only to accountants. It is not sufficient to keep jogging along, not understanding statements. You must ask what they mean.

The figures given in Figure 6.1 (and on any such statement) do not show what outstanding commitments (orders) the library has, and you should keep an account of these. It is never possible for a library to end the financial year with all orders fulfilled (we do not control publishers or booksellers). However, for the sake of the accounts department you will need to know what orders (or invoices) you have outstanding (creditors), and what payments are due to the library (debtors). Again, keeping separate records of these is important information for your managers and for you when you are trying to make a case for more money next year. Also, you may need to adjust your estimates during the year. Keep your managers informed of problems such as the relative strengths of various currencies, or cash flow problems as charged services are not paid for at once.

The amount of record-keeping you will need to do for individual orders and payments will vary depending on where you work. As a minimum you should keep one copy of each order sent out and one copy of each invoice paid. Auditors (the people who check the accounts and accountants) like accession registers and invoice ledgers. Busy librarians do not. You can explain that catalogues take over from accession registers and that copy invoices replace ledgers in which each bill is individually entered. In practice, your accountant will be producing a ledger entry every time they pay an invoice or receive credit.

You should note on invoice copies the date on which you send them to the accounts department for payment so as to help you check statements from suppliers. Statements are sent out by suppliers at regular intervals. If your accounts department does not pay within the time stated on an invoice (e.g. 'Terms net 30 days') you will receive a statement showing invoices unpaid. Beware: statements are often printed on exactly the same stationery as invoices. Look for the word **statement**. Some accounts departments will check statements for you, but if neither of you does and bills are left unpaid, you will receive a beautifully embellished solicitor's letter. It is not worth risking these very often. If you do receive one (even if its contents are erroneous), resolve the problem at once for your peace of mind and the library's internal competency rating.

Every so often your accounts will be thoroughly checked by an auditor. The most common auditing method in libraries is to use an audit trail. The auditor will follow an individual order through from raising the order to receipt and payment. They may well want to see the item itself as well as its paid invoice. They may also consider wider issues such as value-for-money if you have a publications exchange programme or the handling of a Value Added Tax (VAT) on charged services.

It is up to the librarian to show the value of the library service, both in monetary and quality terms. You cannot do this unless you have a clearly worked out budget, careful cost accounting throughout the year, and both of these linked to the stated aims and objectives of the service. Accounting for staff time as a feature of your costs is part of a professionally prepared budget.

◆ Purchasing

PURCHASES

The main purchase for any library is information, which comes in many forms as materials (books, journals, data) and services (online, information brokers). You need staff to exploit this information as well as the space in which to operate and the necessary equipment. All these factors have to be considered as part of your budget.

MATERIALS

Your usual material purchases are likely to be books, journals, conference proceedings, reports and working papers, government publications, and trade/professional literature. It goes without saying that you should try to get the best value for money by obtaining discounts where possible but, on the whole, speed of supply and accuracy are likely to be ahead of price on your list of priorities. (There is more on this topic in Roy Adams' chapter on 'Relationships with suppliers'.)

Find suppliers who can handle your requirements and work out, for example, how to get the latest government report on the day it is published (or the day before, if that is when it appears). This can mean you or your staff going personally, cash-in-hand or paying a courier (also cash-in-hand).

Library users have little idea of the difficulties of purchasing or obtaining obscure reports. If you cannot buy what the user wants, try borrowing from another library. Build up a network of other libraries that will help, and offer help to them in return when it is needed.

Buying individual books and reports is usually a well-accepted practice in special libraries, but ongoing orders for periodicals or expensive annual reference books can be harder to justify. Serials are also an ongoing commitment in staff time for check-in, chasing, binding and circulation. They are vulnerable to cuts. Some libraries 'charge out' periodicals or serials to individual departments which have a particular interest in the subject matter, but this means they no longer belong to the library and control over them is lost (as the items themselves often are too). Try to use prepayment discounts for these items from suppliers such as the Swets and Blackwell subscription services. They will also be able to offer advice on currency fluctuations.

Selection of what materials to buy is in practice the librarian's task. Of course, you should react to suggestions from your library users, but you must keep up with what is going on in your organization as a whole. Try to purchase ahead of need. For instance, my library committee rejected the purchase of expensive statistics on China, but once they arrived one member of the committee used them all the time for a new project. Use bookseller alerting services such as the slips from Bumpus, Haldane and Maxwell. Buy specialist items from specialist suppliers, e.g. Collets specialize in material from Eastern Europe.

Beware of donations to the library. There is no such thing as a free book, despite the well known belief of library users – BLOTSBYTS (books leap onto the shelves by themselves). Donations are a cost to your service.

Of course, the collection you build up is unlikely to consist only of books and journals. You will have to consider such formats as software packages, trade literature and indexes, video, slides, and CD-ROM, as well as in-house databases.

Try to keep records of total materials spending, average costs per item, and how much is spent on each department of your organization. This can be fed into your budget planning next time around together with publicly available price indices.

SERVICES

The services most commonly purchased for special libraries are on-line search services, and information brokerage or information consultants. On-line services are confusing in their different methods of charging, further complicated by their willingness to negotiate terms related to access and volume of use. You may want to account for annual charges to a database host as a materials purchase and actual on-line costs as a services purchase. Of course, on-line services not only provide your clients with more information, but also push up the demand for further information provision, in particular inter-library loans.

Inter-library loan is crucial for small units in the provision of material outside your normal subject area or only needed occasionally, material which cannot be purchased or which is too expensive to purchase. Electronic transmission of requests and the use of available periodical and accession lists should speed up your service. Translations are a specialized area where you may have to purchase outside services.

If there is limited staff (isn't there always?) you will have to use information broker services to cope with 'I need it yesterday' requests. Extensive and expensive use of such services may help make the case for more staff in-house at a later date. Records of such costs must certainly be kept.

You may also want to use consultants to help establish a new service, design or redesign the physical set-up of your service, overhaul your existing service, or indulge in systems analysis. On the whole, this is work you could do yourself if you only had the time.

For bought-in services (in budgetary terms), the question then is do they:

- reduce costs?
- speed access to information?
- provide better quality information?

The way in which you order these considerations will depend on the priorities of the organization for which you work. Payment for an automated library system can also be considered as a purchased service.

STAFF

The cost of staff is usually the largest part of your total budget. At least 50% and up to 80% of the budget can be used in this way. In the budget you will have to consider existing staff and any temporary or new staff you expect to recruit for special projects. Advertising and interview expenses can be substantial. The cost of training and staff development should also be planned, along with any increments or special payments due. Apart from actually paying staff, there are indirect costs such as National Insurance and pension payments which could add another 50% to the staff bill.

Your organization is likely to set salary ranges, hours, special payments and fringe benefits and, of course, holidays. While you may have little say in these beyond the level of recommendations to the personnel department, the advantage to you may be that staff are not considered as part of your annual budget. Nevertheless, you should still keep careful records of grading, job descriptions, incremental or long-service payments, and pension scheme membership.

SPACE

Some libraries and information units are charged by their organizations for the space which they occupy. These charges can include lease, or rent, mortgage, business rates, and heating and power. The advantage of this system is that a clear indication is given of what the library actually costs the institution in space terms. The library manager is unlikely to be able to change the system (although if the lease of your building precludes sub-letting you could try!).

On occasions, these kinds of payments will be indirect, being absorbed by the parent organization, but you should not ignore their existence. You may still be charged maintenance charges even if you are not charged rent. Space charges are an overhead you will need to cover when accounting for your services.

EQUIPMENT

The most obvious equipment purchases for libraries are office supplies, stationery, printing, furniture, etc. However, much more expensive items such as microcomputers, fax machines and photocopiers may also be considered as equipment. You may work for an organization that buys these for you, or arranges fixed or phased payback arrangements so that your budget is not hit too hard all at once. For large pieces of equipment, sometimes known as **capital equipment**, you may have to make a special case for funds. Plan this well ahead to avoid disappointment, and make sure to obtain good prices, and be seen to be doing so.

Much large equipment carries associated recurrent costs such as telephone bills, leasing arrangements for photocopiers, maintenance contracts for computers, and there may also be insurance. You may have to maintain a sinking fund to amortize (gradually kill off the debt for) the cost of equipment, and possibly plan for repurchase.

Library computer systems always have ongoing (and increasing) costs, and you must try to plan for these. They usually appear as an annual charge. If you are allocated money for equipment each year, always make sure to spend it. If you do not it will be assumed that you do not need that amount in another year.

CONTINGENCIES

Last, but by no means least, you will need to leave room in your budget for contingencies and irregular payments. Some examples are:

- Special payments to staff/overtime/overlapping appointments/entertainment
- Interest payments on purchases of capital equipment
- General book fund for immediate urgent purchases (e.g. reference books)

Although it is seldom possible to forecast what immediate needs may arise during the financial year, you should still assume that something unforeseen will arise. However, do not leave any money for contingencies in your budget at the end of the year. You should always be spent to the budget. This is easier said than done, particularly if you are earning money as well as spending, since you will also have to depend on the efficiency of the accounting procedures of your clients. If you have money left over, now is the time to consult your list of what you could purchase if you had the money.

PURCHASING STRATEGY: ON-LINE VERSUS PAPER

The purchase of access to on-line services is viewed as one method of collection management. If you cannot afford the money (or space) to buy printed materials, on-line services can give you access to them, this despite the recent assertion from an officer of the Publishers' Association (UK) that a paperless library is about as likely as a paperless toilet!

The conflict between the purchase of print or on-line can be considered under various headings:

- Does on-line access mean that you can cancel printed subscriptions?
- Are you restricting the number of information users at a time, by only providing one computer terminal or intermediary as opposed to several printed volumes?
- How many of your customers already have their own on-line access and are therefore less likely to make use of the library service?
- Does on-line impose extra stress on your service by suggesting material you will have to obtain from elsewhere?
- Can your budget cope with increased costs of on-line services?
- Can you keep up with the proliferation of databases (20–30% extra per year) and their associated learning curves?
- Do you need to set up a new budget fund or code for on-line?
- Do you need to buy new equipment and furniture?
- Would it be more cost-effective to buy in outside expertise from an information broker or on-line search service?

As you can see, many of the considerations are budgetary, but there is no doubt that whatever kind of service you provide you must make provision in your budget for obtaining material promptly from elsewhere. Inter-library loans are the first obvious route, but you should also have links with other services similar to your own so you can exchange material or simply provide each other with specialist material rapidly. Cooperation breeds cooperation.

◆ Charging

CHARGING FOR YOUR SERVICE

The increasing cost of providing on-line search services has acted as a catalyst in the move towards charging customers for information. Although some would argue that it is a cost-effective means of collection management. This is not the place in which to discuss the pros and cons of charging, but it is important to consider *how* to charge.

Given the substantial historical basis of the free public library service it has taken time for libraries to move towards charging for services, and librarians are seldom trained in the necessary skills. If a special library is a cost centre it may appear to accountants as just one more department amongst many, an overhead of sorts where the library cannot generate its own funds and may not strictly be aware of its own status as an overhead. If, on the other hand, the library is a profit centre, the value of its services becomes more obvious in monetary terms, and it must take active responsibility for overheads on salaries, training, computer and printed information.

The simplest way to charge for information is to 'charge out' the acquisition of materials to departments outside the library. For example, you may purchase a very expensive periodical that is only used by one department (although I think that claims of exclusivity in such multi-disciplinary times are very dangerous), and you could charge the subscription to that department. Another method of charging out would be to charge the direct costs of on-line searching. However, neither of these examples really tackles the actual cost of providing the service. For example, neither takes into account staffing costs.

SETTING CHARGES

Setting a charge for the provision of information must take into account the following factors:

- What is the realistic cost of staff? (This is not just employment costs divided by employment hours.) Assess available hours plus administration and development of service and training of staff. Staff are not 100% efficient all the time, and they do need holidays.

- What is the unit cost for provision of each type of information (e.g. reference, on-line search, abstracts, value-added reports)? Unit costs are not performance measures. Cost does not necessarily reflect value for money. On-line charges are complex, and you may need to fix a price for each piece of information.
- How can you spread costs realistically? If you have high fixed costs, unit costs can decrease with volume of requests, e.g. the second time you answer the same question it will be much cheaper to provide the answer. If you have low fixed costs, the revenue earned can more easily match actual costs. Fixed costs are staff, accommodation, etc.
- How can you set charges? The relationship of costs to 'sales' must not change dramatically over time, which means you should try to set an acceptable charge from the beginning. Dramatic changes in price or complicated pricing will upset customers. You must obviously price at a level your customers can afford, and be able to answer the question 'What do I get for my money?' Some idea of what prices are charged elsewhere would be useful.
- How should customers pay? Retrospective charging or estimation will lead to cash flow problems and invoicing bureaucracy. You may already have to pre-pay on-line service subscriptions. If you charge by subscription this will provide money up front, but your service will be scrutinized on renewal. Obviously, it is easy to charge a subscription for such items as library bulletins. Charging involves a good deal of administrative work in invoicing, etc.
- Where will money come from for development of new services? Variable costs include volume of sales, extra staff, and equipment and marketing. These will need to be budgeted for so that new developing services can 'piggyback' on existing services while they develop. This consideration can underline the tension between serving the institution and encouraging new uses and users of information. Your costs should therefore be related to the aims and objectives of your service.

◆ Conclusion

This chapter has tried to show how to budget, account and purchase for your library or information unit. It advocates an integrated approach to these tasks by linking the mechanics of accounting to the achieving of aims and objectives for the service. There is a conflict in all services between cost effectiveness measured by output or satisfaction, and cost efficiency measured by input with tangible, obvious price tags attached. You have to operate as it were in the centre of this conflict, on the one hand pleasing those with the money, and on the other providing the most professional service that you can. If you know what kind of professional service you should be offering it will be that much easier to budget for it.

◆ References

ASLIB Information **18**(3), March 1990. Special issue on charging for information.
Budgeting: challenge or threat. *Business Library Management* **2**(6), July 1989.
Chapman, E. (1989) *Buying Books for Libraries*. London: Bingley.
Field, S. (1988) Funding, budgeting and acquisition in an industrial library, in *The Eternal Triangle? Proceedings of the 2nd Annual Conference of the National Aquisitions Group*, Oxford: NAG, 56–63.
Midwinter, A. (1990) *Financial Management: A Practical Guide to Budgetary Planning and Control*. Edinburgh: Scottish Library Association.
Roberts, S.A. (1985) *Cost Management for Library and Information Services*. London: Butterworth.
Smith, C. (ed.) (1989) Towards a policy for pricing. In *Proceedings of a Seminar, London, 22 September 1988*. London: Effective Technology Marketing Ltd.
Turock, B.J. (1990) *Creating a Financial Plan: A How-to-do-it Manual for Librarians*, New York: Neal-Schuman.
Webb, S.P. (1988) The value of information. *Outlook on Research Libraries*, **10**(4), 1–4.

7 Relationships with suppliers
Roy Adams

- One or many suppliers?
- Criteria for choosing suppliers
- Contract renewal
- Automating your suppliers
- Remote hosts
- Purchasing automated systems
- Using information brokers
- Who needs a consultant?

The relationship between a library or information unit and a supplier can cover a whole range of associations from a single order that goes disastrously wrong to a long and mutually rewarding association in which the library is provided with material reliably and on time, and the supplier receives a just financial payback. It is the librarian's role to ensure that the organization being served achieves the best possible outcome from the association, although the problem is, of course, that the 'best' is defined by a cumulation of requirements that each supplier must meet in order to have a satisfied client. An unsatisfied client not only produces irritations and eventually a loss of business, but the poor reputation of the supplier may spread to other potential clients.

Some of the criticism may be unjustified, resulting from unreasonable expectations by the library. It is therefore in the interests of the supplier as much as the supplied that the two parties agree on the materials to be supplied, services on offer, and conditions of delivery. While contract law has developed to define many of these relationships, it often manages to achieve the dual sins of being both too detailed and too crude in its methods. For instance, in an obscure on-line service you use twice a year there may be three pages of microscopic detail in a contract, whereas the definitions of service provision between you and your main supplier of books and journals may be very brief and lacking in detail. Can you find your contract now? If you can find it, you keep it with you at all times. But is it still relevant?

Cost differentials are often limited in book and journal supply, and the service elements of the relationship governed by unwritten and changing circumstances. The apparent efficiency of the library can be greatly influenced by the ability of the supplier to produce the items required on time. This chapter considers some of the most important elements in the selection of suppliers, the relevance of the continuing relationship, and the mutual support that produces good quality results. We look at what it is worth in terms of saving the time of the library, saving money, and delivering faster than the next supplier. The problem for the supplier is, of course, that they can provide any level of service that the client requires, but at a cost either in terms of money or as a depletion of facilities. In many ways it is the client's responsibility to make clear exactly what is required in a structured way so that the potential supplier can produce a package that states costs and service, and which can be measured and monitored effectively.

The process of selection implies some form of competition, either directly in terms of a tendering process, or in terms of measuring the comparative performance of different sources. The client therefore needs to be able to determine the value and types of service, how this is to be measured and over what period, and the way in which samples, analyses and the results of analyses are to be determined. Added to this will be the opinions of other users of the supplier, and the ways in which they match or do not match needs.

Our 'supplier' may be one of any number of sources for the materials and services we require. Of course, there is a continued debate in the mind of anyone charged with purchasing – go to source or use an agent. In the end the decision is usually taken out of our control, for which many of us are grateful. Certain sources of supply decide that they trade only directly with the final receiver of the material, a not uncommon attitude among those who produce market analyses, while others insist that an appointed agent must be the access route within a particular geographical area. Between these two extremes the purchaser can, however, exercise considerable judgement on the sources for information and the techniques and methods those suppliers use.

The initial reaction of those who see library systems for the first time is often 'Why use an agent? It's quicker to go direct.' It is only after some thought that the overheads involved in a total 'source from originator' policy appear to be less attractive. We perhaps dismiss this naive approach too easily, since it often emanates from senior members of the organization who may go away unconvinced by a dismissive librarian. Time spent discussing the priorities for employee time not only answers specific queries, but transmits to the receiver that the librarian understands the need to manage their operations effectively.

◆ Single or multiple suppliers?

The decision on the number of suppliers to use, one or many, is often taken from the library, since there are inevitably suppliers who will not deal with an agent and insist that orders come from source. For the majority of orders which pass through the system, however, the client, i.e. the library, does have the choice as to whether only one main supplier is employed, or two or more. The ability to match two suppliers against each other is at first attractive, but will the comparison be fair, since it can be difficult to directly measure success unless they all receive an even distribution of orders in terms of quantity and difficulty? The multiple supplier situation can be difficult to evaluate, but the monopoly supplier is even more of a problem as no comparison can be made except by inference from colleagues whose data will be difficult to interpret. The rationale for the monopoly situation is the greater influence that the client has, but that in turn leaves the library dependent on one source. Any efforts to improve the service of such a supplier are fraught with difficulties, since a basis for comparison does not exist.

The suppliers we deal with here fall into three broad areas;

- suppliers of single order items such as books, reports and similar documents, equipment, etc.
- suppliers of repeat business such as journals and standing orders
- suppliers of services.

◆ Criteria for choosing suppliers

ACCOUNTING AND FINANCIAL CONCERNS

In many ways, the library being served by a trader is not in a simple client–seller relationship. The library serves a company or other organization which is supported by its orders and accounts department. While these are themselves designed to provide a service to other parts of the organization, their relationship with the rest is deeply affected by the reliance which is placed on accounts to ensure that the flow of resources in and out of the organization is regulated to provide for the continuation and development of the company. What others may see as a simple clerical procedure masks the complexities of company law and cash flow. Anything another section can do to minimize perturbations in the systems that govern the financial dealings of the organization will earn appreciation from these custodians of the purse, and be repaid many times.

First, of course, one needs to gain the confidence of the accountants, establishing a relationship in which mutual skills are respected and built up to provide for the smooth running of company systems and the reduction of individual work problems.

On normal order and payment routines, techniques and systems need to be established with primary suppliers that match the requirements of the company's accountants. Every slide in the system produced by a non-standard accountancy procedure results in a disproportional amount of effort for all. Suppliers need to understand the company's accountancy needs in detail, and the consequences to the organization of not meeting them. Such three-way co-operation enables company employees to focus on those areas where compliance with the organization's needs are not so easily established. There will be suppliers with whom it is difficult to build up such a relationship, including the large on-line hosts, government publishers, and organizations which demand direct orders and will not go through agents. With these sources, which often operate within their own intricate and usually mystifying methods, the 'mutual aid method' built up with the internal accounting section when dealing with regular suppliers will smooth the handling of these difficult to administer accounts.

Other aspects of the payments systems that are of concern include the amount of time from invoicing to payment expected by the supplier, any penalties for late payment, and any incentives for early payment. While many companies operate on the basis of paying only at the last moment, in the supply areas in which we exist the cash flow of the supplier may materially affect delivery performance.

Foreign currency transactions are a major problem for companies unused to operating in the international arena, and providing invoices in the local currency for materials from many sources is one of the most 'value added' services a supplier can render. Converting currencies, obtaining orders, and clearing cash through foreign banks (particularly as these transactions are often cash with order) not only save time and effort, but reduce risks for the purchaser. The costs of such activities must, however, be borne by someone, and the purchase price may be heavily loaded to recover the time that has been expended. From time to time correspondence appears in the library press which indicates differences in prices for the same item by as much as 100% for the end purchaser. On sets of expensive specialist encyclopaedia and continuing series this difference can amount to a significant sum.

Understanding the basis on which suppliers charge for foreign material can therefore save thousands over the course of a year. Suppliers with established links in the countries in which the material you are seeking is published stand the best chance of obtaining such material at a good price, and also in reasonable time. How and whether they pass on the financial benefits or costs is a matter of negotiation between them and you. You should at least know on what basis currency conversion rates are calculated, and how any supplement for foreign material is introduced. Without this you cannot even begin to assess the costs and benefits of the service you are seeking.

BIBLIOGRAPHICALLY SPEAKING ...

The timely and accurate provision of material relies to a large extent on the accuracy and completeness of the information generated by the originator of an order and the ability of the supplier to reinforce and supplement this information. Many suppliers see the provision of an accurate and complete bibliographic service as a major feature in their strategy. Evaluating the strength and utility of such services is one of the most difficult aspects of customer/supplier relationships. In many cases the customer may be supporting a service which is not really required. Often the information given on a customer's original order is sufficient and accurate enough to enable the item to be supplied immediately. On others the very nature of the material and lack of information may defeat the intermediate supplier just as much as the originator.

On the other hand, the supplier that can rapidly locate and supply an obscure, urgently required item scores well. Only experience can provide a guide to the benefits using any one supplier can bring to such a situation, although information on the skills and sources available to them will give a strong clue. There is, however, little benefit from receiving a service you do not need, and if you have confidence in your own bibliographic resources you should find a supplier who will offer alternative plus points. A mutual understanding of the bibliographic tools regularly employed by both parties and a common set of codes to denote sources checked will at least prevent needless duplication of effort and eliminate time wasted in repeated checking.

BUT I WANT IT NOW ...

A supplier must decide to what extent the client is driven by price, and to what extent by the level of service on offer. The problem is, of course, that the needs of each client are different, and the needs of those individual clients vary depending on their end users. This is an almost impossible problem for the supplier to solve without adequate information from the client, since without this information the supplier is being asked to make a value judgement about an unknown end use. Tactics employed include librarians trusting that supplier goodwill will be generated by placing regular orders and suppliers making a feature of rapid service at a premium price, e.g. same day delivery of new HMSO (Her Majesty's Stationery Office) materials.

An alternative to either of these tactics is to establish an understanding between the normal supplier and the client on a *modus operandi* for urgent orders. Many delays can be minimized if a basic set of rules is negotiated between both parties on the procedures each will follow if an item is designated urgent. If the proportion of urgent to non-urgent orders is also broadly agreed as a percentage of overall trading, rapid delivery may be achieved when needed at a negligible premium price. The occasion when your Managing Director calls for an obscure document required yesterday is not the time to start talks with your suppliers.

In addition to determining price and delivery such negotiations may cover:

- who in the client's organizations can declare an item urgent
- the level of information supplied about the item
- any special protocols for delivery. For example, should all urgent orders be faxed through to the supplier to avoid any misunderstandings a telephone call might introduce?

Even with the urgent action specialist suppliers, clearance of credit and an understanding of their trading techniques can be as effective as any other element in ensuring prompt service.

BUT IT'S NOT HERE ...

While the aim of all suppliers is to deliver items required at an appropriate time, the efficient notification of possible delays has great value. Not only does it reduce the frustration of the client, but it enables them to plan for the delay. Reports on the factors involved in a delay need to be in a form which is easily assimilated into the client's own record system, and in a form that can be transmitted on to their users with the minimum of effort. The client and the supplier need to establish the events and timescales that lead to the production of reports, and the regularity with which they are produced should an item have a long delay. There should be arrangements made to cover situations where prices are above those predicted by the library.

STOCK EXCHANGE

Most of the time the fact that a supplier holds stock may not be relevant, since the normal distribution system will enable the supplier to order directly from source and to deliver in what the client perceives is a satisfactory timescale. The stockholder has additional overheads in terms of the stock itself and the storage needed to hold it in readiness for orders. By definition, they will have material on the shelves that is going to be in demand and is therefore in the category of 'less difficult to obtain' material. The non-stockholder can concentrate staff on ordering material rather than supporting that which is in stock, and as a result may have a quicker turnaround on the majority of orders not recovered from stock and at a lower cost. The selection of a specialist stockholder thus becomes one of the more finely balanced decision making activities, since their value lies in their ability to 'second-guess' your needs – which they are unlikely to know unless you have been a customer over a considerable period. A sample from some recent orders to your existing supplier can provide an indication of the potential a supplier has in your field for immediate delivery. However, remember that urgently required material may not be mainstream in your subject area, but may be specialist material such as government documents or standards.

An efficient selective dissemination of information (SDI) service on new publications within the library's interest domain provides the supplier's client with an economical method of checking that the library is keeping up with new material. If this information is supplied in a form that matches the library's administrative systems, perhaps as paper slips or a machine readable file, the service can become an integral element in the library's information provision activities.

A good supplier should be able to provide assistance during stock building and editing by the production of lists of suitable material both in stock and not in stock but in print. An inspection service provides this type of support on a continuing basis, although care is needed in establishing the exact conditions under which the service is provided.

The benefits of a book servicing facility will be dependent on the amount of material acquired in a year. For some the amount of in-house time saved by a supplier placing stationery and stamps in new material will be insignificant, while for others the savings enable other tasks to be accomplished in-house that could otherwise not be carried out. Similarly, differences in the charges made for these activities may be a significant element in selecting a supplier. Delivery costs, packaging, etc., all add to costs. In the end it is the price at the bottom of the invoice that we need to concentrate on.

Delivery is a matter not only of efficient service to your clients, but has a direct effect on the allocation of staff resources. A delivery cycle which is unreliable, sporadic and infrequent leaves the purchaser with the inability to plan work loads and causes delays right up to the final payment of invoices. Even if we cannot control individual one-off suppliers, we should be able to obtain a reasonable delivery arrangement from regular ones.

◆ Contract renewal

Few events fill the manager with more dread than going out to contract for the supply of periodicals and standing orders through an agent. Among the most prominent of the more hated experiences is managing the process which stems from using a new agent, i.e. the transition period from the old supplier. While some organizations leave the style and timing for going through the tendering process to the information officer or librarian, in others this event appears to be just the opportunity for the company purchasing officers to show off their skills. If the organization's style is to utilize the talents of purchase/order departments fully in the process, then the secret is, of course, to involve them on your terms. Indeed, such sections have skills that are important and useful, they just perhaps need some moderating.

Seize the initiative by approaching the relevant person early on in the process, and making it clear you value and respect their professional help. A clear understanding of aspects of a tender not directly concerned with price is important. By making a list of these points and placing an estimate of value on them you will be able to more easily isolate the differences between one quotation and another. Having established a document based not only on price but on system responses, such as dealing with missing issues, invoices, credit arrangements, etc., suppliers can be asked to present their offerings. An established track record with similar clients is an important element. Some quantification of the cost of switching from the existing source should be made, and of the help a prospective supplier could give in effecting the transfer. This is a good point at which to discuss the results of any possible change of supplier with the current agent. While the tendering process is being conducted, the existing supplier is much more likely to agree the possible ending of a relationship on amicable terms.

When tenders are examined they can be evaluated against your criteria and the successful agent established. One of the options in this process will of course be a fully estimated and costed alternative to conducting the purchase of periodicals and standing orders directly from source. Once the decision on a supplier has been made, those who failed to get the contract should be informed of the reasons for their failure, provided company policy permits this. Such feedback gives those unsuccessful suppliers an opportunity to improve their techniques and increase the chances of success next time. One of the advantages of having an established cycle of going out to tender and communicating this to suppliers is that those who lose out on the current evaluation know the framework in which another opportunity will arise.

MEASURING THE DIFFERENCES

Determining the 'best' supplier for a service depends on the ability to measure the performance of the organization itself against a set of criteria. The assessment of the supplier's performance against those criteria which are the most sensitive produces a set of **performance indicators**. Performance indicators have been widely advocated by those who control library budgets in all sectors, so developing them for libraries to use in comparing their performance to other libraries gives a new insight into their relevance, as well as helping to define a set of measureable objectives for suppliers to fulfil.

Our supplier performance indicators can be developed from the criteria already discussed. They will enable the library both to compare the supplier against targets assigned to individual companies, and to compare one company with another.

Even with a small throughput of new material the ability to answer the question 'How well does my supplier do?', except in the most general terms, requires the processing power that a computer can give. This sounds relatively easy: buy a package — there are enough acquisition and order modules available for even small operations to implement. Unfortunately, most of these see the type of management information we need as secondary to the task of processing transactions, such as posting an order or invoice to the system. The position is beginning to change, but the requirement for complex analysis of time is still a challenge that many systems are unable to meet.

Even if such analysis is possible, be careful that differences in suppliers are not masking differences in environments and demands. The amount of effort required for such a sophisticated approach needs to be matched by benefits which may not be in the delivery of all materials x days early, but in the arrival of just one important item on time as a result of knowing who best to choose for the order.

◆ Automating your suppliers

It is, of course, one of the tenets of modern library automation that automating the links between supplier and library will lead to improved cost efficiency and service effectiveness. This is simpler to say than to achieve given that there are currently few operational standards to which suppliers can provide a common interface. Some are in the process of development, but until these have reached full international standards status, linking your automated system to that of your supplier is a matter of negotiation. Where you use several suppliers, each of which has a number of other clients, a standard method of communication may seem impossible. A simple file transfer format such as a series of fields in sequential order in ASCII file format may, however, produce an interim measure that provides a pay off in terms of staff time saved at both the library and the supplier, and which more than recoups the effort expended in developing such a system. Not only does such downloading of files in the form of discs or through electronic mail speed up clerical processes, but it leads to greater accuracy by eliminating keyboarding and rechecking data.

◆ Remote hosts

The term **remote database** was coined to define the geographic relationship between the information store and the end user. It is often also an accurate description of the type of relationship enjoyed by the user. Such hosts have very carefully defined terms and conditions of service, originally developed with little thought to the user, which can be imposed quite easily by threat of removing the service instantly using the database password administration system. 'Invalid password' or 'access denied' can be the first indication one has that the organization's accounts system has failed to make a payment on time.

Some of these database hosts were originally targeted on

individuals rather than companies, or were set up for the US market where the use of credit cards for business accounts is much more widespread. The payment method is therefore geared to this, and other methods of handling accounts are treated as secondary. Attempting to persuade your organization to have a charge account or credit card for such payments is probably a challenge which you see as having limited prospects of success, but it is worth thoroughly enumerating the benefits of such a tactic as the advantages to your organization could easily outweigh any company general policy about payments made this way. There is little you can do to establish an easy relationship with these remote on-line suppliers, but some planning may help.

Individual problems can be more easily dealt with if a local agent or office is in place. Failing this, try to establish the name and location of a person who will deal with any problems you have at the host. A fax number will yield great benefits in establishing rapid communications, as will the electronic mailbox of the link person if the on-line host includes e-mail in its facilities.

Changing a supplier's administrative and accounting procedures which are wasteful and inconvenient for the end user by taking up the matter as an individual client is perhaps the method least likely to work. Rather more profitable is to join a user group: both groups designed around particular hosts and more general on-line user groups enable pressure to be applied and problems to be dealt with in a concerted and organized way. Suppliers are then much more likely to act.

◆ Purchasing automated systems

Until a comparatively few years ago the largest contract and purchase that a library needed to be involved in was the periodic review of journal subscriptions. Now, the purchase of automated systems and their attendant maintenance equal and surpass this. The problem is, of course, that while journals are an area every librarian has confidence in, the supply of automated systems produces less confidence and may be heavily biased by company policy on information technology. In addition to the involvement of orders and accounts staff, computing staff may also become involved.

Not that the basic principles of purchase change, but new factors are introduced. A specification of requirements is still needed, and tenders invited and measured on the basis of costs and services, in this case facilities and performance. Questions of deliverables and support are, however, even more important than in normal purchase arrangements. There is also the need to define the requirements for systems now and also over the next five to ten years. There is not usually the luxury of being able to carry out an annual review in this area, and cut or increase facilities to match the budget. Money will still have to be found to support the system in five years' time no matter what level the disposable budget. It is at this point that we need to discuss the full cost of system support over the period of its planned use – its life-cycle cost, including input from your own personnel. While suppliers are often cautious about projecting forward such figures, they become less sensitive to the matter if they understand that every potential supplier has to produce some justified data.

Two of the main reasons that computer system installation plans go wrong are over-specification and 'vapourware'. These exemplify a simple but often repeated problem of not building a relationship with potential suppliers. Both result from the failure to achieve an understanding of the balance between facilities, investment and growth. By over-specifying a system in a tender document, the library may eliminate perfectly suitable and often superior systems from competing. At first sight it may seem a good tactic to specify every possible facility you may wish to use eventually, and require it to be immediately available. In this way, each potentially useful element in the system can be seen to work before purchase. Without such an approach you could be buying 'vapourware', i.e. a part of the system which, although planned, does not exist as a product.

Both approaches lead to failure. The first assumes that your unit will take up all the elements in the system almost immediately, probably something which it is organizationally unable to do. In the period between contract signing and uptake of service, some products may have moved on in specification and so no longer match your needs. One of the rival systems originally rejected may now appear to be more suitable. On the other hand, buying on a company's promises of future products can lead to disappointment if the plans are not fulfilled on schedule.

The careful potential system purchaser discusses the department's mid-term plans and resource levels to build a picture of implementation for the system. In this way, both parties can establish event points along a pathway to full system adoption and mark those points in such a way that each understands the other's role and obligations. Such a policy will also enable each party to assess the needs for hardware growth and upgrade during the life of the system.

Computer systems require a high level of support, both hardware and software, over their life time. The potential purchaser needs to know just how that support is to be offered, and the terms under which it is offered. Some protection needs to be given to the client if the company should fail, such as access to the computer code used and the availability of alternative maintenance sources.

◆ Using information brokers

The information broker's role in an organization's information unit can be ambivalent. On the one hand they may be seen as an aid, while on the other they may appear to be potential alternative sources of information for the parent organization.

The broker has a definite role within an established information unit, able to provide a service within three broad areas; the provision of specialist skills which it is not economic for the unit to support, access to sources that the company may not have directly, and the delivery of information under time constraints that the information unit may be unable to meet because of a sudden temporary upturn in demand.

The cost to an information unit of supporting certain skills with training and practice can be high if the source concerned is little used. Taking all these staff and support costs into consideration, a broker's 'value added' fee may be economical. Brokers acting as third parties can trace information where a direct approach may be rejected.

Although brokers will of course act on a one-off call basis to a standard set of conditions and a fee, building up a relationship with a broker will enable you to assess their talents and be better able to decide when they should be called in. You need to know how each broker handles an enquiry. Do they specialize in certain areas – most do – and what action is taken if an enquiry does not match their skills profile? Some will direct clients to other sources; if so, who do they recommend and why? Do they have reciprocal arrangements with these other sources?

Alternatively, do they sub-contract work to others under their own trading name? If so, to whom, and is the client told when this is done and to whom the work is sent? If the broker uses people who do not work exclusively for them, then who else do they work for, and to whom are they connected? While brokers will not knowingly break a confidence, a chain of people that extends to the interests of a rival company is to be avoided. A chain of sub-contractors will also add to cost overheads and make dealing with any subsequent matters that may arise out of the initial enquiry difficult.

◆ Who needs a consultant?

The role of consultants is often maligned by those who have experienced the arrival, and subsequent departure, of a person who seems full of instant answers but has no responsibility for any outcomes of recommendations. Such experiences are usually the fault of the organizations bringing in the consultant rather than the consultants themselves.

A consultant may be brought in for particular skills, to bring a new approach to a problem, perhaps by looking at a reorganization; or may be asked to give a second opinion on a situation or suggestion. To develop good relations with a consultant one needs to understand the nature of the consultancy, be able to communicate this effectively, and be able to structure the outcome so that any recommendations can be effectively examined by the organization's management, commented on, and appropriate action taken.

The whole process is more likely to develop smoothly if it is the information manager rather than anyone else in the organization who decides that a consultant should be employed within the unit. If this is followed up with a short-list of possible individuals who could fulfil the role, then the initiative, once established, can be built on.

A document setting out the contractual terms of the consultancy and a definition of the area to be covered will enable the short-list of possible consultants to respond with a quotation on the size and cost of the work. When the consultant has been selected they will need more detailed background on the existing situation, the organization, and the roles and relationships between people within it. The success of a consultancy stems to a large extent from building mutual confidence between the consultant and those within the organization with whom they come into contact.

The consultant will understand this, and work towards it as a major goal in achieving the stated aims of the mission. It is those who have never experienced such a situation, or those who have been involved in a poor consultancy, who need support, and it is the section leader who can best provide this through a knowledge of the motivations of those who will be most affected by any outcome. The consultant is only too aware of being both a temporary employee and someone who may change the local environment drastically, both at the same time.

◆ Conclusion

The above discussion has not, as the reader will have noted, reached any definite conclusion. That is deliberate, however, since each user's requirements are different. Below is a list of attributes we might use in choosing a supplier, and which have been discussed in this chapter;

- Acceptability of the organization's methods
- Good invoicing and recording techniques
- Prices that reflect the best in the current market
- A credit system in line with your requirements
- Fast and frequent delivery
- Processing of material to your specification
- Stock held for immediate delivery
- New publications awareness service
- Contacts and relationships with publishers
- Arrangements for imports
- Bibliographic support
- Stock editing support
- Swift response time
- Rapid response facility
- Communications tools
- Chasing material and effective reporting
- Ability to deal with varying loads

- Ability to handle recurrent and standing orders
- Technical support for automated systems.

While the list is not exhaustive, it could be used as a decision table, allocating to each criteria the values:

>Must have
>Useful
>Not wanted

Each potential supplier's services can then be measured against this requirements list.

◆ References

British Library (1989) *Public Library Procurement Specifications and Contract Arrangements.* BNB Research Fund Report 42, London: British Library.

Brownson, C.W. (1991) A method of evaluating vendor performance. *The Acquisitions Librarian,* (5), 37–51.

Bunce, J.P. (1990) Library suppliers as a source of bibliographic information. *Aslib Proceedings,* **42**(2), February, 51–60.

Carpenter, K.H. (1989) Forecasting expenditure for library materials: approaches and techniques. *The Acquisitions Librarian,* (2), 31–48.

Chamberlain, C.E. (1989) The impact of library automation and electronic publishing: towards distributed acquisitions. *The Acquisitions Librarian,* (1), 3–16.

Duston, B. (1990) How to pick an information broker. *Library Management Quarterly,* **13**(1), Winter, 26–27.

Kaplan, P.D. (1990) Years work in technical services automation. *Library Resources and Technical Services,* **34**(3), July, 299–312.

Link, F.E. (1989) Do vendors cost too much for the service they provide? *Library Acquisitions: Practice and Theory,* **13**(2), 125–128.

Miller, R.E. (1989) Acquisition budgets: planning and control for success. *The Acquisitions Librarian,* (2), 1–11.

Saffady, W. (1989) Library automation: an overview. *Library Trends,* **37**(3), Winter, 269–281.

Schcnak, W. (1990) Years work in acquisitions and collection development 1988. *Library Resources and Technical Services,* **34**(3), July, 326–337.

Starkus, T. (1990) Making the scientist an ally in the real research journal funding wars. *Library Acquisitions: Practice and Theory,* **14**(1), 113–119.

St Clair, G. and Poole, J.M. (1989) Bread not butter: funding online searching in hard times. *The Acquisitions Librarian,* (2), 189–204.

Tesfai, K. (1990) Vendor performance evaluation. *Library Acquisitions: Practice and Theory,* **14**(3), 307–312.

8 Records management or information management?

Veronica Davies

- What constitutes a record?
- Impact of legislation
- Records systems and the organization's needs
- Automation
- Integration with information management
- When is a document a document?

Records management may be defined as the systematic control of records from the point of their creation to the point either of their destruction or inclusion in an archive. But what actually is a record? According to Alexis de Toqueville, writing early last century on public administration in the United States, records were paper documents. For Schellenberg in the 1950s, records comprised much the same material, although his definition was more elaborate: records were:

'correspondence, memoranda ... statistical tabulations and analyses, performance and accomplishment reports, narrative reports, and the like that contain the information needed for making decisions; circulars, memoranda, and other procedural and policy directives that serve as means of administrative control; selected records of past actions that serve as precedents ...' (Schellenberg, 1956).

◆ What constitutes a record?

By the 1980s, however, the definition of what constituted a record had changed beyond all measure. According to one modern authority (Emmerson, 1989), records comprised, 'any paper, book, photograph, microfilm, map, drawing, chart, magnetic tape or disk, or optical disk'. Even this definition appeared dated by 1991, since it failed to specify either electronic mail or databases.

As these illustrations suggest, perceptions of what a record actually is have changed radically and rapidly. In the past, records were just papers, and records management might be perceived as a part of archival administration (the two separate disciplines continue to be taught in UK universities as if they really were much the same subject). Nowadays, the record is as likely to be an electronic impulse as a piece of paper, and the records manager is often recruited from the ranks of information scientists or computer systems architects.

Nevertheless, these important changes should not obscure the fact that one of the principal problems facing records managers is much the same as in de Toqueville's day: paper documents in such volume as to be virtually unmanageable. The electronic office has not led to the creation of the paperless office. In fact, since executives have a tendency to constantly redraft on-line and to print off each version for distribution, the electronic office has led to a proliferation of paperwork. Also, of course, it is far easier to compose on-line than to write on paper. The development of modern computerized systems has thus paradoxically created new difficulties in the handling of the most traditional medium of communication.

◆ The impact of legislation

Additionally, we need to consider the impact of legislation. Year by year, UK and European Community (EC) statutes apply to the type of material which has to be retained for legal reasons. Apart from the Companies' Acts, Local Government Acts and Finance Acts, which are enough in themselves, there are at least 20 other statutory instruments covering the retention of organizational records. As companies expand their operations they have to consider the impact of foreign legislation on the type of records they keep. In addition, with the advent of the single European market, companies will need to be able to prove that they have not been infringing European competition law or been engaged in transborder price-fixing. Officials of the EC Commission or of the UK's Department of Trade and Industry have the right to enter premises unannounced and to examine books or other business records. If there are gaps in the accounts then the company is liable for heavy fines and the company secretary risks imprisonment. To offset this dire eventuality, companies are bound to retain much more than is really needed.

◆ Records systems and the organization's needs

The basic aim of records management is as follows: to ensure that the information necessary for running a business can be retrieved efficiently. Most organizations do not bother to think of records management until they either lose a vital contract or cannot find the papers they need in a convenient space of time. Once this happens they define the condition as urgent, recruit or appoint a records manager, and implement a records management programme. The outcome will usually be a disaster: the newly appointed manager will either impose a copy-cat system learned elsewhere, or will read too many textbooks and attend too many expensive conferences urging the introduction of a comprehensive, 'Rolls-Royce' solution. In fact, the 'old banger' which works is just as good.

Most organizations simply need to identify their immediate priorities and develop a system to meet their needs. A minicab office does not need an elaborate system for invoice-control, nor does it require a safe-storage programme for vital records. Many organizations do not need on-line connection to commercial databases, or a highly centralized filing system. Experience shows that most organizations, once they have identified the problem of the paper mountain and published guidelines to good practice, have resolved most of their difficulties. The records manager will therefore spend most of his/her time hunting out opportunities for storage, drawing up forms to facilitate retrieval, advising on how long documents need to be kept for legal and financial reasons, and organizing the disposal of confidential waste. Few should be involved in composing a company-wide filing system, or in hauling filing cabinets into a new central registry.

Contrary to the popular perception, most records can be safely left with the departments that either generate or use them. All that the records manager needs to do is to advise on good practice and provide support with regard to storage and security. Vital records, however, need to be identified and retained under conditions of safety. Often all this requires is a safe and a security classification scheme which is not abused by prestige-seekers. It does not require a vault on the other side of the world.

In addition, if departments are made responsible in the first instance for their records, they can then be billed for storage costs incurred. This has the advantage of obliging departments to determine for themselves what ought to be kept. If the records manager assumes the burden of having to work out what ought to be kept for five, ten or twenty years, he or she will soon be involved in endless wrangles over whether or not the 1982 Christmas party expenses account needs to be retained. This account has, after all, a deeply historical and sentimental value, and may also be useful in plotting long-term trends in consumption. Should it not be kept for just a little longer?

◆ Automation

Some of the most useful advice the records manager can give lies in regard to computerized information systems. There is, of course, a problem with any sort of computerization. Most people think they are experts on the performance of the English football team, and most believe the same with regard to the latest techniques in automation. Men are particularly bad in this respect, since the use of computing terminology is considered *de rigueur* for the thrusting male executive. The records manager will need to be particularly knowledgeable and convincing if he or, especially, she is to cut through the layers of self-defeating presumption.

The first and most obvious benefit of computerization lies in regard to the retention of outgoing correspondence. Letters and minutes drafted on-line can be safely stored in the creating word processor. If the computers in an organization are networked, then internal communications need never be printed on to hard copy, and there can be common access to files through a file server. Since, however, viruses abound (staff will always smuggle in computer games on pirated software) and accidents are commonplace, the printing out of important correspondence should be made mandatory.

As yet, however, there are few facilities for transferring incoming paper correspondence into electronic form. Scanning is slow, expensive and not always satisfactory. A recent development is the digitizing camera which transfers an image on to diskette. This technology is still in its infancy, but in five years' time it will doubtless be commonplace not only in the office but in the home.

In five years' time, however, most organizations will have dispensed with the Post Office and fax and will be communicating one to another through electronic mailing systems and optical fibre cables. Already, for example, universities in the UK are doing this through the JANET network. Once this happens, incoming as well as outgoing communications may all be stored on-line. The records manager of the future will need to be able to advise on consistency of electronic filing and subject-tagging. He or she will also need to consider whether seldom used information is stored in a format where it can be summoned electronically or as a disk/CD-ROM which is kept in a central area and retrieved manually.

Where an organization relies upon a large number of files of a standard type, it is possible to retain these on microfiche or on optical disk. As far as the former is concerned, the lead in this technology was taken at an early stage by insurance companies, library cataloguers and technical suppliers (most notably garages and service stations). The advantage of both technologies is that they reduce volume very substantially, and are easily filed and retrieved, often in conjunction with a colour coding or header system. Both media may also be prepared on-line, and the relevant image may be summoned up electronically. The legal validity of the records so stored, however, gives pause for thought.

The latest technology allows all these various options to be used simultaneously on the screen. With a 'Windows' facility, the operator may summon up information held on disk, on CD-ROM and on microfiche all at the same time. He or she will not have to log-off before moving on to the next option. Crucially, however, the new technology also allows the operator to gain access to outside databases. It is in this respect that the traditional perception of records management is changing the most rapidly.

◆ Integration with information management

In the past, the records manager dealt primarily with internally generated records that were more than often past their very active life. Now, however, as the executive charged with providing 'the information necessary to run a business', the records manager is becoming increasingly involved with providing access not only to the store of information generated within the organization, but also to a variety of outside databases. Databases available include most obviously news services, press digests, and market reports. This commercial information can be integrated into the work being carried out on-line by the operator, and into the internal records of the organization. Thus, for instance, the daily price of widgets (which is available through Reuter's Textline Service) can be included and modified on a spreadsheet, which is then incorporated into the company's own sales records. The records manager thus becomes an information manager, distributing and manipulating information of varied provenance.

Nevertheless, this additional responsibility imposes new burdens on the records manager. Not only will he or she have to be abreast of the latest technology and commercial initiatives, but the manager will also have to assume responsibility for managing contracts with the commercial database hosts, for monitoring costs, and for ensuring that copyright is not breached. The last of these is a potential minefield. To give one example: if the organization contracts to receive a daily review of the international widget market from Textline and this review is distributed to ten widget traders, legally the organization has bought from Textline not one but eleven copies.

As the records/information manager becomes ever more closely involved with the provision of current information, so his or her role becomes more akin to that of the information scientist/librarian. By the same token, the old link with the archivist becomes increasingly tenuous. The archivist was historically concerned with the management of dead records, the records manager with semi-active ones, which were usually internally generated. Now, however, in the wider role of information manager, the records manager is providing current information from internal and external sources.

◆ When is a document a document?

The overlap between records management and information management carries with it a profound philosophical problem: When is a document a document? As data progresses from network to network, as the text expands, contracts and alters, at what point is the document actually formed? Until now we have always known what a document was. It had a clearly visible format, and we could hold it in our hands. These qualities are, however, lost once the document is on-line. Once a message ceases to be printed in paper form and simply flashes on a screen, it loses some of the qualities which in the past made it easily identifiable as something which ought to be retained and 'managed'. As technical drawings are updated on the computer-design system, as commercial data is buzzed around the management-information system, and is integrated with internal sources, when is the stage reached for, as it were, a 'photograph' to be taken of that information for retention?

In the past the transmission of thought to paper was the crucial stage in document production. Now, however, thoughts are transmitted to disk, revised both by the creator and by other staff members, and combined with new information. The text may be constantly 'saved' and 'sent' but it may never be printed out or logged on the company filing system. We are thus moving into a twilight world where the entire documentation process becomes an extension of the human brain. As I have noted elsewhere (Davies, 1989):

> 'On-line documents are the ghosts of a reasoning process still unconsummated. The circuit is the neuron writ large; and the "document" may now be no more distinguished than a thought.'

At what point should these thoughts be isolated from the mental processes which give them their being, and be scheduled for retention? Almost certainly, as the concept of the 'document' becomes extended, we will have to find an alternative definition of what constitutes a document. At some point procedures will have to be laid down or inculcated, so that the creator recognizes the existing text to have acquired a sufficient significance for the process of revision to be suspended and for the text to be frozen in its current form ready for retention. If this is not done, it is entirely possible to imagine a situation when all that emerges as retained text from a project is the final report. The working papers and data, background briefs, terms of reference, policy initiatives and management interventions have all been cut and pasted into the final text, and have lost their discrete identity as individual information items. A conventional audit trail under these circumstances becomes almost impossible.

If the creator cannot or will not do this, or there are so many creators at work that consensus is impossible, the records manager will have to intervene and arrange for the freezing of texts. *Entia non sint multiplicanda sine necessitate*: but, with due respect to Ockham, the necessity is upon us. In law, the distinction between 'corporate records' and the processes which gave these records birth is already blurred. In the United States, the category of **corporate record** is now extended to include all on-line data: messages, notes, and textualized ideas. To what extent do these new categories actually have a real existence? Will the problems attending their reification be considered at all valid in a court of law?

Records management stands today at a critical moment. The idea that records are just paper is no longer true, even though the electronic revolution has paradoxically created not less but more paperwork. The records manager is involved at the hard end of computer technology, and should be familiar with the latest developments and aware of their impact upon the discipline of management. He/she is now as much an intermediary for current information as a person who looks after semi-active documents. Beyond all this, however, the records manager will need to assume a much more active role in getting departments to release information. He/she will have to intervene constantly in the creative process to extract information for retention.

◆ References

Davies, V. (1990) Loose leaves. *Records Management Journal*, 2(1), 28–29.

Davies, V. (1989) Permanent retention of records: planning for the future. In Etherton, J.J. (ed.) *Documentation Control in the Energy Industries*. London: Institute of Petroleum Information for Energy Group.

Emmerson, P. (ed.) (1989) Establishing a records management policy. In *How to Manage Your Records: A Guide to Effective Practice*. Cambridge: ICSA Publishing.

Penn, I.A. et al. (1989) *Records Management Handbook*. Aldershot: Gower.

Schellenberg, T.R. (1956) *Modern Archives, Principles and Techniques*. Chicago: University of Chicago Press.

9 Your political base

Colin Offor

- Know the culture
- Know your limits of authority
- Read the runes
- Participate to the full
- Cultivate the right people
- Be versatile
- Develop your charisma

A young librarian sat at his desk classifying press cuttings. It was nearly 7pm and the offices were quiet — a good time for this chore, and anyway he was meeting someone in the pub shortly.

Suddenly the door opened and in walked the boss. Not The Librarian or even her manager, but the boss. The Chairman. Someone he only knew from photographs in the Annual Report. Our hero had only been with the company for a few weeks and so had read it recently. Recognizing the great man, he sprang to his feet, ready for a serious professional challenge.

'Can I borrow Who's Who?'
'I'm sorry, no. It's for reference only.'
'I can you know!'

Exit Chairman and Who's Who, neither to be seen again for some time.

Thus your author learned very early about **authority** and **influence**, the two key elements of power within organizations. The Chairman had the authority to do (almost) anything within the company. The young librarian had insufficient influence to get his way.

Politics in organizations, the subject of this chapter, is about the achievement and exercise of power. Whether that power is used to advance worthy or unworthy causes, the reality is that all organizations are riddled with politics, because all individuals at all levels seek to influence events to their advantage, and to enhance their position or prospects.

Most people who aspire to power within organizations will tell you that they want it to achieve objectives they believe in. However, the real significance of power is the ability to control one's environment.

In his book *Management and Machiavelli*, Anthony Jay draws a parallel between citizenship of states and working for corporations. The power of governments in developed democracies to make individual citizens happy or miserable is small – interest rates may slightly affect the cost of a mortgage. The building of infrastructure and the establishment of institutions such as the Health Service will raise the general quality of life, but for everybody.

The power of the corporation over the lives of executives is far greater, more personal and more immediate. They can be told to go and live in another part of the country, or another part of the world. They can be publicly exalted in the eyes of their colleagues, or humiliated. They can be promoted or passed over in favour of a subordinate. All these specifically and personally affect them. The junior manager in Shell or ICI, says Jay, lives in a state of voteless dependence on the favour of the great, just like the sixteenth century Italian.

However, if you become respected and successful within the organization you may begin to be involved in the control of it. You have what some people call **power**. Your life is still partly regulated by the actions and decisions of others, but now a part of it is regulated according to your own choice and by your own decisions. What you really have is **freedom**.

In most organizations, power is held in relatively few hands. Organizations are not straightforward pyramids as often portrayed. Between the broad base and the narrow point there is an interruption – a set of shoulders (see Figure 9.1).

At those shoulders are many senior managers, generally capable, dynamic and thrusting and with power in their departments or divisions. But the next step towards real power in the organization as a whole is limited to a few. These 'shoulders' are prominent factors in the frustration often called 'mid-career crisis'. They are also effective triggers of the intrigue usually called company politics. Clever organizations go to considerable lengths to channel this into creative rather than destructive activity.

I am not sure whether or not to be flattered by being asked to

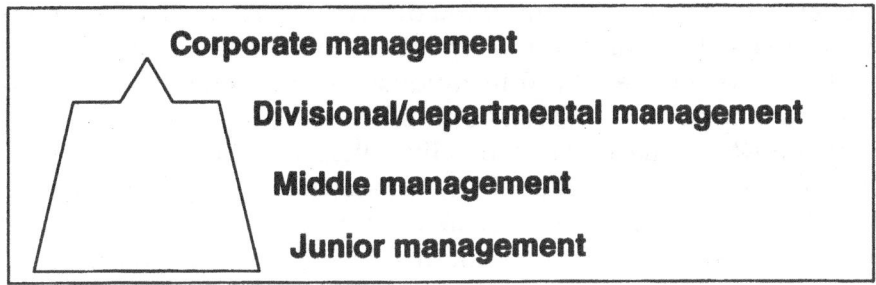

Figure 9.1

write about politics; e. e. cummings wrote that 'A Politician is an arse upon which everything has sat but a man.' Even dictionary definitions imply something less than noble, with adjectives such as manoeuvring, manipulating and scheming.

Idealists may like to believe that by working hard and doing their job professionally and well, their importance will be recognized, and they will be rewarded with respect and regard. But generations of information workers have discovered, to their cost, that in the real world, rewards often do not go to the deserving, but to the politically enterprising.

I remember being appalled by the obvious crawling of a colleague who, while still a graduate trainee, invited the MD home to dinner. Nothing improper, you understand; respective spouses were to be there. To the surprise of almost everyone he accepted. Although good at her job she was not exceptional, but after that no one was at all surprised by her rapid career progress.

Power is also important for good professional reasons as well as for personal satisfaction and advancement. It will determine how close you are to ultimate decision makers on matters ranging from annual budgets and staffing, to very survival. Too many information managers find that they are unable directly to plead their own case on such matters in the real decision making forum.

Clearly the study of politics in organizations is a large field, and many good books have been written on the subject. I have already referred to my own favourite, *Management and Machiavelli*, which though now over 20 years old is a valuable and entertaining read.

For the purposes of this chapter I shall consider techniques, attitudes and activities which advance a professional or personal cause by means other than the excellent performance of one's duties, and the normal promotion of a service. And I shall try to do it with specific regard to the situation of most librarians.

Before we look at those techniques, let us examine those two elements of power, **authority** and **influence**.

Authority is the power officially delegated to an individual. It encompasses the resources of money, assets and people over which one has discretion. It will in many regards be conditional – for example, requiring higher participation in the hiring and firing of staff. As such it is important to understand the limits of your authority and that of those whose authority includes you.

Generally, in an organization of any significance, this will be spelled out in a formal job description although in practice it will often implicitly be added to without formal recognition.

Authority gives you the legitimate power to achieve tasks by utilizing assets and resources within your disposal. For librarians it is generally likely to be insufficient for the achievement of goals, because in a formal sense it will be narrowly drawn. For strategic advance the participation or co-operation of people outside the sphere of authority is often required. What you need goes beyond authority to influence.

Influence is rather mystical. It is the set of qualities and attributes, including authority, that attach to an individual and which motivate others to participate in the achievement of one's goals, whether obliged to or not.

These qualities and attributes range from friendship, personal loyalty and self-interested dependence, to functional significance. Let us look at a few which have particular relevance to librarians.

In many large organizations there are executive recruitment cohorts. For example, a group recruited in the same 'milk-round' as graduate trainees go on induction and training courses together, play squash or golf together and form bonds which last, even though competition between them increases as they progress through the organization. Professionals, recruited to specific posts often in mid-career, not having the shared organizational experience, can never quite break into these groups.

Dependence is often a reciprocal arrangement. From the senior partner in a dependence relationship there is the gift of cultivation and mentorship and the introduction into higher circles. In return they receive services and, frankly, flattery. Services are often in the form of beating the queue for attention, for help with chores such as speech or report writing, committee work, and so on.

Influence also attaches to functional significance. For example, a company in a phase of successful expansion may well see its finance director as an administrative functionary, with an important but not critical role. In a phase of crisis he may well have the most powerful voice, being the man in control of the key resource, cash.

Now many in the profession will maintain that information is power, that information is a key resource in organizations, and many other such grand assertions. But in practice it is those who can utilize information not those who manage it who gain from that significance.

Nor does the information manager generally have the power to influence matters such as status and territory; in that regard she/he may be less influential than the car fleet or office services managers.

Perhaps the most significant contributors to influence are personal qualities – that indefinable set of characteristics often described by that overworked cliché 'charisma'. A related quality is often referred to as the 'bastard' factor. Someone who has both the power and the temperament to squash careers is highly influential in almost any organization.

These examples illustrate why influence is difficult for librarians to achieve. While politics may be important in stretching the limits of one's authority, they are absolutely central to the establishment of all important influence.

Bearing all these factors in mind, what can you do to increase your formal authority, have greater freedom of action, influence events in your own favour, and enhance your perceived significance?

In a brief chapter I make no pretence that the following is a comprehensive list of activities and techniques. Nor do I give any guarantees of success. That will, to a large extent, depend on the strength of your determination, character and personality, and the responsiveness of those around you.

Seven seems to be a magic number, so here are my seven key rules:

> Understand the culture
> Read the runes
> Know your limits of authority

Participate to the full
Cultivate the right people
Be versatile
Cultivate your charisma

I was tempted to add an eighth – *Make yourself indispensable* – but then I remembered that once, when trying too hard to negotiate a pay rise, I was told 'Be careful, Colin. Remember that the graveyards are full of men once regarded as indispensable!' Think about it. Nonetheless, if you uniquely have something – a skill or a resource – which is in demand, simple economics dictates that your value will rise.

◆ Know the culture

The corporate culture is probably one of the most significant determinants of approaches to power and influence. It is something which is related to, but separate from, formally stated corporate objectives, mission statements, and even conduct guides.

The nature and objectives of the organization can, of course, significantly influence the culture. I well recall the culture shock of moving from an advertising agency onto the staff of a university. At first life seemed to live up to the expectations of public repute: dirty, knife in the back politics in advertising, gentlemanly scholars resolving issues through debate in academia. Those who have experience of university politics, or have read C.P. Snow's *The Masters*, will know how naïve that was.

I spent a long time working out why it should be that below the polite surface, university struggles were infinitely nastier than anything I had seen, or have seen since, in business. In large part it is the nature of the organization itself. Lacking in a definable objective – who arbitrates in a tussle for resources between say, the French and History departments? At least in business the balance sheet acts as a final arbiter.

Jay likens universities, and other institutions like the BBC, to the Frankish monarchy, placed in the midst of ancient baronies to which the population gives loyalty. The King moves against the barons at his peril. The university colleges, or the BBC's departments, are self-sustaining baronies unresponsive to a central direction.

Of course, cultures in companies vary too. To understand why, let us consider who has power in organizations, and why. A small family firm is like a feudal estate, since both are entirely and personally run by the head of the family. But as the organization grows and professional management comes between owners and operatives, authority is delegated. Even so, in a few large organizations there are individuals who have real undiluted power, a Robert Maxwell or an Arnold Weinstock, for example. But in most, direction and culture arise from the interaction of influential men and women, all of whom are working on their own agendas.

While the corporate culture may be conditioned by the type of organization and its objectives, it is more than these. It is a complex mix of all of those practices and attitudes that are held to be not just good but which enable someone to be regarded as 'one of us'. And being 'one of us', as certain UK cabinet ministers discovered in the 1980s, is critical to participation in decision making.

The culture can be monitored by watching what thrives; who is rising within the organization? What characteristics does he display – is he hard or soft? What style does he adopt – planned and thoughtful, or instinctive and 'shoot from the hip'? If the organization regards these values in its stars, those with aspirations do well to adopt as much of them as they possibly can.

In some ways the professional brought in to a specific service function is, as we have already seen, unlikely to be completely part of the mainstream management. However, he or she can utilize the characteristics of the culture to his or her advantage.

Talking the same jargon, reading the same papers, sharing broadly in the same aspirations, living the same lifestyle, participating knowledgeably but not heretically in discussions of corporate policy are all part of being in tune with the organizational culture.

It is important because working with the grain in large and small matters makes the achievement of goals not just easier, but sometimes just possible.

I recall an instance where a new dynamic librarian took over the rather tired and reactive information service of a City company in London. The culture was very anti-bureaucratic. Memos longer than one side of A4 were frowned on. Meetings were discouraged, but when necessary were crisp and decision-oriented. Centralized services were kept to a minimum and had low status. The spending of money on internal niceties was a cardinal sin.

For good professional reasons, and to make a speedy reputation for being dynamic and proactive, the new librarian launched a current awareness bulletin. He had it professionally designed and printed. It was a model of its kind. The first reactions were encouraging. 'Phone calls praised the service and the initiative behind it. Then came the summons to his boss. He had had a 'phone call from on high complaining about the unnecessary filling up of in-trays, demanding to know how much it cost and who had approved it. This was not, he was told firmly, 'our way of doing things'.

◆ Read the runes

As a profession, information workers are constantly highlighting the importance of good intelligence in strategic planning. I am less convinced that in planning to achieve their own objectives within organizations they have learned the lesson which they preach.

I know of one librarian who quite openly confessed that she found the quarterly presentation of management accounts to the staff boring, and found any excuse not to attend. Being too busy doing her proper job was how she put it. Looking around at her narrow world she saw the use of her services increasing and contentedly assumed all was well. Her redundancy seemed to her to come out of the blue.

Organizations give out many signals that point to the way things are going. Reading the implicit signals in the financial figures is just one.

Management restructurings often reveal a great deal about the climate and priorities that the company faces. Which departments are achieving status? When the finance and treasury functions are to the fore, be careful! When R&D and service departments are advancing, the company is probably taking a long-term expansionist view.

Remuneration structures are another useful indicator. Traditionally, the actions that were most rewarded were those which directly benefited the performance of the company – increased sales or decreased costs. But better educated managers of the 1980s recognized that executives read such signals only too well, and followed where the credit was due. So more complex sets of performance measures were introduced. The theory can be summed up as 'What gets measured is what gets done'. So what is measured can indicate what the company is prioritizing, say, quality of service or whether it is more concerned with volumes or margins, or is being innovative or conservative.

The agendas of management committees, management 'awaydays', staff conferences, or even departmental meetings are often the early indicators of the issues which are currently exercising the organization.

Businesses tend to go through cycles with regard to service departments and central costs. For a time they are regarded as poor practice disguising true margins. Then costs are allocated, and internal charges are introduced. Eventually, someone notices the costs of administering the system, and the difficulty that arises in spreading costs if one department will not agree and they become part of some central budget. To ensure you can use whichever situation is imposed on you – you are unlikely to be able to influence the decision – to your own advantage, you have to know what the prevalent view is, and be prepared. Watching how other service departments are dealt with, and listening to or even prompting management discussion of the topic, is an important element of preparation.

Knowing where the organization is going, how well or badly it is doing, and how its management practices and priorities are changing, allows the librarian to adjust his/her stance accordingly. Obviously, it is bad politics to press for a straightforward increase in budget when cash is tight and the creditors are pressing. You will appear to demonstrate an ignorance of the company's priorities. Presenting your budget application in relation to the achievement of those priorities will, even in difficult times, give off all the right signals of someone in tune with the organization and its objectives.

◆ Know your limits of authority

The formal limits of authority as set down in the job description frequently remain unaltered for years, while its real scope expands over time by practice. The politically ambitious will always be seeking to expand those boundaries, and having done so to consolidate their position.

Influence arises from one's ability to spend money, to hire and fire staff, and to control assets. If you do not have such authority it should certainly be a priority to achieve it. A campaign to achieve such key responsibilities needs careful planning.

It is good management practice to prepare all the data which justifies your case. But it is politics which will decide how, when and to whom you present it. The homework that needs to be done includes understanding the individuals whose current authority you want to have delegated to you, and particularly the triggers that are likely to make them and the organization receptive to the idea.

A proposition phrased in terms of your professional or status requirements is likely to have considerably less impact than one which appears to offer advantages to the organization or, more probably, the individual.

Like a good salesman you must understand and address his/her needs and concerns, and anticipate and prepare answers for any objections he/she may have. Utilizing the concept of 'back pocket' information helps. If you put all of your case on the table in one go you have no data with which to deal with resistance. And the manager will resist. It is, after all, his/her job to test the proposal and be reassured that the organization will benefit. If you can save some powerful arguments backed by data to respond to that resistance your case will be infinitely stronger than if you had presented it all in one go.

On the matter of budgets, the wise manager in any department will always ensure that somewhere hidden within it there is some element of discretion. Call it miscellaneous or contingency, if you are allowed, although often activating contingency lines requires higher approval. Add a percentage here or there, but find some way in which to give yourself room to manoeuvre. Your budgetary authority is largely illusory if you must spend the last penny exactly within pre-agreed budgeting lines.

In smaller matters it is worth remembering the dictum that 'it is easier to be forgiven than to get permission'. If you ask your manager whether you may attend a particular conference, or send one of your staff on a training course, for example, he/she will see it as their responsibility to question and require justification. They may even turn you down occasionally just to assert authority.

However, as long as there are no positive injunctions against such activities, the chances are that if objections arise after the event an open handed apology will be generously accepted, especially if you haven't overstepped the budget, which is what gets managers into trouble.

As a manager in business, assume that you are paid to make and take responsibility for decisions. So unless you are obliged to seek permission, don't. It may be politic, though, to ask for input or advice. This often arises in hiring staff – you may ask your boss to meet your final shortlist and give his/her impression of the best fit with the company's style, but make it clear that the final decision is yours, or you will have given away authority – always a mistake.

Nonetheless, one must have a good sense of judgment. You must not break specific regulations or injunctions. Whilst everyone will privately acknowledge that 'rules exist for the guidance of wise men and the obedience of donkeys', few managers can afford to be seen to waive them in public, and breaking them does give grounds for disciplinary action in most companies.

It is important that any excursion into new territory takes into account not only the cultural and organizational priorities as discussed above, but also the personal sensitivities of your boss and those who may see what you are doing as encroaching on their territory. Organizing a discussion of information problems that impinge on someone else's department could be seen as highly threatening. Overstepping the bounds of acceptability can be a seriously career limiting exercise.

◆ Participate to the full

Visibility is an important weapon in the political armoury. Being there not only means knowing what's going on, but increases your acceptance as part of the team.

A good strategy is to identify the management group or level that you regard as your proper peer group. Press for opportunities to attend training courses, seminars and conferences with them, especially residential ones. These will help bond you into the group. As a service department manager you may not progress to higher reaches of management, but some of these colleagues will. There are few things quite as useful as being on social terms with the Chief Executive.

Be prepared at such gatherings to discuss broad strategic issues of relevance to the organization. Just because you are a specialist does not mean you cannot have a valid opinion on marketing, management, finance or corporate direction, but be sure to do sound homework. Asking questions or voicing opinions in such groups exposes you to scrutiny.

Be careful and also be tactful. I once attended a company dinner at which the Chairman gave the after dinner speech. It was usual form for questions and answers to be taken afterwards. One questioner took the opportunity to lambaste the company's brand new advertising campaign in none too polite terms, and to ask whether in future the Chairman shouldn't have the final approval on the public face of the company. Of course, he had approved the campaign, and his reply was barely printable. I doubt whether the Chairman would have remembered the incident for long, but everyone else at the dinner did.

Generally, people hesitate to participate in management discussions because they think that their questions or ideas will expose ignorance, be regarded as heretical, or worse, regarded as silly. You might try the tactic of discussing agenda items or conference themes privately in advance with someone you know who understands the issues thoroughly. Be frank about why you are doing it. Usually they will be flattered to have been asked, and will respect you for making the effort. If you do it over lunch or a drink you don't impinge on their work schedule, and the social atmosphere allows you to test any thoughts outside the context of a formal meeting.

Even if you feel uncomfortable, force yourself to participate in the social life of the peer group. Have lunch with them. If it is a squash, golf, or pub culture, join in. If you behave as though you belong in the group you will be accepted as one of the group, both by them and by superiors. Everything that identifies you with that level of management helps your campaign to be accepted as management.

◆ Cultivate the right people

There are some executives and managers who believe that it is their job to serve some entity called the company, as if it existed separately from the people who own and run it. Canning once expressed the idea about governments as 'the idle supposition that it is the harness and not the horses that pull the carriage.'

Directors, when they appoint managers, are backing people, not strategies or plans. It is the quality of the people that will determine whether the company succeeds or fails. Likewise, it is people who control our destinies in companies.

It behoves us to recognize the implications of that. I give you what may seem to be a trivial example. In deciding priorities between two urgent requests, which is more important: the Managing Director's request for information for his son's homework, or the researcher's need for vital data input into a laboratory test? This is an example of a real dilemma faced by many librarians.

The puritan would, of course, choose the researcher. The realist, the ambitious and the professional, would choose the MD. This is not just the 'brown nose' syndrome. Certainly, impressing the boss has its advantages, but in reality it is rare to get any direct exposure to such senior managers. A helpful approach and good service when such opportunities do arrive stores up goodwill in vital quarters that could pay untold dividends in future resource allocations.

But the position is rarely a simple and static one. After all, that researcher you let down might one day become your boss. Now, of course, as a professional you will always give every user your best service on every occasion. But who do you go out of your way to influence? For whom do you go that extra mile?

Anyone with experience in special libraries knows only too well that there is a range of reactions to the service. The vast majority of users and potential users just take the library services for granted, or ignore them. At one extreme, however, there are the fans and advocates, and at the other the positively hostile.

Can you just ignore the antagonistic? It certainly is very tempting, especially if the consensus appears to be on your side. But there is a great danger here. People who are actively hostile generally are highly political. They are looking for causes, otherwise why would they bother? It is likely that their hostility centres on the allocation of resources – space or money, which they feel could be better applied, or saved. So, should they gain ascendancy, you will immediately be on the defensive.

It may be the least comfortable option, but certainly the most potentially productive, to devote effort and energy only to those who like you least. The strategy should be pursued on a broad front. The head-on response to criticism, the active delivery of the best possible service, is an essential part of it, but the most you are likely to achieve is grudging acceptance.

However, if you look carefully at such ambitious people you generally find that they too depend on supporters and mentors. Convert these from the apathetic to active supporters and you may well curtail their potential to harm. It does no harm either to cultivate secretaries.

It is tempting to try to spot the rising and falling stars. In stable times there is, in most organizations a consensus view of the company's position, direction and priorities. In this climate, those who advocate the party line and who perform are cultivated as senior management looks to breed successors in their own image. It is possible then to see those individuals promoted ahead of their recruitment cohorts. They are the ones given strategically important jobs. In one company for which I worked a sure early indicator of someone being groomed was a sponsored spell at Harvard Business School.

Sometimes, however, this consensus can give rise to corporate mythology. When the organization collectively starts to believe too much in its own PR it can get out of touch with reality. When this breaks through and performance starts to suffer, then it is often the heretics and mavericks who can break through and be regarded as visionaries. These too can emerge where there is a change of corporate structure such as a move from private to public company, or a threatened or actual takeover.

An organization for which I worked for many years was, when I joined it, imbued with a *pro bono publico* ethnic. It was, in its own terms, successful. It was relatively small, very friendly and comfortable. The culture was businesslike but forgiving. One year the company made its first ever trading loss. A Director told me 'Don't worry, our balance sheet is so strong we could make losses for twenty years before it really matters.'

But within the company there was a small number, not at that stage a group, of fairly junior managers who had been imbued with the Harvard hard-nosed approach to business. They judged the company's performance purely on return on investment and shareholder value criteria. They were outsiders then. One in particular ran a regional office. He was good. He produced results, but he had a reputation as a hard, unforgiving man. Definitely not 'one of us'.

A changing market, an economic recession and a possible flotation later and he is heir apparent to the Chief Executive, and few of the old 'us' survived.

Look out for the change of boss, especially if the old one was a mentor. I am sure that a contributing factor in my own involuntary departure from one of my employers was that I ignored this particular situation. I was recruited by the manager to build and establish the service in which he firmly believed. Consequently he was very supportive. In many ways to be otherwise would be an acknowledgement of misjudgment. His successor was polite but distant. In retrospect, there were small signs, which I missed at the time, that he had rather less commitment than his predecessor.

Eventually times got rough. My new boss, a good politician, did exactly the right thing and made the cuts of his choice before any were forced upon him.

What were the signs, and could I have done anything differently if I had recognized them? Well, the signs were no longer having the relaxed informal relationship in which my former boss asked for my opinion. Not being asked to take on projects which would naturally have fallen within my province. Finding that he had discussed sensitive issues with my subordinates without my knowledge. Actually, by this stage, I was fairly sure I had a problem.

I would imagine it is easy to be wise in the abstract and after the event. A head-on confrontation could well have preempted the inevitable. In retrospect, I think the best strategy would have been to seek his approval for the participation in a review of the service. At worst this would have made no difference. At best there is a reasonable chance that having had an input into reshaping the service he would have had more commitment to it.

◆ Be versatile

Is business the right place in which to stand on your professional dignity or pride? I am reminded of the Vicar of Bray who held his living for half a century by being twice Protestant and twice Catholic. It was Plautus who said that 'From whatever direction the wind is, the sail must be shifted accordingly'.

I am most certainly not advocating servility. Librarians who are one-man (or more usually one-woman) bands are often imposed upon to take on quasi-secretarial functions. I even know of one highly paid senior professional who was asked to make tea for a meeting because the secretary was away. This poses a real dilemma, and one which executive women are better qualified to advise on than me. In this instance, the person concerned complied because there were clients present, but afterwards told her boss in no uncertain terms that if it ever happened again he could expect her immediate resignation.

But responsiveness to changes in climate, priorities, structure and style is a legitimate professional attitude and one which can be used to manipulate influence.

Organizations are continually in a state of change. To assume that you live in a stable state where established practices and relationships endure is to believe that organizations are somehow immune from the normal rules of nature. Organizations, like organisms, have an inherent determination to survive, and will mutate and evolve in order to do so. So the wise manager is flexible and versatile.

At budget time, for example, to present even a well reasoned bid for substantial increases when the company is in difficulties is clearly unreasonable. Even so, it is not necessarily right to volunteer cuts. What is definitely right is, knowing the situation, to have prepared a strategy which minimizes the impact of such cuts on the service, and to present that as a positive contribution to coping with the situation.

I well recall one librarian proudly boasting that he had told his employers that there was no way he would cut back on his budget, and if they forced him to he would make the cuts hurt the users as hard as possible. There was a sort of logic in the hope that users might pressurize the company to change their minds. But of course, he overestimated his own significance and the real impact was for them to see him as part of the problem instead of part of the solution.

There are creative ways in which to preserve services in hard times, such as revenue earning, capital investment in systems to reduce recurring fixed costs, and increasingly contracting-out. To be the proposer of such moves instead of the reluctant implementor will show you up as opportunity- rather than problem-oriented, definitely a career enhancing attribute.

Such versatility is not just a useful strategy for the hard times, though. An expansionist approach of seeking ways to increase the contribution that the information service can make to corporate and management goals enhances the manager's role as a player on the corporate stage.

Frequently, librarians are deterred from pursuing such approaches because they lack what they see as essential skills. However, it should be remembered that managers do not need to have all the skills of those they manage. There are examples of librarians who have gone down the systems route and become responsible for information technology. There are those who have taken the service route and incorporated economic and market research and analysis. If you have the idea, run with it, take and keep control of it. Keep and promote a broad vision of the information concept, and be prepared to manage its application.

Frequently, this may mean employing people more qualified and in some senses 'better' than you are. I am reminded of David Ogilvy's advice to his managers: 'If we always employ people smaller than we are we will end up as a company of midgets.'

◆ Develop your charisma

Since charisma is, like beauty, in the eye of the beholder, there is a sense in which I might be accused of asking the impossible. However, as with beauty, there are devices and artifices which can, with skill, improve the appearance of even the most plain if they choose to use them.

Some of those devices are common to charisma in business. Appropriate dress, hairstyle, choice of accessories and so on give the appearance of seniority and success. It is easy to denigrate such apparently superficial matters, but whether we like it or not, we all make judgements based on the signals that appearance and bearing convey.

Personal attributes such as a confident style, whether you feel it inside or not, and a measured purposeful tone of voice, convey a sense of direction, and the inevitability of success. In meetings, the natural leader does not take part in the fierce arguments of those who are too obviously fighting a self-interested corner. They save their contribution, rise above the debate, and resolve issues in line with corporate objectives.

While all these are necessary, they are not sufficient, especially for librarians who are not naturally expected to be influential. The cultivation of prominence involves being prepared to take unexpected initiatives, to propose solutions and innovations, to take the stage and present a case with apparent ease and humour, to appear at home with even the most elevated company.

All of which requires hard work and preparation – none of which must be allowed to show.

At the end of the day you may think that all of this is irrelevant to the practice of those professional skills you have learned and honed. But as Emerson observed, 'in politics and in trade, bruisers and pirates are a better prospect than talkers and clerks.'

10 Time management

Beryl Morris

- What is time management?
- Time management strategies
- Specific skills
- Where do we (YOU) go from here?

Time management is one of society's buzz topics and the number of books and courses on this subject grows every day. However, it is also one of the manager's most important skills, hence the inclusion of this chapter in the book.

This chapter looks at what time management is and why it matters. There is an attempt to analyse the key principles of time management, together with examples of tips and techniques which work in practice. It is perhaps important to stress that time management is not just work related: it is also important to effectively balance home and work. Finally, there is a brief list of references which allows the readers to take some of the points further if they wish, together with a list of some of the time management systems available. Incidentally, the chapter assumes that readers have some control over their work and the way in which they work. Without that assumption, the chapter is meaningless.

◆ What is time management and why does it matter?

According to writers such as Lakein (1973) and Adair (1987), time is our most precious resource, for once it has gone it has gone for good. Adair goes further and suggests that time is even more valuable than money, and deserves to be treated with more respect.

Poor time management techniques are regarded as a major cause of stress, and the cost of ineffective ways of working is reckoned to be astronomical. In the past, this has perhaps been hidden in many library and information units, but the move towards fee-based services and recharging is causing organizations to look critically at the use of time. However, like all management techniques, time management is not a panacea. If your workforce is to achieve maximum effectiveness, it needs more than just time mangement.

Time management is an essential management skill, as it enables the manager to be in control of themselves and their circumstances which should, theoretically, result in less negative stress. It should also lead to better credibility in the organization as things will get done. This, in turn, should lead to more confidence as an individual and as a manager. Time management means making time for the important as well as the urgent, and for anticipating and planning for events rather than always responding. Time to plan as well as to do should in turn lead to better quality decisions and actions. Finally, good time management techniques enable the individual to create quality time for themselves and the things that matter. More about this aspect later. In addition, there is one last but very important point which relates to one's role as a manager. People who cannot manage themselves should not attempt to manage other people. If you have worked for a poor time manager in the past (or possibly even at the moment) you will know what I mean!

Time management involves several stages. First, it is important to identify your approach to time management and analyse where your time goes. Second, it means identifying any problems and areas that need attention. Finally, and this is the really hard bit, it means considering what you are going to change. This may not be earth shattering, often the changes needed amount to small and apparently simple steps, but they can make a lot of difference. We will talk about action planning later, but for an example of a typical form, see Appendix 1.

TIME ROBBERS

If you ask a group of workers in any organization, what causes them to manage their time less well than they might, the answers usually include telephones, staff queries, meetings, and similar activities. Writers on time management such as Adair (1987) and Garrett (1986) suggest that there are five major time robbers. See if they apply to you.

The first is not as you might expect, telephones and people, but

lack of a plan, i.e. not knowing what you want to achieve. This makes it difficult to prioritize, to identify what needs to be done, and perhaps more importantly, what can be left.

The second time robber is **interruptions**. This includes enquirers, telephones, staff and non-work examples such as children and neighbours. It is important to value your own time, for without that others will not value it either. However, the trick is to be ruthless with time but courteous with people.

The third time robber is the **inability to say no**, and for many people this is more of a problem outside work than within it. It also relates to the first point, not knowing what you have to achieve.

The fourth time robber is **your own standards** which can make it difficult or impossible to delegate, and for some people means that they never let go.

Finally, the fifth time robber concerns **crises**. Sometimes there is nothing you can do, because according to Murphy's law, if it can go wrong it will. However, many crises are the result of poor planning or anticipation, and may in fact have been avoidable. There are also some people who live their whole life as a crisis. You will know if that sounds like you!

YOUR APPROACH TO TIME MANAGEMENT

Identifying your approach to time management demands honesty and the willingness to change if necessary. Saying there is nothing you can do is negative and defeatist. Time management texts always start with helping you to analyse where your time goes, and suggest that this needs to be systematic as our memories are liable to distort the truth.

There are a variety of approaches to analysing where your time goes. The time log such as that shown in Figure 10.1 is the most common approach. This needs self-discipline to start and most people find it very time consuming at first but feel that it gives them an invaluable insight into where their time goes. Often the ten minute tea break turns out to be 30 minutes, the so called quick meeting has, in reality, taken all day, and most worryingly, the time devoted to planning and anticipating is almost negligible. It is worth keeping the log for at least a week to see where patterns occur. Then the questions that should be asked include does the time allocated actually reflect the organization's and your own priorities? Are there any tasks which could be delegated? Is there

Time Log		
Start time	Activity	Duration
0845	Arrive - make coffee	5
0850	Read through day file	10
0900	Telephone call from Dave	2
0902	Day file	5
0907	Chris stops for chat	8
0915	Day file	8
0923	Go to Kay's desk - not there - leave note	7
0930	John asks advice on detail	13
0943	Kay rings - discussion about cladding	6
0949	Penny brings post - chat	6
0955	Go through post	14
1009	Ask Penny to do letter - reply to contractor	9
1018	Continue reading post	12
1030	Ring QS - response to letter	5
1035	Make coffee - chat to Peter	15
1050	Write minutes of site meeting	9
1059	Phone call from tile supplier - argument!	-5
1104	Loo	5
1109	Site meeting minutes	16
1125	Charles rings about squash match	5
1130	Site meeting minutes	17
1147	Tile supplier rings	3
1150	Site meeting minutes	7
1157	John asks for more advice	15

Figure 10.1

scope for simplification or a lowering of standards, and are there tasks that need not be done at all?

Other approaches include listing the tasks involved in one's job, estimating the time they will take, then comparing this with the actual time taken. This is very instructive, as we invariably underestimate the time needed to complete tasks, sometimes by up to 50%. Diaries can also be used to record significant events and contacts, and making a retrospective analysis of one's diary is not only useful, but it can prove to be fascinating.

The other aspect of taking stock is to analyse your approach to work. We all work differently, and the danger with time management advice is that it becomes too dogmatic and ignores our own personal preferences. To maximize our effectiveness we need to determine our own approach and build on that. To adopt someone else's approach will be doomed to failure.

The sort of questions you need to ask yourself are as follows (you must answer honestly for it to be worthwhile!):

- Do you usually leave things until the last minute?
- Do you find it hard to get down to work?
- Are you able to stick at a task for very long?
- Do you work better in some places rather than others?
- Do you work better at certain times rather than others?
- Do you always do the important things first?
- Could certain skills such as reading and keyboarding be improved?

Do you usually leave things until the last minute?
Does this sound like you?

> ' He slept beneath the moon,
> He basked beneath the sun
> He lived a life of going to do
> And died with nothing done. '

People who procrastinate always stress that they work better under pressure, and certainly for most of us an element of pressure makes sure that we stick at the task in hand. However, leaving things too long often leads to poor quality work. If we have underestimated the complexity of the task we may have to ask for an extension of the deadline, which inconveniences others and makes us look inefficient. We also leave ourselves no time to plan or prepare, which makes for a less effective approach and often creates panic for other people. Finally, we create unnecessary stress for ourselves which in the long-term can harm our health and our relationships with others.

Do you find it hard to get down to work?
There can be a number of reasons for this. Having no plan or list of priorities can make it difficult to decide what to do first. Also, if your work space is untidy and messy, it can make it impossible to work effectively. Good time managers are supposed to have only one item on their desk at a time, but this may be a pious hope for most of us.

Are you able to stick at a task for very long?
This may not be a problem as some people need variety in their work, and for most people their concentration span is fairly limited. According to Minzberg (1973), the manager's work is characterized by variety, brevity and fragmentation so that an acceptance of this can be helpful. However, if you have to put things down after a short period, it is important to devise strategies which enable you to pick up where you left off. Also, we would all agree that if something is interesting or challenging, we can amaze ourselves with our dedication. A manager's task is to maximize this interest on behalf of all their staff as well as themselves.

Do you work better in some places rather than others?
This question asks if you know where you work well. Some people work well in a noisy environment where there is a considerable amount of hustle and bustle, others need absolute silence to get down to work. Clearly, it is impossible to optimize the environment all the time, but where work requires concentration it makes sense to get away from too much noise and interruption. Conversely, if the environment is going to be noisy, targeting that period to do work which demands less concentration makes good sense and is best use of the time available.

Do you work better at certain times rather than others?
Knowing your best time is also important. According to the literature, we are either a lark or an owl, i.e. we work better early in the morning or later in the day. Think about a task you have to achieve; would you rather get up early and get it out of the way? In

that case you are a lark. Or would you prefer to burn the midnight oil? In which case you are probably an owl. Again, you are not going to be able to suit your body clock all the time, but if you can target difficult or detailed work at a time when you are at your peak, it will be so much easier, probably quicker, and of better quality.

Do you always do the important things first?
This is to some extent a trick question, as it relates to a number of issues, including the point above about your best time. For example, if you are an owl it might make sense to leave the important things until later in the day. Similarly, many people find that tackling a couple of quick and easy tasks gives them the confidence to attempt the more difficult things. What is important is that time is made for the important things, as if these are neglected they may become crises.

Your organization may also determine when certain things happen, such as no telephone calls before lunch, to take advantage of cheaper rates. This has to be taken into account when planning one's time but if such rules create major difficulties they should be carefully scrutinized.

Could certain skills such as reading and keyboarding be improved?
Finally, time management is not just about time, it is also about an effective use of relevant skills. If you know that your keyboarding skills need attention, for example, part of your action plan should be to improve them.

PRINCIPLES OF TIME MANAGEMENT

Time management involves a number of principles, considered in the following section.

First, contrary to popular belief, time management is not necessarily about working harder. As a nation we are obsessed with effort rather than achievement, and tend to admire the person who works a twelve-hour day rather than the person who can achieve the same amount of work in eight hours. Time management should mean working fewer hours, but being more effective during that time. Similarly, there is a fear that helping staff to become better time managers is always exploitive – it is if the workload continues to increase until staff drop with exhaustion. However, if staff too are able to use their time more effectively, and reap the benefits already outlined above, they will be more fulfilled and will have a better quality life as a result.

There are a number of important issues with respect to time management. The first is that it need not be expensive. At the end of this chapter there is a brief list of some of the systems available, but these can cost several hundred pounds sterling. Some of the most effective systems rely on a small notebook and diary. The secret is making time management a habit, and making sure that the system you design reflects your own needs and approach.

The second issue, as we have already seen, is about achievement rather than effort. Lakein (1973), whose work on time management has become a classic, suggests that good time managers are effective rather than efficient. Efficient is defined as *doing things right*, effective is *doing the right things*! This implies that good time management may mean not doing something at all, or at least, doing it less well than before.

As an example, libraries and information units sometimes have practices and procedures that have existed for years. If queried the answer is usually 'We've always done it that way.' Being effective may involve taking a long hard look at all activities, and determining which are essential and which are less so.

Finally, in all things there is a need for balance, and time management is no exception. Managing your time does not mean ruthlessly jettisoning all existing practices, neither should it mean being rude or discourteous with staff or customers. As we have said already, the trick is to be ruthless with time, whilst being courteous with people. Ways in which you can do that will be considered below.

◆ Time management strategies

1. LIST OBJECTIVES

If you do not know where you are going, how do you know when you have arrived? Knowing what you want to achieve is essential to good time management. Objective setting happens in many organizations, and is important in giving people a sense of direction and achievement. Pointers that help you to set objectives include the goals of the organization, (what is the company really aiming at?), the goals of your department or section, your job description (see the chapter by Sue Hill and Alison Jago if you do not have one), and your own personal goals. It would be ideal and probably unrealistic to expect a perfect match between your goals and those of your organization, but an awareness of what you are aiming at helps you to make informed choices about the work you do and how you do it.

2. SET PRIORITIES

Having identified your goals it is usually easier to decide on priorities, although, as we have already seen, there is a tendency to do the urgent at the expense of the important. Prioritizing involves a number of aspects, including making time to plan, having a system that does not allow things to slip, regular monitoring and, probably above all, confidence in your own judgement. Incidentally, your priorities may have to take account of the priorities of others, such as your boss!

3. WRITE IT DOWN!

Some people are able to remember what they need to do in their heads, but as we get older our memories become less effective, often at the same time as our lives and work become more complex. For all writers on time management, making a note of what has to be done is a key element. Not only does this fix the tasks in our mind, most people would say that being able to tick something off the list is very satisfying.

However, a list on its own is little use, and tends to impose its own order. Effective time managers ignore this and determine their own order in accordance with the importance/urgency of the task; the amount and quality of the time available and other considerations. Lakein (1973) recommends designating tasks A,B,C, etc. whilst others prefer a numerical approach which signals what needs to be done first. (Try using pencil to accommodate unforeseen changes!)

4. EATING ELEPHANTS – MAKING TASKS MANAGEABLE

This is my favourite time management strategy, and is enormously helpful in dealing with tasks which in themselves are very complex or large. It is also a very useful approach for procrastinators as it gives them less excuse for putting things off.

Elephant eating, or the Swiss cheese approach as Lakein (1973) calls it, involves breaking a task down into 'bitesize chunks'. This not only makes it less daunting, it enables elements of the task to be completed so that it diminishes all the time.

Researchers at Glasgow University have found that students who approach problems in this fragmented way are able to tackle complex issues that defeat other students. It also enables you to keep track of where you are up to with a project, and acts as a useful reminder if other people are involved.

To illustrate elephant eating in practical terms, let us take the annual report. This is a complex and lengthy piece of work, and the tendency for many people is to put it off for as long as possible. However, with elephant eating it becomes much more manageable. An example of this applied to an annual report is shown in Figure 10.2, together with the use of a pattern note or mind map which helps to determine the total task, and is particularly useful if you tend to think visually.

5. WHAT IS THE BEST USE OF MY TIME NOW?

It is worth asking this question on a regular basis. It is partly related to the point about our concentration span, but also reflects the need for everyone to switch off now and then. Clearly, it has to be played by ear to some extent, but if the best use of your time now is to switch off for a few minutes, then so be it.

Related to this aspect, and an important part of stress management, is the concept of 'me' time. This, too, has become something of a buzz word, and relates to the need we have for time to recharge the batteries and make quality time for ourselves. We all have different ways of using our 'me' time; some indulge in sport, others watch plays, cinema or television, others use friends or family to wind down. Particular favourites include having a bath or shower, pampering yourself in some way, or having a good laugh.

It is important that our busy schedules leave some time for ourselves and the things that matter, otherwise illness, etc., will

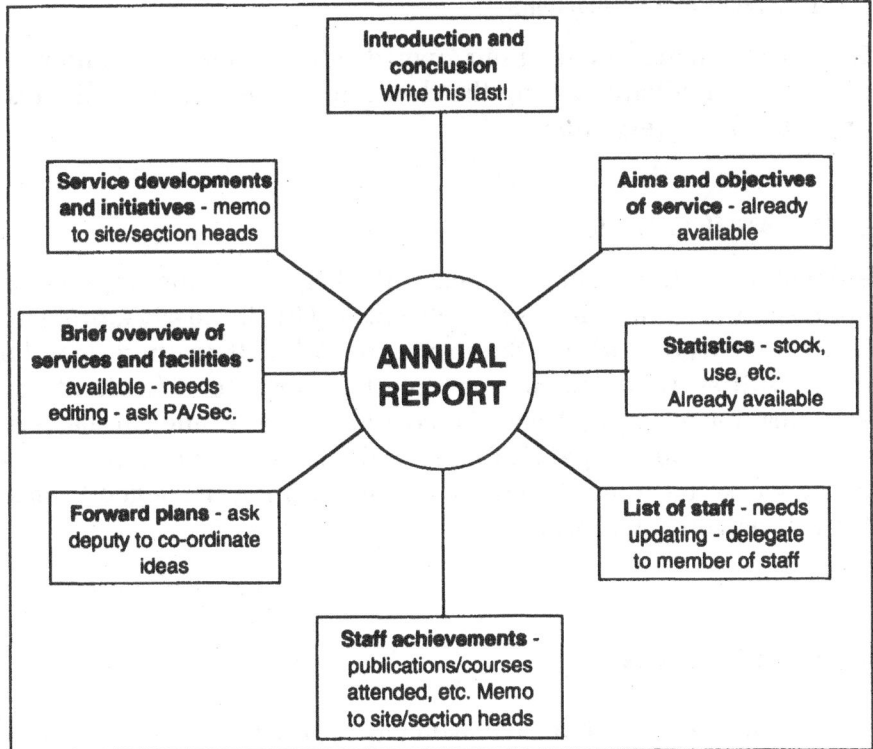

Figure 10.2

result. 'Me' time also helps us to see things in perspective, which is another crucial element in being in control.

6. DO IT NOW

According to Lakein (1973), procrastination is the thief of time. As we have already seen, if we leave things until the last minute we run the risk of poor quality work, and increase our stress levels into the bargain. Edward Bliss in a useful book entitled *Do It Now* (1983), suggests that procrastinators should identify all those tasks they are putting off and resolve to do at least three at the start of each day. In this way the list becomes manageable, and you become much more confident in dealing with tasks that you thought were difficult. Remember Franklin's words: 'One today is worth two tomorrows.'

7. SET AND KEEP DEADLINES

Good time managers set their own deadlines, but they know to make them realistic. Saying the deadline was too short will work once, but not every time.

8. ORGANIZE OTHERS

Related to the time robbers listed at the beginning, the importance of delegation cannot be over emphasized. This is clearly a problem for people who work on their own, but even then there may be opportunities to delegate some of the work, to consultants or agencies, for example. Here, the costing of one's time can be very revealing. If you are paid £15 000 and spend several hours a day doing work at a much lower level, this does not make good sense for you or your organization.

◆ Specific skills

As we said above, time management is about developing skills which enable you to make the most effective use of your time. Some of these are considered below.

DELEGATION

Delegation may not save the organization time overall, but it does ensure that tasks are carried out at the right level, and makes more effective use of the resources available, i.e. staff. It is also an important aspect of motivation as it implies recognition and respect.

The reasons for not delegating are well known. Sometimes the manager feels that it is quicker and easier to do the job themselves. This is a particular problem for people who have set up their own business or section and who are then reluctant to let go. Other reasons include a member of staff being given the responsibility for a task, but not the resources to enable them to do it, lack of adequate training or briefing, and the inability to let go.

Delegation means to entrust, and that means passing on the

resources and the power that is needed to get the job done. It also means paying attention to basic matters such as communicating what the job is and what standards are expected, training that might be necessary, and praise and thanks for a job well done. Incidentally, delegation does not mean abdication. As the manager of a library or information unit, you are still accountable for what happens, which means maintaining control without too much interference. Not an easy task, but one that is essential to a good time manager.

Related to delegating is the need to let go. The old maxim where if you want a job doing you give it to someone who is busy is good sense, partly because they will probably use their time well, but they will also know when to stop.

The concept of 'good enough' is a difficult one for many people to accept as often we have been encouraged to be 'perfect' in our education and upbringing. Yet a task only has to be good enough for its purpose, and we may spend a long time refining something when it is not really worth the effort. This applies to non-work tasks as well, a classic example being cleaning, which some have developed to a fine art whereas others will stop once it is acceptable.

The principle of 'good enough' relates to a concept known as the Pareto principle, i.e. the 80/20 rule. Named after an Italian economist, this states that significant items in a group form a relatively small part of the total. In time management terms, this means that 80% of your telephone calls will be to approximately 20 numbers, and that 80% of your really productive and creative work will be done in 20% of your time. It is worth looking at your list of to do's (see Appendix 1) to determine which of the points will yield the most effect.

ORGANIZATION

People who are disorganized may not be poor time managers, but do not inspire confidence. Part of good organization is to handle paper only once if at all possible. Sorting your mail into priorities helps, as does actioning, i.e. answering or delegating as much as possible. Managers who have achieved this discipline reckon that they save themselves at least an hour a day, which adds up to more than 200 hours a year!

Similarly, establishing effective procedures such as bring forward systems is also important, as is proper use of clerical and secretarial support where it exists. As an aside, one of the greatest difficulties for secretaries is watching their boss do work that they are capable of doing themselves! This is not only poor use of the manager's time, but also leads to frustration and lack of motivation on the part of the secretary.

Other important aspects of organization include critically evaluating your work area and making sure that the things you need on a regular basis are close to hand. Physical comfort is also important; it is difficult to be effective if the surroundings are dingy and dismal and everyone is suffering from backache due to poor furniture or lighting. Finally, most writers on time management advocate clearing your desk (possibly into neat piles) at the end of the day. This makes psychological sense, and also provides a good foundation for work the next day.

PLAN YOUR DAY

We have already seen that writing things down is an important part of managing your time effectively.

According to most books on time management, compiling a programme for each day is an essential discipline. In fact, a consultant named Ivy Lee received a $25 000 fee for suggesting that Charles M. Schwab, a major US steel producer, compile a list of the next day's tasks each evening before he left work. In the 1920s this was a considerable amount of money, but Schwab said that it was the most valuable advice he had had in his business career!

Most writers echo this approach, and also advocate that lists should be compiled the previous evening. If postponed until the morning it has been found that the list tends to reflect urgent items at the expense of the important ones. Also, psychologists suggest that if we fix problems in our minds, we are able to work on them in our subconscious. This could sound like a plea for procrastination, but it is not.

The list should obviously include appointments, essential tasks, telephone calls and other items, and should have some indication of priority. Writers like Adair go a stage further, and suggest that each task should have a time limit. This may be difficult at first, but should come with practice.

Your daily list should also take your best time into account, so that you try, wherever possible, to target the difficult/important tasks for when you are at your peak. It should also, whenever possible, include periods of uninterrupted thinking time, for it is usually this aspect which is neglected.

Questions to ask when your list does not seem to go down at all include: Are you trying to do too much in one day? Did you tackle at least some of your priorities? Did you have all the available information? Did sufficient planning precede the task? A common reason for tasks not being achieved is interruptions. This aspect will be considered below.

DEALING WITH INTERRUPTIONS

Most managers attribute their lack of time management to interruptions. Indeed, research into managers' use of time has shown that some managers take upward of 40 telephone calls a day and have contact with dozens of people.

As we have already seen, the trick for dealing with interruptions is to be ruthless with time, but courteous with people. This means having times of the day when you close your door or go into 'Pope status', i.e. only the Pope can disturb you. It may also mean doing deals with other colleagues so that they answer the telephone while you get on with some work. It goes without saying that for this to be successful, it should be reciprocal! Some people find that working somewhere else in the building gives them time away from interruptions and allows them to do difficult or detailed work. If this strategy can take account of your best time as well, so much the better. Incidentally, these approaches will not be feasible for everyone – if you work alone, for instance – but are worth considering.

Recognized damage control methods for dealing with interruptions include setting a time limit, e.g. five minutes now or half an hour tomorrow; setting the scene by saying that you are busy or are expecting a visitor. Other techniques include keeping people standing, they should eventually get the message; have a prominent clock; meet in other people's offices – it is easier to leave; use active listening to get people to the point and avoid too much smalltalk. We all need to work out our own strategies in this area, and of course to be aware when others are using them with us!

SAYING NO (OR NOT YET)

Another important aspect of time management is knowing what not to do which means learning to say no, or at least putting your own *caveats* on things you are asked to do by others. Otherwise, you will become a servant to the priorities of others. This not only makes you a poor time manager, but can also be very stressful, as you are no longer in control of what you do.

Some people find saying no very difficult. It is bound up with our fear of not coping or of being disliked. However, as all the books on assertiveness will tell you, we have the right to say no without feeling guilty. Learning to say no or not yet is a very important aspect of time management, and should be practised when necessary. This, of course, applies to non-work activities as well as work, and also means that we have to accept no from others without making them feel guilty.

MANAGING MEETINGS

Meetings, like interruptions, are regarded as a major time waster by most managers, and if we use the cost analysis mentioned earlier meetings can become very expensive indeed.

However, meetings are essential to communication within the workplace, they create a sense of belonging and commitment, and enable us to involve staff in the decisions which affect them.

Managing meetings effectively includes determining their purpose and paying attention to what they are meant to achieve, as well as who should attend. Good meetings practice is also important. This means considering the location, timing, room layout, etc., as well as making sure that everyone is adequately briefed and has been able to do the necessary preparation and thinking. Preparation is the key to successful meetings, which means a comprehensive agenda, dispatched in good time with enough information so that people know what is expected. Items such as staffing, budget, etc., are not usually helpful on their own, and need some elaboration such as an indication of what sort of decision is required. It goes without saying that the skill of the Chairperson is also important, as is good minute taking and follow up. A key question to ask of any meeting is, of course, is it necessary? If the answer is no, you know what to do!

Many of the books listed at the end of the chapter contain

information on meetings. In addition, there are dozens of books dedicated to this topic.

COMMITTED TIME

For many people, a large part of their day is already committed with travel, stints at the information or reference desk, chores, etc. A good time manager uses this time proactively, i.e. they will make constructive use of this time, even the fewest minutes. Adair (1987) calls it redeeming time, cheating the system and snatching a small victory.

Let's start with travel time. Arnold Bennett (1902) was very critical of those who wasted their travel time by reading newspapers or just wandering about. Bennett, and also Anthony Trollope, used their travel time to write, and although we may not all be budding authors, work such as keeping up to date, jotting down notes, etc., can be usefully carried out on some journeys.

Waiting time, such as when a visitor is late, can also be used for small tasks such as the odd letter or memo. This is where elephant eating can prove useful, as it provides dozens of small tasks that can be accommodated as necessary. Waiting time at stations, airports, etc., provides a marvellous opportunity for people watching, important for those in a service role. Bearing in mind the need for balance and 'me' time, such time can also be used for switching off, for reading a book, or just for thinking. Time management is not about making every second count – it is about making good use of the majority of them.

A SENSE OF BALANCE

According to Adair (1987), it is not easy to become efficient without becoming odious. Certainly, with an emphasis on time management, it is easy to become obsessive and a time bore such as the prig described by Arnold Bennett (1962). Also, it is important to be flexible, and not to become a slave to your programme. A daily list is a servant not a master, and should never be regarded as being written in concrete. Time for the unexpected such as an important 'chat', an impromptu social event, etc., is also important. In fact, most writers see time management as a way of making time for the things that really matter such as family, friends, and you.

Related to this, and an important although perhaps unexpected aspect of time management, is the need to take care of your health. The reasons are very simple; if we are over-tired or feeling unwell we cannot work at our best. What we are aiming at with time management is making quality time for the things that matter. This means paying attention to basic things such as adequate sleep, and making sure that you switch off early enough to be able to go to bed relaxed. It also means looking at our diet and trying to achieve a common-sense approach, which means balance rather than the latest fads and fancies. Similarly, most of us need to take more exercise. Every week, we read articles criticizing our sedentary lifestyles, yet we still don't make the time to exercise. Regular and often are the keywords, and if we are able to find something we enjoy doing, we are more likely to keep with it. Even walking more at work, or using the stairs rather than taking the lift, is a start, and we can develop from there.

Finally, as already stated, time to switch off is important. Not only does it help us to recharge the batteries, it enables us to see things in perspective, which is another crucial element in managing our stress. Having pastimes and hobbies that allow us to forget about work is important, as is having strategies that help you relax.

Similarly, making time to get away altogether is vital. People who maintain that they do not have the time to take a holiday are not only foolish, they are also storing up trouble for themselves in the future. I was particularly saddened by a friend who said that they would not be going on holiday, as it involved too much administration! When holidays become a chore, perhaps it is time to take stock with a vengeance! Recognizing the symptoms of stress is important, and clearly taking steps to do something about the causes is vital.

◆ Where do we (YOU) go from here?

As stated at the beginning of this chapter, time management is not easy. To make more effective use of your time you need to resolve to make changes to the way you do things and stick with them. However, it is not, as we have seen, a question of working harder; it is about working smarter, i.e. becoming effective, not just efficient.

Here are some suggestions which have worked for others.

TIME MANAGEMENT TIPS

- Develop a bring forward system so that papers, etc., are where you expect them to be
- Use handwritten replies to memos unless forbidden by the organization
- Make sure that key dates are in the diary well in advance
- Anticipate hold ups, allow lee time with reports, etc.
- Do things like shopping at less busy times – it saves hours

Finally, two quotes from John Adair's book:

'It is not enough to be busy. The question is: what are you busy about?' (Henry Thoreau)

'There's never enough time for everything
Help me to do a little less, a little better' (unattributed)

The most effective time management system for you will be the one you develop for yourself. However, there are a number of tried and tested systems available. Here is a brief list, there are, of course, many more.

Personal organizers
These consist of a smallish ring binder with a series of inserts covering diaries, addresses, planners and numerous other items. You can even buy Filofax or Lefax novels if you wish.

The advantage of these systems is that everything is together in one place, and can force you to be organized whether you want it or not. However, they are expensive and can become cumbersome. They are also regarded as being potentially dangerous because if lost or stolen they reveal a lot of information about you, possibly including credit card numbers and personal details. Also, you may lose all your important documents in one go. In fact, in the US there are Filofax counsellors for those who have mislaid their Filofax. If you would be devastated by the loss of your personal organizer, make a copy of everything in it and try to keep some of the contents separately.

Time Manager International
This is a Scandinavian system that aims to help people achieve their goals by organizing their time effectively. The system is fairly

complex, and relies on a diary that identifies plans on an annual, monthly, weekly and daily basis. Needless to say, the planner is quite large!

TMI run a course on time management and then sell you the system at the end of it. The package is not cheap, but some people find it has revolutionized their life.

For more details contact:

TMI
50 High Street
Henley in Arden
Solihull B95 5AN
United Kingdom
Tel: (+44) (0)5642 4100

Psion

The Psion is a small portable computer about the size of a calculator. It enables you to enter appointments, etc., as well as adding up your shopping. It is not cheap (from £100–200, $170–300), and to my mind very fiddly, but again some swear by them.

A-Time

A-Time is a recently developed time management system. Again, it consists of an A5 ring binder which comes with an assortment of pages – diary, planner, appointment schedules, address and telephone pages, and maps. There is also an archive box and the usual essential items such as a hole puncher (including a portable version), the credit card and diskette pages, even a wine guide.

The organization runs time management courses for managers and secretaries as well as a more general management course. A video training pack was launched in September 1991 which includes a video and individual workbook, but not the personal organizer, which has to be bought separately. Priced at £29.95 ($50), the pack is cheaper than other versions but the organizers are expensive, starting at £79.95 ($110) for the vinyl version and upward of £170.00 ($250) for the 'Diplomat' in leather. Timelink is a software version of the system, and comes with specially punched computer paper.

Further details are available from:

Time/System
40 West Street
Marlow
Buckingham SL7 2NB
United Kingdom
Tel: +44 (0)628 476071

◆ References

There are hundreds of books giving advice on time management. The following contain practical ideas as well as supporting the text.

Adair, J. (1987) *How to Manage Your Time*, Aldershot: Gower.
Bennett, A. (1962) *How to Live on Twenty-four Hours a Day*, New York: Cornerstone Library.
Bliss, E. (1983) *Doing It Now*, London: Macdonald.
Consumers' Association (1988) *Understanding Stress*, London: Consumers' Association.
Garrett, S. (1986) *Manage Your Time*, London: Collins.
Lakein, A. (1973) *How to get Control of Your Time ... and Your Life*, Aldershot: Gower.
Minzberg, H. (1973) *The Nature of Managerial Work*, New York: Harper & Row.
Seiwart, L.J. (1991) *Time is Money: Save It*, London: Kogan Page.
Shaevitz, M. (1984) *The Superwoman Syndrome*, London: Pan Books.
Treacy, D. (1991) *Clear Your Desk: The Definitive Guide to Conquering Your Paper*. London: Business Books.

◆ **Appendix 1**

Things to Do

11 Self-development

Feona Hamilton

- Thinking ahead and making an action plan
- At last – a management post!
- Developing management skills
- Passing on your expertise
- Read all about it
- The forgotten art

It has recently become fashionable to spend time either developing your body or – if you're at a certain age – at least trying to maintain some sort of muscle tone and suppleness of movement. This very positive attitude to our bodies is a good thing, and there is every reason to encourage it. However, there is no such widespread acknowledgement that the same also applies to our minds. The more common attitude is to think that once the degree is obtained, once the magic letters are in place, there is no need to worry any more. This is wrong on two counts at least: it is very arrogant to think that learning the theory (and a six week vacation job) will equip us for all the years of practice; and it can mean that you are soon left behind by new developments and new techniques.

In the information profession, ignorance is not bliss, it's the way to being dropped, passed over and bored out of your mind. Any information professional should, by nature, have more than his or her fair share of curiosity, and because there is such emphasis on finding out and passing on information, it should be one of the easiest professions in which to develop your natural abilities to their fullest extent.

The term **self-development** or, as it is sometimes known **personal development**, is used to cover all the means used to advance yourself along your chosen career path after leaving full-time education and starting full-time employment. Once begun, self-development really never stops – unless you choose otherwise – until you come to a full stop yourself. Many people become addicted to it, or to certain aspects of it. Many Open University (OU) graduates in the UK, for example, continue watching OU broadcasts long after they have finished their degrees. The opportunities for guided self-development, such as further education courses, distance learning programmes and adult education classes, have never been greater.

These avenues to learning are only one, relatively small, part of the whole. In this chapter I consider more the types of self-development that are available to anyone who works in a special library or information centre specifically. This type of development depends on you seizing opportunities that may be presented within your organization, during your day-to-day life in the office, as well as taking up the more conventional options of attending structured courses.

◆ Thinking ahead and making an 'Action Plan'

It is never too early, or too late, to give some thought to what you want to do next. If you chose to obtain a library or information science qualification, your next moves may be decided for you, as there may be requirements laid down by various professional associations which have to be fulfilled.

If you had not thought it necessary to become qualified, you should have given some thought to your natural abilities and inclinations and planned a career path accordingly. Since the types of information work available are so many and varied, you will have built in a certain amount of flexibility so that you can change to something different if it is more attractive. As an example, some people find that they are actually more interested in how the computer works than in supplying on-line searches, so they may move from an information service into a computer centre. Others may discover that they prefer moving from place to place rather than staying in the same surroundings, so they move to selling information products. Others still prefer books to people, and would rather be in the cataloguing department than on the reference desk. Your curiosity may lead you to try working with different subject areas from your original interests. That's what being in information is all about – flexibility and variety.

ACTION PLANS

The structured way to do this self-analysis is to take a long, hard look at yourself, and to try drawing up an action plan for the future. As a potential or actual manager, you should already have a considerable list of skills and expertise on which to work. Take, as an example, answering a research enquiry, and break it down into its component parts, showing the skills needed to deal with each step:

1. Finding out what's needed: interview
   listen
   comprehend
   estimate costs
   make accurate notes
2. Find the information: knowledge of sources available
   research skills
   on-line searching
   use hard copy
   understand specialist terminology
   use external sources
3. Supply answer: analyse results
   write report
   supply actual costs
   send to client
   keep to deadlines

Not all information work needs all skills, but it is quite a list, nonetheless. Given more general expression, if you are an experienced information specialist (but not a manager yet) you will have gained the following skills:

- communication (interviewing, report writing)
- research (on-line and hard copy searching)
- analysis (looking at search results)
- financial (estimated and actual costs)
- organization (order of searching and meeting deadlines)

and much of it by the peculiar process of osmosis which seems to be the main informal learning method in this profession.

Since most people in an information centre have wide-ranging responsibilities, as well as those of answering enquiries, a variety of other skills should also be there. Think of the routines gone through for acquisitions, classifying and cataloguing, filing returns, circulating journals, scanning newspapers, current awareness services, etc. Just a few examples of the different tasks undertaken by an information department demonstrating many different skills.

The point of all this is to note down all the things you have to do, with all the skills that you need to undertake them successfully, and then to analyse them in two ways:

1. How good you are at doing them (1–4, poor to excellent).
2. How much you enjoy doing them (1–4, loathe to love).

You are advised not to use an odd number for analysis, like 1–5, so that you can't just tick the middle one. You're looking for a more detailed analysis than simply 'average'.

The results should clearly indicate where there is room for improvement. Using this and – if you have them – the results of the last performance appraisal interview you had, you should be able to draw up some short-term goals (to improve certain skills and, perhaps, gain new ones in your present position) and some longer-term goals (where you hope to be in two, three, or five years from now).

Long-term planning will include whether you wish to remain where you are, or whether you wish to move on. It is important to realize that while loyalty to the organization is praiseworthy, it should not be taken to excess. Yes, you should feel some commitment, especially if you are benefitting from training which you are receiving at their expense. But remember one thing – most organizations do this because it benefits them, and not for any other reason. So take advantage of any benefit offered by the organization, do your best while you're with them, but move on as and when it's right for you and your career, without feeling guilty.

◆ At last – a management post!

Reading this book intimates that you have now reached the third stage of self-development. You may be qualified as a librarian or information scientist, you have decided which type of information work interests you, and you feel ready for some management content in your job. This can be a sticking point in some careers unless you realize two things:

1. You will not be able to spend nearly as much time involved in information related tasks if you have staff and resources to manage.
2. You will need to acquire a whole new range of skills that are not specifically related to information management.

Think about it carefully. There are no half measures.

Finding your first post with a management component may be as easy as simply being promoted into a job because the person who was there has left, or it may involve moving to another place altogether. If you are promoted within the organization and you enjoy working there, that's the least intimidating way to do it. But if your present job no longer stretches you, or there are no prospects of promotion, then a move may be the right course of action. However, if you move make sure you really do move to a better position. Sideways moves can be beneficial in that they provide extra experience, but they can also damage career prospects.

Internal promotion should offer you the possibilities of gaining management skills automatically. In a good information centre you should have picked up some management concepts from the previous incumbent, since you were there working together. Your own staff training and assessment should have included time spent with your manager, being told how various management tasks are carried out. Finally, your appraisal interviews should have given you some idea of the areas which you need to develop, and how much progress you have made so far.

◆ Developing management skills

There is a range of management skills which are core skills – i.e. needed by all managers, at whatever level. The emphasis on each individual skill may vary from job to job, but they will all be needed, and they can all be learnt. Some people contend that 'Managers are born and not made – it's all a matter of instinct and common sense.' Well, that may be so in some cases, but I believe that most managers are made, not born. The best ones may be those whose instincts play a large part in their decision-making, but they will benefit by being taught how to make good decisions initially.

The core skills are:

- personnel management (i.e. dealing with staff)
- financial management (i.e. dealing with money)
- project management (i.e. dealing with plans and deadlines)
- communication skills (i.e. speaking, writing and listening)

not necessarily in that order of importance.

Personnel management is the most difficult area of all, simply because you are dealing with other human beings.

Good managers are those who: encourage initiative in their staff; delegate responsibility; supervise unobtrusively; organize routines and make sure they are implemented; communicate well; train and develop their staff; encourage attendance at professional events (conferences, user groups, etc); expect staff to work with and not for them; and lead by example; among other things.

Bad managers are those who: take all the decisions themselves; impose those decisions on others; refuse to listen to new ideas; discourage professional involvement; shut themselves away; and fail to communicate.

Watching and learning from experience should help you to avoid being a bad manager and to acquire the skills that will enable you to be a good manager. For other methods of learning, read on.

Financial management skills are mainly concerned with budgets – drawing them up and keeping close to them. 'Budgets' is deliberately in the plural – there's a lot more to it than simply drawing up the annual budget for the running of a library or information service. That budget, unless you are starting up a brand new service, may already have been drawn up by a predecessor. It will need to be considered each year in case there have been alterations to the service that involve cutting some items and adjusting the amounts available for others. The organization's financial circumstances may also affect it (Liz Chapman's chapter on budgeting goes into more detail).

The challenge starts when budgeting for new projects that you have to sell to the organization as a vital necessity. These might include such items as:

- computer equipment
- a new on-line service

- new journal titles
- more shelving or space
- extra staff
- more bookstock

Looking at that list, isn't it interesting how priorities have changed? The computer came into my mind first, the books last. In the special libraries field this is probably the usual order now. The accuracy, currency and coverage offered by on-line services and CD-ROM means that computerized services are now the most widely used means of accessing information.

Extra expenditure has to be justified. If you are working in a library or information centre which charges for its services – and more and more do – it is easier to justify additional services when you can at least recover costs. If you can actually make a profit, so much the better. Something which is a cost alone, such as new shelving, is more difficult to justify.

Projects have always been part of your working life, even if you didn't realize it. Organizing a search strategy to provide in-depth information on an industry sector, for example, is a project. The difference between these sort of projects and those dignified by needing 'project management' is not very great. Many consultants, project directors and project managers would be surprised if they were told what skills were needed to organize a complex information search.

Project management skills include:

- putting the original proposal together, showing how you propose to carry out the project, plus the equipment needed, the time and staff needed, and the estimated costs
- organizing the day-to-day work needed to actually carry out the proposal
- analysing the results
- writing and presenting the report

so it's mostly a mixture of research and communication skills.

Communication skills are not specifically limited to managers, of course, but they are in this list because if you haven't developed them already you must do so now. Being able to get your ideas across to the relevant people is a skill that will stand you in good stead all through your career. Persuading people that what you are saying makes sense is an ability that will ensure you are noticed quickly. Being able to make a presentation to senior management, or the Board of Directors, is a good way to raise your own profile, as well as that of the information service.

FORMAL SELF-DEVELOPMENT

Where do you find the means of developing such skills? If there is an in-house training facility, then use it. Some organizations, especially the larger, multinational companies, have excellent training facilities. Management training may be offered automatically, either as a series of introductory courses for new managers (i.e. either those in their first management post, or managers new to the company), or as courses aimed at those who have been recommended for such training before actually taking up a management level post. If you are offered the chance to attend any courses of this nature, do so.

When you attend this kind of in-house training you may well find that it is highly participative, and that you are expected to keep a log for the time that you are on it. Often, such courses are run at a separate training centre – perhaps a country house that has been transformed into a training centre – and they last for five residential days at least. These are the best type of courses – being away from the office and your home, with nothing to distract you, is a good way to learn. You will also make some very useful contacts from other parts of the company, and also gain a support group that will function when you all return to your desks. In some companies, such groups are encouraged to have regular social meetings to enable the contacts and the support to continue.

If you are part of a smaller organization, or work where there are no training facilities of this nature, it should be possible to find relevant courses to attend. Many learned societies and professional institutions run management courses that are open to anyone willing to pay the fees. Some such institutions run courses in their own specialisms aimed at those from other professions. Thus, accountancy bodies offer courses in financial matters for non-accountants and make the point that non-members and those who are not accountants are welcome. As they often offer a wide range of courses in other skills such as personnel management, effective communication, and chairing committees, such bodies are often a very useful source of training. The professional associations within the information profession itself also offer management level courses. These concentrate on management skills, aimed specifically at the information manager.

As well as courses, a long list of useful texts are available for the aspiring manager. But it must be said that management skills can only be fully learned by practising them – reading comes second as a learning method. (Sylvia Webb also discusses managers' training needs in her chapter on Staff Training and Development).

INFORMAL SELF-DEVELOPMENT

Any means by which you add to your knowledge of management techniques, apart from attending formally structured training courses as a learner (see below for attending in other capacities), comes under the all-embracing term 'informal self-development'. This includes:

- self-assessment
- learning by watching
- learning by doing
- staff meetings
- other discussion groups
- joining special interest groups
- training others
- public speaking
- writing
- ... and reading.

Self-assessment is not only relevant at management level, of course, you should have been doing it all the time. Spend some time regularly – at least three times a year – going through the process outlined above in the section on 'action plans'. Give honest opinions about how well, or badly, you are doing in carrying out your tasks. Assessing your own progress involves asking other people if they have spotted weaknesses in your performance, as well as strengths. It's difficult to decide whom to ask, but if you have a deputy with whom you have a good working relationship, try asking him or her. Also ask the users – most of us have users with whom we are particularly friendly. Tell them what you need from them and take them out to lunch for a discussion.

If you've picked the right people, the result should be useful input into your self-assessment. You may also find you have a spin-off, because your deputy will feel flattered that you trust him/her enough to ask their opinion, and the users will appreciate that you're trying to improve the way you perform at work.

Learning by watching the correct methods used by others – and then trying to do the same, or similar, yourself (learning by doing) – are both instinctive methods of self-development which everyone uses. We also all use the opposite – watching someone make a complete mess of some task, and vowing never to do that ourselves. Both are as valid as each other.

Staff meetings are an opportunity to practise skills as well as learn new ones. The skill of listening to what other people are saying and really taking note is a vastly under-rated and under-used skill. It is increasingly being realized at last that nearly everyone can make a contribution to the successful running of an information service, whatever their position in the hierarchy. New members of staff can be especially useful in a staff meeting. Encouraging them to comment on existing services and to ask why some task is carried out as it is (or even why it's done at all) can be a great eye-opener, and lead to improvements. Managers are no longer expected to be the only people involved in decision-making – a team effort often achieves spectacular results.

Anyone intent on self-development should be involved in professional activities outside the information service itself. This profession is particularly good at setting up groups, networks, associations, and the like. The hours spent attending such meetings are well worth the effort. If you can also gain a place on a committee or the council of one of the professional associations, this can prove extremely worthwhile. Getting onto committees and councils is not as difficult as it may seem, since many people shy away from such public exposure. It's simply a question of joining the association, special interest group, user group, or whatever, and going to meetings regularly. During the course of those meetings, you will get to know the other people who are active in that group. When the time comes for committees to be elected, put yourself forward by letting it be known that you are interested.

◆ Passing on your expertise

It may be that you have read the last paragraphs nodding in agreement all the way through because you already do all this. Is there anything else left? Yes, there is – what about passing on your experience to others? It can be done by lecturing on short courses, or writing books, or speaking at conferences and meetings. Choose whichever you're most comfortable with – but remember your aim is self-development.

Neither of these areas are particularly easy to break into – speaking on courses and at meetings tends to be done by the same people over and over again. The problem is that until you've been tried out, people are hesitant about taking the risk. One way in which to get started is to offer to speak about your particular job to a special interest group to which you belong. In that way you can give a short paper (perhaps 15–20 minutes) and follow it with a discussion or question and answer session. The advantages are that you will be with people you know, in an informal atmosphere, talking about something you are very familiar with. Making mistakes under these circumstances is not the major disaster it could be at an annual conference, for instance. If you can get someone to listen and then give you their honest opinion it will be an even more useful exercise.

As a result of this type of public speaking you may be offered the chance to contribute a case study or lecture as part of a short course. If the chance doesn't come, then write to the appropriate person and ask if you can lecture for them. If you can list any kind of related experience – public speaking, teaching in-house – that will be an advantage. If you really enjoy this kind of activity you can build up your expertise to the point where you can design and run entire courses yourself. You may even find that this is the start of a whole new phase in your career as an information professional.

Developing the skill of writing about your particular areas of interest can also be an enjoyable experience. You won't make a fortune – especially if you limit yourself to the professional press – but you will have the satisfaction of seeing your thoughts in print. The most important thing to remember when writing is to study the market, i.e. don't send an article on records management in a bank to a journal which specializes in pharmaceutical information management. It is a good idea to either telephone the editor first, or to write a letter outlining the idea and ask if it would be of interest. If you get the go-ahead, make sure you submit your article in the right manner (ask for a style sheet) and on time. As with public speaking, one thing can lead to another – if you want it to.

◆ Read all about it

Earlier in this chapter I stated that reading comes second as a learning method, compared with the 'practice makes perfect' approach. This is true, but that doesn't mean that reading is not important. If you've ever thought 'all I get for my subscription to . . . is a journal', you haven't realized just how useful a journal can be. Journals or newspapers (and their on-line equivalent) are often the first places to find reports of recent developments in subjects of interest to you in your job. The same holds true of developments of interest to you as a manager. New philosophies of management, which we will all apply unthinkingly within a few months or years, will get their first airing in the pages of a professional institute's journal, or even on the front page of a newspaper's 'Appointments' section.

When you have attended a course on an aspect of management you will often find a list of recommended reading attached to the course notes. This is how you add to what you have learned, by reading about the subject in more detail. Short courses are just that – short – and there isn't time to do much more than give an outline of the subject to be covered in each lecture. Those books in the reading list have not been selected at random. Finally, keep an eye out for other, newer titles which are published in later years. Attending one short course does not make you an instant expert!

There are literally hundreds of books that have been written on the subject of management, and a bibliography would be as long as this entire book itself. For your own self-development, try and achieve a mix of the standard text and the more light-hearted approach. The former category would include anything by Peter Drucker and some handbooks, like the Gower *Handbook of Management Skills*. In the latter category are books like *Parkinson's Law* or *The Peter Principle*, and series like the BIM's *Effective Management Skills* series. Visit any large bookshop, or a specialist business bookshop for a full range of management titles.

◆ The forgotten art

At this point I thought I had virtually finished this chapter. I had to go out to a business lunch, so I switched off the computer, switched on the answerphone, and went.

During lunch, I was forcibly reminded of the forgotten art – social graces. Unfortunately, this well-meaning and very experienced information manager lacked these particular skills. Greeting people, carrying on a social conversation, ordering a meal, paying for it, knowing when and how to begin discussing the business in hand and, finally saying goodbye. Someone who has reached a level of responsibility needs to have found out how to behave in such circumstances.

◆ Conclusion

The point of all this heckling and urging to attend courses, join associations and become a lecturer is to show you just how much more you can get out of life than simply going into work every day. Self-development is your chance to make the most of your abilities and interests in the way that you choose. So, you don't have to trample on other people's dreams to get to the top, and you don't have to be ruthlessly ambitious. Not developing existing natural abilities and following your interests is a terrible waste of talent. It also means that life is less exciting, because there are no challenges and no stimuli. Having some kind of plan to give you direction means that you have the satisfaction of being able to look back and see that you have made progress. Making progress means that you get more satisfaction and a larger salary. It's sometimes very hard work, but it's not dull. And, as I wrote at the beginning – it's never too late to start.

◆ References

Baird, R.B. (1990) *Corporate Directory of Career Change and Outplacement* (2nd edn.), Executive Grapevine.
Calvert, R. et al. (1990) *First Find Your Hilltop*, London: Hutchinson Business Books.
Francis, D. (1985) *Managing Your Own Career*, London: Fontana.
Freedman, H.S. (1989) *How to Get a Headhunter to Call*. New York: John Wiley.
Hamilton, F. (1990) *Infopromotion: Publicity and Marketing Ideas for the Information Profession*. Aldershot: Gower.
Stewart, D.M. (ed.) (1987) *Handbook of Management Skills*. Aldershot: Gower (new edition in preparation).

Studner, P.K. (1989) *Super Job-search*, New York: Mercury Books. UK edition adapted by Professor M. McDonald, Cranfield School of Management.

Webb, S.P. (1991) *Personal Development in Information Work.* (2nd edn.), London: Aslib.

12 Management concerns for the minimal staff library

Guy St. Clair

- Mission
- Self-management
- The value of networking
- Professional considerations
- Interactive support

In the last decade or so, library management for the minimal staff library – the library staffed by one or two people – has been recognized as a subject for study in the profession. For some reason, during the development of library management as a subset of general organizational management, there was a tendency within the profession to focus attention on the concerns of the medium- to large-size library, and librarians and information professionals employed in minimal staff libraries were expected to adapt what they could to their particular situations. Such is not the case today, and there is now a strong body of literature analysing the management of the one- or two-person operation.

This chapter looks at the particular requirements for management success in a minimal staff library. These include understanding the librarian's role in the organization (and the role of the library in the organizational mission), self-management, and the value of skilful networking (both within and outside the organization), which includes the implementation of proven techniques for the involvement of other staff, management employees, and senior management in support of the library and information centre.

Many people are employed in minimal staff libraries, particularly in the special libraries community. There are, of course, one- and two-person libraries in other types of libraries as well. Their management concerns, too, have not been addressed by the profession, for most measurements of libraries are by staff size or materials expenditures, and of those groups and organizations which measure by staff size (the Library Association, UNESCO, the American Library Association), the minimum size category is usually for those libraries 'with staff of three or fewer'. Such measurement does not distinguish the many librarians who are employed in minimal staff libraries, i.e. those with one (the vast majority) or two employees, and thus their specific management concerns, until recently, remained unaddressed.

Minimal staff public libraries are often branch libraries of a larger system, or are very small one- or two-person libraries serving communities with a limited population base. The minimal staff academic library is typically a departmental library, sometimes attached to the main campus facility and sometimes not. These academic minimal staff libraries may be as varied as the single-staff special collection located within the university library's central building or the one- or two-person libraries, such as those serving an observatory staff or an oceanographic institute, located some miles distant from the main academic centre. School libraries with one or two employees are administratively part of a school system and sometimes even part of an organized and geographically defined multi-type library system. All three of these types of minimal staff libraries – public, academic and school – derive their managment direction from the organizations or community authorities of which they are part. Or, as is all too frequently the case, these minimal staff librarians do without management direction at all.

If they are not satisfied with the guidance they receive, many minimal staff library employees turn to the literature and continuing education programmes of the special libraries field and then adapt special libraries management techniques for their particular libraries. It is in this branch of the profession that the major body of work in the management of the one-person or minimal staff library has been done. This is not surprising, since the work of the special librarian is often characterized by a level of accountability which is not necessarily found in the other branches of the profession and which, by being part of the library manager's routine, demands a higher level of management skill. While the public, academic and school librarian is primarily concerned with the teaching of library procedures (an educational role which has come about from the profession's long connection with the teaching community) the special library or information centre exists to provide specific information in response to specific queries.

This difference was spelled out, perhaps unintentionally, as recently as March 1990, when Patricia Glass Schuman (1990) published an article on library technology in which she asserted that 'Our business is not information. Our business is to facilitate understanding through knowledge.' Indeed. In the public, academic or school library, teaching the people who come to the library how to use the facility, how to understand the myriad resources available to them for the answers they are seeking, and to guide them toward those sources which will in fact facilitate their understanding through the knowledge gained from using those sources, is a fundamental part of the mission of the library.

But for the special librarian the direction is different, and this distinction has been recognized by Elizabeth Ferguson and Emily Mobley (1984) in their work on the special library. For them, a special library is defined as:

> '... characteristically a unit or department of an organization primarily devoted to other than library or educational purposes. A special librarian is first an employee, a staff member of the parent organization, and second, a librarian. "Special" really means library service specialized or geared to the interests of the organization and to the information needs of its personnel.'

Ferguson and Mobley further characterize the special librarian, which for our purposes includes most of the people who work in minimal staff libraries, as both a professional librarian and a company manager (or, if the parent organization which the library serves is a not-for-profit or non-profit entity, 'organizational' manager rather than a 'company' manager):

> 'It is a question of two allegiances – one to the organization and one to his/her profession. On the one hand, allegiance to the library profession is very much involved in a librarian's competence on the job; and this competence can only be maintained by strong professional connections and by keeping abreast of current developments in a fast-moving profession. On the other hand, allegiance to the organization is implicit in the library's mandate to provide information service that supports the company's work and furthers its goals. Identification with the company is in the nature of the job ...'

Although the term is used frequently in the profession, the special librarian is most often defined in terms of what he/she is not: the special librarian is not a public, academic or school librarian (although, to be fair, many academic, public and even some school librarians engaged in managing libraries with special subject collections are special librarians as well, because of the specific nature of the materials and the information they manage). A better definition has recently been developed in America, where the Special Libraries Association (SLA), an international organization of these information professionals, is headquartered. A special library, according to SLA (1990), is 'an organization that provides focused, working information to a specialized clientele on an ongoing basis to further the mission and goals of the parent company/organization.' Special librarians are 'information and research professionals who provide focused, working information to a specialized clientele on an ongoing basis to further the mission and goals of the parent company/organization.' The terms **special librarian** and **information professionals** are often used interchangeably.

These distinctions between special librarians and others in the profession have been recognized by others in the profession, in other types of libraries. Joseph Blumenthal (1988) at the University of California at Berkeley has suggested that for libraries to succeed in the future they will all have to adopt the techniques and methodologies of special librarianship:

> 'Librarians will become more like special librarians. They will deal more in information and less in simply saying, "Here's the bibliographic apparatus; it's up to you to find out which things you want." In certain situations, they may come to function more as part of the research team.
>
> '... There will be different protocols for accessing data in these different spheres or circles, and librarians will be kept busy trying to translate those protocols into simpler language for the researcher and trying to train people to use, to access, these different spheres of information.
>
> 'The better librarians are at doing this, the more their services are going to be in demand. So to the extent that we and our successors are good, we will be building demand for our services.'

Thus, library leaders such as Patricia Berger (who served as President of the American Library Association from 1989–1990) have suggested that differences between types of libraries will be eliminated: '... the distinctions we have known in the past among the various kinds of libraries in this country will tend to disappear.' (Berger, 1988).

If so, it is toward the results orientation of special librarianship that library management seems to be directing itself, and a major component of this direction has to do with the accountability of the library manager. Today's minimal staff library manager does not have any choice but to perform his duties with an absolute commitment to excellence, for his supervisors and managers, and most especially those who use the library, cannot make their decisions without the confidence that the information provided by the library or information centre is absolutely correct. This does not mean that the special librarian abrogates his/her responsibility to lead the user to understanding, to facilitating that *'understanding through knowledge'* which Schuman seeks. Instead, it means that the special librarian, as a special librarian, assumes the additional responsibility of strict accountability *as well as* providing the humanizing influence which, in Schuman's terms leads to understanding.

Given the environment in which the one-person/minimal staff library manager works, we recognize that the job requires special management considerations, primarily because the library manager is operating in an environment of professional isolation. He/she is the unique library or information professional in the organization, and his/her role, as library manager, is obviously influenced by this isolation. He/she is required, as has been described elsewhere (St. Clair and Williamson, 1986), to recognize this professional isolation and to master it. In so doing, the one-person/minimal staff library manager can, despite the limitations of environment, create from those very limitations the assets that will turn the library or information centre into the major resource for the organization that it should be.

◆ Mission

The first step in this process is to obtain a clear understanding of what the one-person or minimal staff library is supposed to be doing, and what it should not do. A look at the library's mission is called for at this point, and certainly such an approach is the advice of Shirley Echelman (1974), in her famous essay on managing the library as a business. According to Echelman, the special librarian (and, it might be added, most especially the manager of a one-person or minimal staff library or information centre) has two responsibilities:

1. '... to establish and maintain liaison with other department and division managers, to ascertain needs and evaluate trends, and to direct the work of the library so that it meets current needs and is prepared for changes in direction before they occur, and
2. ... to manage the operations of the library.'

The order in which Echelman lists these responsibilities is significant, for it suggests that for the successful librarian, a passive, reactive style of management is not appropriate. For the librarian to know what services should be being offered to his users, it is necessary to go into the workplace and find out what the users expect from the library and its services. Only then, after this initial responsibility has been recognized and steps taken to meet it, can the librarian concentrate on managing the operations of the library or information centre.

For example, the librarian who has just been hired to manage the one-person information centre in a small financial firm, a company with just eight or ten senior employees and an equal number of people in support operations, discovers during the first few days on the job that several of the senior employees use external sources for some of their specific information needs. When asked about this, each of the employees refers to the fact that the previous library manager didn't 'have time' to provide this information, which is needed on a recurring and timely basis. Yet the library has the capability for providing this information. After interviewing the employees who use the information, the library manager re-arranged procedures in the library to accommodate these searches and provides them regularly for the users, thus saving the company a considerable amount of money for the outside service.

Sometimes the failure to respond to an opportunity for service for the parent organization is nothing more than a tendency, on the part of the library manager, to become so caught up in routine 'operational' demands that the real purposes of the library get lost. It might not be inappropriate to inject a negative consideration here, in the form of cautionary advice. Far too often, it seems, librarians and other information professionals tend to dismiss the importance of others in the organization or company who can advise the library manager. According to Arley Ripin MacDonald (1983), there is frequently a tendency with 'librarians and information professionals . . . to hold aloof, or distance themselves from groups outside the library context . . . .' Yet it is to these very people that the proactive, truly service-oriented minimal staff library manager will go, for these people, while they may not have the advantage of his/her sophisticated understanding of the management of collections and information, will have another valuable advantage: they understand exactly how they will use the information which the library provides for them, and thus they have a direction and a core of understanding which the library manager, in his/her objective search for the information, will not have.

In fact, one of the most important but frequently neglected factors in managing the one-person/minimal staff library is the role of the users. As we work out the library's mission statement in relation to the mission of the organization, it is tempting to think in terms of organizational goals, but according to Janice Ladendort (1973) in a paper on the evaluation of information services:

> 'No manager who wants to be successful can ever afford to forget one basic principle: There is never any such thing as an organization; there are only groups of people engaged in a continuing process of organizing.'

Which simply says to the library manager that he or she is going to be dealing not with an amorphous or vague organization, but with people. The organizational mission, in fact, has to do with the efforts of these people, so the library manager's efforts must be directed toward the staff and determining, *with them*, what their informational needs are.

Specific steps in this process have been identified. In a programme for the UK's Library Association Industrial Group in Edinburgh, Joan Williamson (1988) suggested that, among other things, the library manager should interview a representative sample of users by means of a questionnaire or a personal visit to find out what their work entails and what their information needs are. As in much of our work in library and information studies, there is some divergence of opinion about the value of user studies, but for the minimal staff library manager, certain basic information is necessary to provide services for users which will be relevant to their work. And to obtain this information, he/she will be required to ask his/her users and managers. This procedure, which can be formal or informal, will determine what services and programmes the library should offer.

For example, Rita Evans, Information Specialist at Dolby Laboratories in San Francisco, makes serious efforts to let the staff know what she can do for them. As described in a recent profile (1990), Evans 'speaks at the monthly engineering meetings, sometimes brings in material about a new reference source, sometimes talks about a new on-line service. She also publishes a monthly acquisitions list, and as new people come on staff, Evans makes it her business to visit them in their offices and offer an in-depth visit to the library. These invitations for tours are almost invariably accepted, and in the course of getting to know the new employee, Evans puts together an informal profile so that she can route materials to the person without being asked. She also makes a special effort to do an on-line search on some subject of particular interest to a staff member, and then provide him/her with the results of that search. Evans finds that this is the best way to demonstrate what on-line searching is about. Otherwise, if she attempts to explain it, without a product in hand, the user can become confused and not really know what to ask for.'

This interviewing and profiling of users and potential users will require a certain flexibility of approach, for the librarian may feel the necessity to change the library's direction as the organization's mission changes. It does not show weakness if the librarian varies programmes from time to time, dropping unnecessary services and adding new ones. Such flexibility simply reflects the library manager's understanding of the varying patterns of organizational goals, and of the needs of the people who are there to implement these goals.

For example, a rather major change in direction occurred not too long ago at one of the art institutions in Arizona. This museum, which had been established some years ago as a local fine arts collection, had been built up from the personal collection owned and donated by one of the prominent citizens. It was a small but very general collection. Recently, through donations of large gifts from newer citizens in the community and because of recognized demographic changes in the population base, the museum has begun to collect contemporary Mexican art. This meant that the manager of the museum's minimal staff library (one professional librarian and two volunteer assistants) was required to re-think not only the library's acquisitions programme, but has had to work with the curators in the new collection to educate himself and his volunteers in the types of research materials they must have in the library to support the museum's new work.

In thinking about a mission statement for the minimal staff library, the library manager might turn to Ellis Mount (1983), who recommends a 'common-sense goals statement.' These goals, Mount asserts, will be:

> 'directly related to the implementation of the goals of the sponsoring organization. It also is necessary for the goals to be clearly stated for all to see, particularly top management. A top executive could understandably question the value of supporting an information service if its goals were largely unrelated to the overall goals of the sponsor.'

Thus, for Mount, the library goals statement will include a description of the user base, the types of materials expected to be obtained and/or retained for the users, and a short statement about the uses of technology. User needs are paramount, and the library manager's supervisor must be in full agreement.

Williamson, too, offers direction in determining the value of the information which has been elicited from these user studies, and recommends that, with user information in hand, the one-person or minimal staff library manager prepare a statement for management. The statement will define priorities and objectives for the library/information unit and, after discussing the findings with management, the library manager and her supervisor will agree on the services to be offered.

◆ Self-management

The one-person or minimal staff library manager next learns the basic concepts of self-management. This is an idea which is gaining importance in the workplace today, as we are called upon to increase our productivity but are frequently not given additional staff or resources to bring about that increase. In fact, one firm which concentrates on advising professionals about their career patterns has identified self-management as the key to a successful career:

> 'Regardless of what your field is, you must be able to manage resources. The most important of these resources is yourself. Workaholics and neurotics are notoriously bad self-managers. Good self-management

means working fewer hours, because you are getting more done in less time. It also means gaining a good understanding of your limitations and potentials, and determining the role you want work to play in your life, thus freeing yourself from the anxiety of dealing with cross-purposes and unrealistic, self-imposed demands . . .

'Self-management is a career skill that will become increasingly important in the professional world as the pressure for efficiency grows, stakes are raised and competition gets hotter.' (Calano and Salzman, 1988)

This is obviously not the kind of language we in the library community are accustomed to hearing, but for the one-person or minimal staff library manager, faced with clear accountability and the demand to provide the highest quality library services (frequently with limited resources), such considerations must be made. If the library manager doesn't perform, and perform well, he may very well find himself without a job. So a commitment to self-management is vital to both the user and the librarian.

For many who work alone or with minimal assistance, self-management (which includes basic time management concepts) is crucial, for this is the only way one can 'do it all'. There are hazards in aspiring to 'do it all', for it is probably impossible, and the conscientious one-person or minimal staff library manager must understand at the very beginning that there are dangers in trying to do too much.

However, having recognized that in the one-person or minimal staff library there are limitations, there are certain directions one can think about to accomplish as much as possible with the limited time and resources available. The first key, as far as most library managers are concerned, is planning, which flows directly from the development of a mission statement for the library.

The library manager, who in consultation with his/her management and users has established a statement of the library's goals and mission, has already placed rational limits on his work. The library manager can now look ahead, to think about goals, then devise the necessary procedures. Then, and again in consultation with management if necessary, the library manager determines strategies for accomplishing the things the library is going to achieve, and once the strategies are implemented, they are monitored and evaluated as the work proceeds.

There are, as far as planning is concerned, a variety of points to consider. The first is to be alert to changes in constituent users and their needs. The example about the art museum described earlier is a case in point. A sensitivity to technological developments and the impact such developments can have on library planning is also important, and certainly today, with the incorporation of CD-ROM products into the library's holdings, we can assure management that, for the investment of not a large amount of money (in organizational terms), the library can provide information services of the highest calibre.

Plans, of course, are most vulnerable to economics: changes in funding levels, the inflation rate, materials costs and, for the library that has more than one person, personnel costs. Political factors, such as changes in management and changes in support formulas or levels of support, can have serious effect on a planning programme, and changes in the parent institution (such as the recent wave of mergers and acquisitions in the corporate world) can also drastically alter your planning.

Certainly, as a part of planning, the one-person or minimal staff library manager must develop a sense of priorities, not only for the day-to-day tasks but for major long-term projects as well. The librarian must have a sense of what is important and what is not, of what tasks must be undertaken in the course of the day's work, and what tasks can be set aside until another time or, better yet, not done at all. There are obviously some tasks in the one-person or minimal staff library which will be done every day. The library manager does not have any choice in deciding whether or not to perform them. The same is true of those tasks that have built-in deadlines, tasks like quarterly reports, or the provision of data for an employee who has a Friday morning deadline. But part of successful self-management is to look at those tasks which one performs alone and to determine when (if ever) they must be performed.

All of us have some tasks that we find ourselves doing automatically, and sometimes we look at one of these and wonder why we are doing it. In such cases, an objective look at the value of the task might be in order.

The best quick guideline for determining what *not* to do comes from Michael LeBoeuf, in one of his well-known time-management texts. LeBoeuf (1979) suggests that, in addition to having a 'to-do' list, there should also be a 'not-to-do' list, including such things as:

1. All low-priority items, unless high-priority items have been completed.
2. Any task whose completion is of little or no consequence – when you have something to do, ask yourself the worst thing that could happen if you didn't do it.
3. Anything you can give someone else to do.
4. Anything just to please others because you fear their condemnation or you want to put them in your debt – examine your motives.
5. Thoughtless or inappropriate requests for your time and effort.
6. Anything others should do for themselves.

Another key to success in self-management would be an acceptance of, and the support of one's management in accepting, the value of what might be called 'private time' in the workplace. One of the greatest concerns of one-person or minimal staff library managers is the necessity to be constantly 'on call'. Certainly, as practitioners in a service profession, library managers want to be available and to serve their users whenever needed, but they also, if they are to manage their libraries efficiently and effectively, must have time when they will not be interrupted, when they are not expected to be available for what, in the larger library community, is known as 'public service'.

The establishment of private time begins with the assessment of the users' needs, the very basic interviewing that goes on early in the process when the librarian is learning how the organization's staff uses the library, and when those services are most in demand. Here, again, the value of limitations is recognized. There is no need for the library to be open for the convenience of all users (certainly no library staff is on duty for that occasional scientist who works into the night in his laboratory and who just might need a citation or to check a reference book at 10.30pm!), and the same standards can be used to determine when the library can have some 'down time' during the regular workday. If the library manager works, for example, from 9.00am to 5.00pm and there are few users before 10.30 or so in the morning, why not approach management and suggest that the library be open to users from 10.30 on Tuesdays and Fridays? If your manager agrees, and if the new library hours are publicized, with an accompanying explanation, well in advance of the new service hours, this will give the library manager three hours a week for those tasks which she would perform best without interruption.

Of course, such an ideal scenario can be helpful only up to a point, for the librarian is there to be interrupted, and interruptions are part of a service profession. But for the one person or minimal staff library manager who must have some uninterrupted time, changing the hours of opening can be one solution to the problem. The major point must be repeated, however: such change must be done with the cooperation of management and must be well publicized in advance.

Once it has been recognized that the one-person minimal staff library manager cannot 'do it all' and that his first responsibility is to determine, with management, what services and programmes are to be offered for the users, his life at the library will be made easier if such basic self-management concepts as planning, a developed sense of priorities, and a commitment to private time are built into his working situation.

◆ The value of networking*

One theme is constant in all conversations and writings about the one-person or minimal staff library: success depends upon the level of commitment, by the library manager, to the concept of networking.

Networking is not a new phenomenon in the library world. Particularly in special libraries, the branch of the profession in which most one-person and minimal staff library managers operate, networking has been not only a means by which the librarian expands his/her resources, it has been a vital lifeline for surmounting the obstacles of professional isolation. While the limitations of the very small library or information centre can be seen as an advantage, in that these limitations permit the library to excel by specializing, those same limitations mean that the librarian is without professional colleagues in the immediate workplace.

The definition of the one-person library used by the newly

---

* Parts of this section originally appeared, in a slightly different form, in *Special Libraries*, **80**(2), Spring 1989, pp. 107–112.

established Solo Librarians Caucus of the Special Libraries Association reflects this absence of professional collegiality in the workplace. The word 'solo' was chosen, according to the organizers, because it conveyed an 'image of featured artists with talents exceeding those of the accompanying group', and this thinking led to the caucus's even more precise organizational definition: the solo librarian is the 'isolated librarian or information collector/provider who has no professional peers within the immediate organization.' (The Specialist, 1988) This, of course, defines the librarian who is managing a one-person or minimal staff library, and it is this manager who benefits from even the most basic networking efforts.

And they can be basic. Networking is defined in its simplest terms by Beth Wheeler Fox (1988):

> 'Do you ever eat lunch with a neighboring librarian or call with a question about the best supplier of catalog cards? If so, you have just created an informal network. Librarians routinely need to know how to resolve an enormous variety of questions. Quick answers are rarely available. A search through library literature would provide many answers, yet the item in shortest supply is time . . . Networking allows us to share this type of knowledge with one another.'

Such networking might be described as 'informal', or, better yet, as 'interpersonal', as it takes its value from relationships between people. The successful one-person or minimal staff library manager recognizes this, and instinctively seeks to become part of an interpersonal network (although each individual will decide for himself or herself the extent to which he or she will take advantage of the network). Ferguson and Mobley (1984) found networking to be an almost natural characteristic of special librarians:

> 'Networks emerged from the tradition of cooperation among libraries, and special library cooperation is an integral part of this history. It is almost too obvious to say that special librarians have always been involved in informal cooperative efforts . . . Special Libraries Association chapters themselves come close to being networks in that they provide an ideal framework for such efforts.'

Ferguson and Mobley give credit to Edward Strable, who in 1980 coined a special term for these informal networks: **resource sharing creations** (Strable, 1980). He went on to identify several characteristics for these interpersonal networks: that they aren't really organized, but just 'come into being'; that they are usually found in metropolitan areas; that one doesn't really join but just sort of melds into [the network]; that there are no written rules ('although codes of conduct are severe, automatically sensed, and carefully adhered to by all'); that illegal and unethical methods are not used; and, most important, that the product of these networks is 'usually' information. Strable also found that 'In the exchange of information, the similarity to the "old boy network" is very apparent'. (Strable, 1980).

It is in this similarity to the 'old boy/old girl' networks that interpersonal networking is most striking. But where this term carries dangerously elitist connotations, the concept here is pre-eminently egalitarian: in the library and information management profession, literally anyone has the potential to be an 'old boy' or 'old girl'. Rather than leaning on past or inherited relationships – school, professors, and so forth – one-person minimal staff library managers have the opportunity to make virtually every colleague a new link in an on-going chain of resources. If success in one's work is defined in terms of excellence of service – which assuredly is the only criterion we can permit ourselves in describing our success – does it not naturally follow that all efforts and techniques, including shared information, determined by personal relationships with professional colleagues, are appropriate for the attainment of such excellence? While there might be some need for care, and while decision-making, particularly in what are characterized as 'judgement' calls, might require highly cautious analysis, the personal relationships, the 'old boy' and 'old girl' networks, do not necessarily have to lead to abuse. If these networks are not manipulated for personal gain, but enable us to offer the best service we can in our libraries and information centres, they do not characterize one-person or minimal staff library managers as elitist. In point of fact, they define their excellence.

Networks are no more than *connections*, an idea prominently promulgated in *Managing the One-Person Library* (St. Clair and Williamson, 1986), and certainly applicable to the successful management of a minimal staff operation as well. Special librarians have long taken advantage of such cooperation, and Herbert S. White (1984) has attributed this tendency to the fact that special libraries are characterized by their 'small size, the limitations of their collections and the uniqueness of some of their problems'. These same characteristics have contributed equally to the success of informal networks, those interpersonal **resource sharing creations** Strable identified. The members of informal networks are people who share a vision of what their library service can be for their users and for the organizations which support them.

Today that vision is changing, as was most clearly stated by Michael Gorman in a particularly important article published in 1986. Gorman's (1986) thesis is that 'libraries and cooperation cannot be separated', that cooperation is 'not an activity libraries may or may not choose to engage in', and it is his assertion that what we think of as a library is in fact a 'fusion of all libraries through cooperation'. It is also, Gorman states, 'library service from the library user's point of view' because:

> 'to any library user, the question is not a building, or a collection, or an administrative structure. It is "Are the materials and services available to me, when I need them?"'

Gorman (1986) advocates returning 'library service to the local and small units favored by library users', and he suggests 'selflessness' as the new ethic of librarianship:

> 'Selflessness in librarianship would not only be "right" but also would be of practical benefit – to librarians, individual libraries, and, most importantly, to the users of libraries.'

What does this mean to the one-person or minimal staff library manager? Simply that he must recognize the value of these connections and commit himself to seeking out those personal relationships which might have been forgotten. And, while becoming re-acquainted with some of the tried and true techniques for seeking those relationships, the one-person minimal staff library manager might come to recognize some new ways by which the profession, and his/her job, can benefit from interpersonal networking: membership (and participation) in professional associations, recognizing the value of cross-disciplinary interests, seeking out those librarians and information professionals who work in types of libraries different from the one in which he/she is employed. These are all avenues which lead to the successful combination of resources which overcome the problems of professional isolation.

◆ Professional considerations

A frequent concern of one-person or minimal staff library managers has to do with professionalism and the placement of the library or information centre in the organizational structure. And one of the most frequently asked questions about one-person librarianship (which, for our purposes, could also be asked about the minimal staff library, since it is rare that a library of two employees has both positions filled with what we call 'professional' librarians) is whether a one-person librarian can be a 'professional' librarian.

To answer these questions we must first define our terms. In the United States and Canada, a professional librarian is one who has completed a programme of graduate studies culminating in the awarding of a Master's Degree in Library Science. In the UK, a chartered librarian is one who has been recognized by the Library Association as having completed the studies necessary for work as a professional librarian, often including a Master's Degree as well. In the United States, however, there is no enforcing mechanism other than the accreditation of the graduate programme by the appropriate committee of the American Library Association, and without a licensing or examination arrangement, such as those required in the legal or medical professions, the term 'librarian' is frequently attached to information and library workers who have not completed graduate studies.

There are a variety of reasons for this looseness in terms, but for our purposes the primary one might seem to be that those organizations and companies which are small enough to require only one or two people to work in the library are, because of the size of the organization itself, frequently managed by people who are not knowledgeable about the distinctions between 'professional' and 'non-professional' work in a library or information centre. And as people come into the workplace with certain skills in information work, skills acquired on the job or in continuing education programmes or similar situations without having done graduate work in library and information studies, the distinctions are further blurred. Thus confusion reigns, and the question of who is and who is not a 'librarian' becomes one of some significance.

Can the non-degreed library manager be a 'librarian'? Probably not to other librarians, because in most of the Western world the successful completion of a graduate degree in library and information science is the accepted criterion to be a librarian. Nevertheless, there are many information workers, particularly one-person and minimal staff library managers, who are called 'librarians', and they see themselves as professionals. They make great efforts to attend continuing education programmes, to participate in the activities of professional organizations, and otherwise be part of the profession. Therefore, they are able to work as library managers without, in the strictest sense of the term, being 'librarians'.

Can they be effective library managers? That depends on their commitment to professionalism, on how much they are willing to do on their own, without the status of a graduate degree, and particularly on how seriously they take their roles as managers. Not all one-person or minimal staff library employees are considered managers, but those who see *themselves* as managers, those who organize themselves and their work so that they are working in the management milieu, can certainly be so recognized. The term 'management' is usually used to refer to those administrative staff whose duties include supervising others, but Helen J. Waldron (1982) has stated that anyone finding him/herself in a special library situation (which is the case of most one-person minimal staff library managers), even a very small one-, two-, or three-person operation, is forced to be a manager whether he/she likes it or not. This can be, Waldron says, 'a frightening experience, but it can also be a very exhilarating one – depending on how much the librarian knows'. And it might be suggested, with reference to the value of networks and interpersonal connection, *who* the librarian knows as well.

One way of defining a library manager is to look at the work he or she does, and this is certainly the approach many take who study library management. Miriam Tees (1984) has listed the roles of a manager as those of 'planning, organizing, staffing, directing and controlling'. Similarly, according to Ellis Mount (1983), the library manager's responsibilities are:

1. Relating to top management
2. Planning
3. Budgeting
4. Organizing and staffing
5. Supervising
6. Marketing
7. Evaluating operations

Thus, except for the information professional who is in a totally isolated one-person library, managerial concerns include these responsibilities, and even the one-person librarian, while not directly supervising others, will come into contact with others to whom he/she must convey a businesslike and professional attitude, qualifying him/her, as well, for the managerial role.

There is yet another fact which stands in the way of librarians being accepted as managers. Tees (1984) points out that some may question the ability of librarians to manage based on perceived personality traits of librarians (which, she is quick to point out, does not describe all librarians, 'many of whom differ from the norm'), but there is, indeed, some evidence 'to back the notion that librarians do not have leadership qualities which are useful for managers'. Tees supports the contention of Charles Davis, who has stated that while leadership is necessary for librarians, it may be easier to train people 'in management techniques than [to] make leaders of people without inherent leadership qualities'.

Leadership is not a quality often looked for in the one-person or minimal staff library manager, but it is a quality which lends itself to the successful operation of that library – certainly more than in larger libraries. The distinctions between leaders and managers has been frequently studied, but one approach which is useful in discussing one-person or minimal staff library management appeared in *The Times* [London] in 1986:

> 'A distinction has been made in recent years between a leader and a manager. Those who made it, and those who subscribe to it, claim that this is not an esoteric division: the effectiveness of an organization can depend upon knowing which one of these two different creatures it needs.
>
> 'In brief, leaders are defined very much as they have always been – innovators, risk-takers, creators of excitement, guides to The Way.
>
> 'Managers, on the other hand, are viewed as bureaucrats. More and more the traditional view of the manager as a dynamic leader is being challenged. He is being seen, not as an initiator, but as one who reacts to keep his organization balanced and to keep the number of possible options to a minimum.
>
> 'Given the need for change, the manager will do his best to adapt his own behaviour – a need which in recent years has led to a proliferation of "management" courses which have behaviour modification as one of their primary goals.
>
> 'The leader, on the other hand, seeks to change the circumstances. Managers adapt to their inherited surroundings, as one eminent writer has put it, "like a chameleon." Organizations need such adaptable people, of course.'

After several years of increased attention to the management of the one-person or minimal staff library, it appears that the successful library manager in a one- or two-person operation combines the characteristics of both the leader and the manager: he/she is going to be a good library manager, in the best sense of the term, in that he/she is going to be organized and is going to work hard to keep the library and its services balanced. Yet today, as librarianship and the information profession go into the twenty-first century with all the excitement and innovation that that idea implies, the one-person or minimal staff library manager must also be innovative and willing to take risks. The days of the librarian who sits passively and waits for enquiries is gone, certainly in the world in which today's one-person/minimal staff library manager operates. The organizations which support us, and whom we support, will no longer accept that kind of library management, and the one-person or minimal staff library manager is now required, by the very circumstances of information management in the profession today, to understand and to demonstrate both leadership and management.

Organizational placement for the library or information service can sometimes be problematic for the one person or minimal staff library manager. Mount (1983) has suggested that:

> 'there are no hard and fast rules about the best organizational placement of the library or information center since personal differences between top management personnel may have more significance than the rank of the person.'

However, Mount (1983) has also suggested that there are a variety of considerations in determining the place of the library in the organization:

> 'In addition to the rank and title of the one to whom the library manager should ideally report, other factors to consider are the personality and interest (or lack of interest) a particular person in top management may have for the library. It has been argued that an enthusiastic supporter of the library can accomplish more for it than someone higher up in the organization who is lukewarm in his or her support of the library.'

Joan Williamson (1988) has also observed that management is the first source for support for the library, and she does not hesitate to suggest that obtaining this support is not a passive activity. Prior to the interview stage of the 'market survey' which will be used to determine library programmes and services, Williamson identifies two steps which must be undertaken by the library manager: he/she must win the backing of at least one strong person in the organization, preferably at the management level, and he/she must get supervisors and management involved in his/her decisions about the organization of information. Such steps will, it is hoped, lead to management support for the library's work, and will serve to ensure that the library or information centre is not seen as an 'overhead' expense simply to be tolerated, but as a department which contributes directly to the corporate profits or other success of the organization's specified mission.

◆ Interactive support

For most one-person or minimal staff library managers, the question of support for the library is a vital one. Because the parent organization in which such a 'small' library or information service is located frequently is managed by personnel who are unsophisticated about the value of a library, the library manager often finds himself or herself in a defensive position, having to convince management, other staff and library users that the work of the library is necessary for the successful achievement of the parent organization's mission.

It is certainly best to build up library support before it is needed. And while there are a number of accepted procedures for achieving this, the most useful direction, it would seem, has to do with establishing what has been referred to as 'the credibility of our product – information – as part of effective decision making'.

It is vital for the library manager to understand that he/she provides the information that the decision makers in his/her organization must have. Morton (1983) sees communication as the vital link in this relationship:

> 'I refer to knowledge and information separately, although I believe they are part of the same decision making continuum. It is the function of today's information manager to serve as the catalyst for the change information undergoes on the way to becoming knowledge. And knowledge – or the lack of it – is the vital ingredient in sound decision making ... The all-too-often missing link between the two is communication. Information without communication is about as useful as one chopstick. Without a receptive audience, information cannot become knowledge. Therefore, those responsible for information's acquisition, treatment, storage, retrieval, *and* communication

become crucial to the successful decision making process within their respective organizations.'

How we achieve this level of communication is based on a number of factors, but the most successful include an understanding, by the library manager, of the corporate culture of the parent organization. It also includes an understanding of others' perceptions of the library and library services in general, and the providing of excellent service, including (as Helen J. Waldron (1982) has characterized it) 'specialized and personalized' service, leading to 'harmonious' relations within the organization. Finally, it includes a number of accepted procedures which have been seen to work in the profession at large, or in other professions or industries, and which can be successfully adapted in the information service provided by the one-person or minimal staff library manager.

Corporate culture is a relatively new field of study, particularly in library management, but it has been thought about for a couple of decades in the business community. Silverzweig and Allen (1976) identified corporate culture in 1976 and described it as '... a set of expected behaviors that are generally supported within the group ... unwritten "rules" that have an immense impact on behavior ... (and) which affect every aspect of organizational functioning'. Writing in *Library Management Quarterly*, Marlene Vogelsang (1989) described corporate culture as 'the shared values and assumptions of the employees' within the parent organization, and it is those shared values that give corporate culture its 'strength and power'. Further, Vogelsang suggests that, since corporate culture is based on the values of the people who make up the culture, 'acknowledging culture acknowledges the importance and value of people in the organization.' In a similar vein, John Kok (1980) has gone so far as to suggest that 'No single factor has a greater influence on the special library manager than the parent organization's attitude toward information.'

The library manager must consider how the corporation perceives the work of the library and its information service. It is important to recognize – and to accept – that people who are not involved in information services (even people who use information provided by the library or information centre with some frequency) do not have an understanding of what library management is all about. Nor should they. The one-person or minimal staff library manager is the unique information professional in the organization, and it is his/her responsibility to operate the information services. Nevertheless, the library manager can do his/her work more successfully if aware of how he/she is seen by others. For most people, the library or information service is taken for granted, to be there when it is needed but not necessarily thought about otherwise.

This point was effectively made in a report on the value of the information professional (Special Libraries Association, in 1987) wherein several reasons were listed for explaining why library services are often undervalued:

1. Library products and services are given away – they have no value attached.
2. Librarians are not skilled politically or in implementing public relations efforts.
3. Information provided is not measurable.
4. Information provided is not used up.
5. The librarian's creative work – adding 'value to the otherwise inert material in the collection' is invisible both to our supervisors and our users.

Once the library manager has acquired an understanding of the corporate culture within the organization, and has determined the parent organization's attitude toward information, he/she can begin to think about taking steps to ensure that management understands the value of information, and the library.

The first of these steps has been identified by Helen Waldron (1982) who suggests that the library manager must provide a 'very specialized and personalized service, which is both a philosophy and a practice'. The library manager is a provider of information, and the user wants the information, not to be told how to look it up. Such practices, Waldron suggests, lead to the establishment of 'harmonious relations – with users, with peers in the organization, and with management strata above and below'. Such harmonious relations clearly lead to positive reinforcement for the library and its services and, in the organizational structure, go far toward validating the service to the organization as a whole.

For example, Doris Johnson (1987) at Northeast Utilities in Hartford, Connecticut, recognized 'an on-going need to quantify the benefits' of the company's Research Information Centre, and she designed a six-question survey which was sent to the centre's more active users. 'The response was amazing . . . 75% in just three days ... The number of hours which the Centre saved these employees in a one-year period was impressive', with such figures as '50–60 hours' and 'over 120 hours' reported. While Johnson noted that it is 'difficult to actually pinpoint the dollars and cents saved', one can survey man-hours saved and put salary dollar values to them, thus coming up with a figure which management will understand.

Where this approach is leading, it seems, is to establishing the value of the library, to establishing that the library and its services are seen as absolutely necessary to the organization. In an article on organizational placement, White (1973) recognized that decisions about placement of the library or information centre in the organization's structure were out of the hands of the library manager:

> 'If the librarian can count on one thing, it is that the people who will ultimately make these major decisions (and this group includes neither the head of administrative services nor the director of research) will act selfishly. They will vote in favor of dispensing with services they do not use, and keeping services they do use.
>
> 'The library's strategy, in terms of self-protection and survival, must be geared to making itself indispensable to these people – whether or not they ever ask for information (and they probably do not), whether or not they take an interest, and whether or not you are chartered to serve them ... The time to start this program of ingratiated irreplaceability is now – when trouble starts it is too late.'

White acknowledges a concept from B.E. Holm (1986) who had written that 'the major advantage of an information function is that it can find answers for the inquirer more rapidly than he could himself'. To this White adds '... it can also provide answers which the inquirer needs but has not thought to request'.

Another approach to establishing the value of the library in the organization and using that value to gain management support for the library and its services is, of course, based on the excellence of the services and programs which the library provides. This is not a new idea. In fact, Ellis Mount (1983) has suggested that excellence of service is directly related to the support the library receives:

> 'To maintain the support of management a special library/information center must perform well in meeting its goals. It is therefore necessary for the manager to take periodic looks at the service, whether through surveys or interviews, to see how it is doing.

'The job of a manager in establishing good relations with top management is to provide good service, and to see that top mangement is made aware of it through judicious marketing or promotional efforts.'

It is important to recognize, however, that the standard of excellence must be shared by both the minimal staff library manager and the corporation or organizations's senior management. This, of course, is one of the primary reasons the librarian must take a fairly assertive stance in getting to know management personnel, and why the library manager is obligated to play a proactive role, and not a reactive one, in the organization.

For example, when Marylou Pierce Fox was the library manager at Arthur Andersen & Company's San Francisco office, it was her philosophy of librarianship and its value to the corporate community which enabled her to do what she had to do for AA&Co. 'A really excellent library,' she said, 'is not defined as much by the number of books on its shelves as by the quality and responsiveness of its personnel. . . . we provide a full range of services, from a quickly located reference resource to an in-depth search through the library's numerous database sources.' Her manager, John Greene, was in agreement about the excellence of the library's services: 'San Francisco is known to have one of the finest libraries within the firm,' he commented. 'It consistently has provided the highest level of service to our people and, as a result, has made a direct impact on the quality of client service in our Northern California practice.' (*The One Person Library*, 1987).

And after establishing that excellence of service ensures support for the library, Mount brings up an additional point which the serious one-person or minimal staff library manager must recognize, and accept:

'While the service-oriented manager wishes to help all clientele of the unit, it is only common sense to make sure that top management personnel are given the best service possible. One way of looking at it is that their needs are apt to be more significant for the overall good of the organization than the needs of those in lower positions. The manager must use good judgment when the needs of a lower echelon person conflict with the requests of higher ranking personnel.'

Mount is not alone in suggesting that some users should receive a higher level of service than others. This is a difficult concept for many in the library profession, for it implies a discrimination which runs against the grain of many. As practitioners in a service profession in which egalitarian concepts are frequently held up as the ideal, many library people are uncomfortable with the notion that some receive different service than others, yet as John Kok (1980) has so abruptly put it, 'Equal access for all users has no place in a special library.' The effective one-person or minimal staff library manager is expected to recognize where support comes from, for without that support she cannot provide the services she has been hired – as the unique professional – to provide.

For example, the library manager in a public relations firm has recognized that there is a certain partner who has information needs requiring special effort, and she does not hesitate to take the extra time, even put in the extra hours, to see that the data this partner needs is available when he needs it. Then, when there is a new CD-ROM product which will not only be useful to him in his work but will definitely benefit the firm's library in its efforts to serve other users as well, she does not hesitate to tell this partner about it and let him know how much time and effort the new product will save him, to say nothing of what it will save the company. Then, when he is called upon to make a decision about the product and the services it can deliver, he is in a position to make an intelligent decision and one which not only benefits him and his clients but the library as well.

Thus, the successful one-person or minimal staff library manager sees this different level of service for certain users as an investment in gaining support for the organization's information programmes, and although he will handle this part of his work tactfully, he will incorporate it into his management style. He does not play petty politics and, when there are attempts to minimize the role of the library in the organization, he makes sure that management personnel think of the library/information centre as a 'management' information service, so that the people who benefit directly from the library will feel some responsibility for its continued role in the organization.

Finally, one of the ways in which to involve others in support for the one-person or minimal staff library is to look at the group of people who are naturally drawn to the library and its services. This group has been identified by Doris Bolef (1988), who sees it as a valuable source of support:

> 'Often a group of patrons form a "belt system" around a library. Usually highly literate and interested in libraries, having used them all their lives, these patrons provide support essential to the library's wellbeing. They help open the channels of communication both ways,

formal and informal. They serve as sources of invaluable information to the [library] manager about the organization and where it is going. At the same time, through them the [library] manager can spread the work about the library's programs, especially new or changed ones. Such patrons should be continually courted and the number increased with no departmental favoritism. It goes without saying that members of this group receive a higher level of service.'

Sometimes these relationships are formalized in a library committee. These working relationships have been cogently described by Jane Katayama (1983):

'The principal purpose of the committee is to advise, support, and guide the library director and to serve as a linkage among the users, the library, and the management. It is essential to distinguish between advisory functions, which are in the domain of the library committee, and the administrative functions, which belong to the library manager. The library manager should not surrender managerial responsibilities. ... An active, interested committee can provide the library with meaningful support, sound advice and guidance, and act as liaison between users and management. ... The relationship among library committee members, senior management personnel, and the library staff can best be described as a synergistic one, each bringing expertise and knowledge to a common goal – that of contributing to the fulfillment of the organization's mission.'

The difficulty with these arrangements is that the library manager is, in effect, reporting to two authorities, although it is clear that as the unique information professional in the organization, the library manager, even in a one-person or minimal staff operation, has a role of considerable influence. These people – the committee members Bolef's 'belt system' – are laypeople, not trained in the intricacies and procedures of library and information management, and they will come to rely on the library manager for his advice and expertise.

For example, David Ross was Librarian/Archivist at The New York Psychoanalytic Institute for several years, and during that time he worked closely with a library committee, composed of specialists in their field. As in many private organizations, Ross reported to the committee in library (not adminstrative) matters. The committee's role was primarily advisory but, when necessary, policy matters were discussed. Its chairman was supportive of what was done in the library, and Ross, as a member of the library committee, attended its meetings and had a weekly meeting with its chairman. The committee members were dependent on Ross for the professional information they needed – the information that only a professional librarian could provide – to enable them to make the correct decisions affecting the Institute's library (*The One Person Library*, 1987).

In the final analysis, the successful library manager in the one-person or minimal staff library is one who is skilful in meeting the service needs of the library, including an understanding of the library's role in the organization, self-management, successful networking, and determined interactive relationships with other staff, management employees, and senior management in support of the library and information centre. But that still is not quite enough. The successful one-person or minimal staff library manager will also have the confidence that what he or she is doing is worth doing, and worth the support that the company or the organization is investing in the library's resources. Such confidence comes only from understanding that, despite the setbacks, despite the cuts in funding, the seemingly ongoing efforts to undermine the role of the library or research centre, it produces services and products that are vital to the organization and its mission. It is a very personal thing, this confidence, but it is not an option. It is required for those who are going to succeed in the information profession, today and in the future. It has best been described, not in the library literature, but in business, by John Nathan (1989) in an interview:

> 'I've been in the presence of some powerful and original business thinkers, and I've been very impressed.... From what I've seen, [these people] are insulated to a remarkable degree against self-doubt, which is the source of power in many men who are able to control their worlds ... They seem to have a highly articulated vision of the world they inhabit and of how they want it to be ... they have the energy to put in realization the smallest detail. It's an important empowerer; it allows you to communicate your vision to everyone around you with maximum efficiency and persuasiveness.'

◆ References

Berger, P. In Riggs, D.E. and Sabine, G.A. (eds.). (1988) *Libraries in the 1990s: What the Leaders Expect*, Phoenix: Oryx Press.

Blumenthal, J. In Riggs, D.E. and Sabine, G.A. (eds.) (1988) *Libraries in the 90s: What the leaders expect*, Phoenix: Oryx Press.

LeBoeuf, M. (1979) *Working Smart*. New York: Warner.

Bolef, D. (1988) The special library. In Katz, B. (ed.). *The How-to-do-it Manual for Small Libraries*, New York: Neal-Schuman.

Calano, J. and Salzman, J. (1988) How to get more done in a day. *Working Woman*, April, 99–100.

Coming of age. *Inc.*, 11(4), April 1989.

Echelman, S. (1974) Libraries are businesses, too! *Special Libraries*, 65(10/11), October/November.

Ferguson, E. and Mobley, E.R. (1984) *Special Libraries at Work*, Hamden, CT: Shoe String Press.

Fox, B.W. (1988) *The Dynamic Community Library: Creative, Practical and Inexpensive Ideas for the Director*. Chicago: American Library Association.

Gorman, M. (1986) Laying siege to the fortress library: a vibrant technological web connecting resources and users will spell its end. *American Libraries*, May.

Holm, B.E. (1968) *How to Manage your Information*, New York: Reinhold.

Johnson, D. (1987) The information center: necessity or luxury. *The One-Person Library: A Newsletter for Librarians and Management*, 4(1), May, 2–3.

Katayama, J.H. (1983) The library committee: how important is it? *Special Libraries*, 74(1), January.

Kok, J. (1980) Now that I'm in charge, what do I do? *Special Libraries*, 72(12), December.

Ladendorf, J. (1973) Information service evaluation: the gap between the ideal and the possible. *Special Libraries*, 64(7), July.

MacDonald, A.R. (1983) *Managers View Information*. New York: Special Libraries Association.

Morton, P.A. (1983) The information manager: a link in effective organizational decision making. In Koenig, M. (ed.). *Managing the Electronic Library, Papers of the 1982 Conference of the Library Management Division of the Special Libraries Association*, New York: Special Libraries Association.

Mount, E. (1983) *Special Libraries and Information Centers: An Introductory Text*. New York: Special Libraries Association.

Profile: David J. Ross (1987) *The One-Person Library: a Newsletter for Librarians and Management*, 4(4), August.

Profile: Marylou Pierce Fox (1987) *The One-Person Library: a Newsletter for Librarians and Management*, 4(6), October, 2–3.

Profile: Rita Evans (1990) *The One-Person Library: a Newsletter for Librarians and Management*, 7(2), June.

Schuman, P.G. (1990) Reclaiming our technological future. *Library Journal*, 115(4), March 1.

Silverzweig, S. and Allen, R. (1976) Changing the corporate culture. *Sloan Management Review*, Spring, 33–49.

Solo librarians caucus takes flight. *The Specialist*, 11(12), December 1988.

Special Libraries Association. (1987) *President's Task Force on the Value of the Information Professional*. Final report, Washington: Special Libraries Association.

Special Libraries Association Strategic Planning Committee (1990) *A visionary framework for the future: SLA's strategic plan 1990–2005*, Washington: Special Libraries Association.

St. Clair, G. and Williamson, J. (1986) *Managing the One-person Library*. London: Saur.

Strable, E.G. (1980) The way it was. In Gibson, R.W. (ed.). *The Special Library Role in Networks*. New York: Special Libraries Association.

Tees, M. (1984) Is it possible to educate librarians as managers? *Special Libraries*, July.

Vogelsang, M. (1989) The reflection of corporate culture in the library/information center. *Library Management Quarterly*, **12**(2), Spring.

Waldron, H.J. (1982) The business of managing a special library. In Jackson, E. (ed.). *Special Librarianship: A New Reader*. Jefferson, NC: McFarland.

White, H.S. (1984) *Managing the Special Library*. White Plains: Knowledge Industry Publications.

White, H.S. (1973) Organizational placement of the industrial special library: its relationship to success and survival. *Special Libraries*, **64**(3), March.

Williamson, J. (1988) On OPL ailments and cures. *The One-Person Library: a Newsletter for Librarians and Management*, **4**(12), April.

Willis, R. (1986) General appointments. *The Times* (London), 18 September.

GENERAL READING

The One-Person Library: A Newsletter for Librarians and Management (1984–). OPL Resources Ltd, PO Box 948, Murray Hill Station, New York, NY 10156, USA.

St. Clair, G. and Berner, A. (1990) *The Best of OPL; Five Years of The One-Person Library – A Newsletter for Librarians and Management*. Washington: Special Libraries Assocation.

Index

Absenteeism 36, 38
Academic libraries, minimal staff 194
Accession registers 104
Accounting 102–5
  invoices 104
  record-keeping 104
  statements 104
  suppliers 117
  see also Costs
Acquisitions. See purchasing
Action plans 180–2
Advertising
  in staff recruitment 9–11
    design 10
    newspapers 9–10
    professional journals 9–10
    response 10
    timing 10–11
  information services 70
Application forms 12
Appraisal. See Performance appraisal
Attitude scales 62–3
Audit. See Information audit
Auditors 104, 105
Authority 139, 142, 147–9
Automated systems
  costs 126
  deliverables and support 126–7
  facilities and performance 126
  life-cycle cost 126
  overspecification 126
  purchasing 125–7
  specification of requirements 126
  'vapourware' 126
  see also Computer systems
Automation
  records management 134–5
  suppliers 124

Bibliographic services, suppliers 118–19
Book servicing 121
Branding 69–70
Brokers. See Information brokers
Budgeting 97–102, 147
  background 97–102
  contingencies 109–10, 148
  incremental 100
  line-by-line 99–100
  method used for 99
  performance 100–1
  staff costs 108
  zero-based 101–2

Capital equipment 109
Career path 180
Career structure 43
CD–ROM 76
  accuracy, currency and coverage offered by 185
  awareness of new products 218
  storage of seldom-used information 135
  Windows facility 135
Charging for services 111–12
Complaints 74
Computer centre 76
Computer skills, acquisition of 77
Computer systems
  installation problems 126
  library housekeeping 77
  new difficulties arising from 132
  purchasing 109
  support requirements 127
  see also Automation
Consultants 107, 128–30
Contingencies, budgeting 109–10, 148
Corporate culture 144–6, 214
Corporate information strategy 96
Corporate mythology 152

Corporate records 138
  legal aspects 138
  new categories of 138
Costs
  automated systems 126
  database monitoring 136
  information 91–5
  information audit 91–5
  information brokers 127, 128
  information services 91
  information technology 91
  library services 105
  on-line search services 111
  spreading 147
  staff 108
  staff recruitment 20
  suppliers 121
Crises 159
cummings, e.e. 141
Curriculum vitae 12
Customer care 73–4
  as promotional tool 73
  complaints strategy 74
  staff training for 73
Customer needs 55–6
  functional activities 56
  marketing issues 55–6
  non-functional activities 56

Data Protection Act 1984 24
Database management system (DBMS) 86
  Delta 4.3 86–7
  Delta 5 87
  non-relational 86
  relational 87
  transactional 86
Databases 136
  commercial information available on 136
  contracts with hosts 136
  for information audit 87–9
  record files 87
  remote 124
  see also On-line services; Remote databases
Decision packages 101–2
Delegation 168–9
Demotivating factors 36
Disabled Persons (Employment) Acts 1944 and 1958 24
Documents 136–7
  alternative definition 138

  legal aspects 138
  new concept of 137
  on-line 137
  problems of terminology 136
  production 137

80/20 rule 169
Electronic mail 131
Electronic office 132
Employment Agencies Act 1973 25
Equal Pay Act 1970 25
Equity theory of motivation 31

Financial year 102–5
Ford Motor Company 33
Foreign currency transactions 118

Group discussions 61, 62

Human relations school of management 27
Hygiene factors 29, 31

Induction 41–3, 70–1
Influence 139, 142–4, 148
Information
  as company asset 75
  charging methods 111
  core commodity 75–6
  cost of 91–5
  setting charges for provision of 111–12
Information audit 75–96
  analysis phase 93–5
  confidentiality 87
  costs 91–5
  external consultant 80
  goodwill 75
  interviewees 84–5
  interviews 81–6
  methodology 79
  preparation for 80
  presenting the report 95–6
  project introduction 79
  proposal for 79–80
  purpose of 77–9
  questionnaire forms 81
  requirements for 80
  security levels 87
  setting up databases 87–9
  staff needs 79
  style of interview 85–6
  timescale 79

title of proposal 79
writing the report 93–5
Information brokers 127–8
  access to sources 127
  confidentiality aspect 128
  costs 127, 128
  delivery of information under time constraints 127
  need to know methods of working 127–8
  provision of specialist skills 127
  purchasing the services of 107
  role in information unit 127
Information centre
  activities of 76
  budget 91
  current situation 76
  development of 76
  joint systems 76, 77
Information management 77
  integration of records system with 135–8
  new concept of 136
  see also Documents; Records management
Information professionals, distinction from special librarian 196
Information resources 78–9
  index 88
  questionnaire on 88
  value of 92–3
  see also Information audit
Information services
  advertising 70
  costs 91
  non-functional values 56
  split with information technology 76
  valuing 92–3
Information strategy, formulation of 96
Information technology
  company policy on 125
  costs 91
  joint systems 76, 77
  split with information services 76
  use of internal and external sources 136
  see also Automation; Computer systems
In-house newspapers 72
In-house training 32, 186

Interviews 12–18
  bad first impressions 14
  closing 17–18
  contacting candidates for 13
  duration 15
  information audit 81–6
  note taking 16–18
  physical environment 13–15
  planning 12
  procedure 15–18
  second 17, 18
  shortlisting candidates for 12–13
  showing work environment 17
Invoices. See Accounting

JANET network 135
Job applications, confidentiality in 14–15
Job description 5, 6–7
  samples 21–4
Job dissatisfiers 28–9
Job enrichment 34
Job offer 18–19
Job rotation 34
Job title 7
John Lewis Partnership 33

Lateness 36
Leadership 35, 211
Legislation, effect on records management 132
Library housekeeping, use of computers in 77
Library management with minimal staff 193–222
  academic libraries 194
  definition 205
  interactive support 213–20
  library hours 204
  management techniques 194
  mission of 197–201
  networking 205–8
  organizational placement 212
  private time 204
  professional considerations 208–13
  public libraries 194
  results orientation direction 197
  role of librarian 197–201
  school libraries 194
  self-management 201–5
  selflessness concept 208
  'to-do' and 'not-to-do' lists 203–4

225

user needs 204
user role 199
Library service
  cost of 105
  value of 105

Management courses 186
Managers
  elimination of demotivating factors 36
  leading by example 35
  MBWA 34–5
  oversupervision 35
  personal development 52
  role in staff motivation 34–6
  staff concerns 35
  training and development needs 38, 51–2, 186
  walking the job 34
Market penetration 66
Market pricing 66
Market research 59
  qualitative and quantitative techniques 61
Market segmentation 59
Market surveys 68
Marketing 54–74
  definition 55
  key aspects 55–9
  strategies and plans 60, 63–6
  see also Promotion
Marketing mix, concept of 65
MBWA (Management by Walking About) 35
Meetings 172–3
Microfiche, advantages of 135
Mid-career crisis 140
Minimal staff library. See Library management with minimal staff
Monthly statement 103–4
Motivational factors 30

Networking 205–8
  commitment to concept of 205
  informal or interpersonal 206–7
  one-person or minimal staff library 205
  special libraries 205, 207
  value of 205–8

Objective setting 164–5
On-line services
  accuracy, currency and coverage offered by 185
  and records management 136
  costs 111
  documents 137
  financial sector 77
  purchasing 110
  reliance on, at cost of hard copy 77
  remote hosts 124–5
  searching 76
  see also Databases; Remote databases
Optical disks 135
Organization 169–70

Pareto principle 169
Performance appraisal 33, 37, 45–7
Performance measures 66
Performance related pay 33
  see also Poor performance
Periodicals 122
Person specification 5, 8–9
  desirable attributes 9
  essential attributes 9
  samples 21–4
  Seven Point Plan 8–9
Personal development. See Self-development
Personal organizers 175
Personnel department
  cooperation with 5–6
  relationship with 6
Personnel management in development of management skills 184
Peter Principle 37
Planning Programming Budgeting Systems (PPBS) 101
Politics in organizations 139–56
Poor performance 36–8
  detection and causes 36–8
  stages in addressing 38
  tackling problem of 38
Power 140, 141
Pricing 66–7
Priorities in time management 165
Procrastination 161–2, 167
  effect on quality of work 161–2
  reasons for 162
  stress resulting from 162
  see also Time management
Profitability 56–9

Project management 184, 185
Promotion
  marketing 67–74
    objectives 69
    techniques 69–74
  personnel 183
Public libraries
  charging for services 111
  minimal staff 194
Public relations 71–3
Public speaking 189
Purchasing 105–10
  automated systems 125–7
  bought-in services 107
  computer systems 109
  decision to go to source vs agent 15–16
  donations 106
  equipment 109
  materials 105–7
  non-book materials 106
  obscure reports 106
  on-line versus paper strategy 110
  records of spending 107
  selection 106
  serials 106
  services 107–8
  space 108
  supply of periodicals and standing orders 122

Questionnaires 62–3
  forms 81–4
  on information resources 88

Race Relations Act 1976 25
Reading in self-development 190
Record files 87–9
  defining format 87
  method of devising 87
Record-keeping for accounting 104
Records
  corporate 138
  definition 131–2
  perceptions of 132
Records management 131–8
  and on-line services 136
  automation 134–5
  basic aim 133
  basic procedure 133–4
  changes in 132
  implementation of 133
  responsibility for 133–4
Records manager, role of 133–8
Records systems 133–4
  automation 134–5
  development of 133
  organization's needs 133–4
  responsibility for 133–4
Recruitment agencies 11–12
Recruitment law, UK 24
Recruitment. See Staff recruitment
References, candidates' 19
Rehabilitation of Offenders Act 1974 25
Rejection letters 12, 19–20
Remote database 124–5
  definition of term 124
  local agent or office 125
  payment methods 125
  user groups 125
  see also Databases; On-line services
Remote hosts 124–5
  conditions of service 124
  password 124
Rewards 33

Scottish Tourist Board 74
Selective dissemination of information (SDI), new publications 121
Self-actualization 28, 33–4
Self-analysis 181
Self-assessment 187
Self-development 179–92
  formal 186–7
  informal 187–8
  management post 182–3
  opportunities for 180
  use of term 179–80
Self-management 201–5
Serials 136
Sex Discrimination Act 1975 25
Special librarian 194–7
  accountability of 194
  definition 195–6
  management skills 194
  responsibility of 197
Special libraries
  definition 195
  management techniques 194
  networking 205, 207
  purchasing in 106
  results orientation 197

techniques and methodologies of 196–7
Special Libraries Association (SLA) 196, 215
Staff costs 108
Staff magazines 72
Staff motivation 26–39
  manager's role in 34–6
  poor performance 36–8
  practical methods of 31–4
  strategies for improving 39
  theories 27–31
Staff recruitment 4–25
  advertising 9–11
  alternatives to advertising 11
  costs 20
  information for candidates 12
  mistakes 20–1
  recruitment agencies 11–12
  search techniques 9
Staff selection 15–20
  interviews 15–18
  making the offer 18
  rejection 19–20
Staff training and development 32, 33, 40–53
  evaluation 49–51
  external courses 51
  feedback 50
  for managers 38, 51–2, 186
  identifying needs 44–5
  importance of wider professional involvement 49
  long-term 43–4
  methods 48–9
  objectives 48
  observation and counselling 50–1
  organizational impact on planning 47–8
  scheduling 48–9
Standing orders 122
Statements. See Accounting
Stress 162, 166, 167, 174
Suppliers
  accounting 117
  agents 115–16, 122
  and client needs 119–20
  areas covered by 116
  automation 124
  bibliographic services 118–19
  book servicing 121
  client needs 119
  contract law 114

contract renewal 122–4
costs 121
criteria for choosing 117–22
delivery service 121
file transfer format 124
financial concerns 117–18
foreign currency transactions 118
goodwill 119
inspection service 121
measuring the differences 123
notification of possible delays 120
order/payment routines 117–18
overheads 116
payments systems 117–18
performance indicators 123
periodicals 122
relationships with 114–30
selection 115
service elements 115
single or multiple 116
specialist stock holders 121
standing orders 122
stock holders 121
tenders 122
urgent orders 119–20
SWOT analysis 64

Team working and social needs 32
Tenders 122
Theory X, Theory Y 30, 37
Theory Y 30, 37
Time management 157–78
  approach to 159–63
  committed time 173
  effective strategies 174–7
  health issues 166–7, 174
  learning to say no 172
  'me' time 166–7
  planning 170–1
  priorities 165
  procrastination 161–2, 167
  robbers 157–8
  strategies of 164–8
  tips 175
  use of lists 165
Time robbers 158–9
Training. See Staff training and development

Value of library service 105
Valuing information services 91–2

Writing skills 189